Muhammad Ali

In the series *Sporting*, edited by Amy Bass

Thomas Hauser, *The Boxing Scene*

David Wangerin, *Soccer in a Football World: The Story of America's Forgotten Game*

Grant Farred, *Long Distance Love: A Passion for Football*

Tommie Smith, *Silent Gesture: The Autobiography of Tommie Smith*

Michael Ezra

Muhammad Ali

The Making of an Icon

T TEMPLE UNIVERSITY PRESS
Philadelphia

Temple University Press
1601 North Broad Street
Philadelphia, Pennsylvania 19122
www.temple.edu/tempress

∞The paper used in this publication meets the requirements of the American National
Standard for Information Sciences—Permanence of Paper for Printed Library Materials,
ANSI Z39.48–1984

Library of Congress Cataloging-in-Publication Data

Ezra, Michael, 1972–
Muhammad Ali : The making of an icon / Michael Ezra.
    p. cm. – (Sporting (SPRT))
Includes bibliographical references and index.
ISBN 978-1-59213-661-2 (hardcover : alk. paper)—
ISBN 978-1-59213-662-9 (pbk. : alk. paper)
    1. Ali, Muhammad, 1942-   2. Boxers (Sports)—United States—Biography.   I. Title.
GV1132.A4E97 2009
796.83092—dc22

2008034323

2 4 6 8 9 7 5 3 1

For David Katzman

Beloved mentor and living proof of the very best the world has to offer

Contents

Acknowledgments   ix

Introduction: Why Another Book about Muhammad Ali?   1

PART I   Louisville Sponsoring Group

Louisville's Favorite Son: The Professional Debut   7

Choosing Management: The Courtship of Cassius Clay   14

The Early Bouts, 1961–1962   29

Clay vs. Moore: The Seminal Text   40

The Most Hated Man in Boxing? The Early Bouts, 1963   49

Damage Control through Moral Authority: The Louisville
Sponsoring Group's Specialty   62

The Relationship between Cassius Clay and the Louisville
Sponsoring Group: A Summary   67

The Commercial Elements of Clay-Liston I   80

PART II   Nation of Islam

Main Bout Inc.: How Commerce Affects Culture   93

Carving Out Moral Authority: Ali's Race Man Phase   120

PART III Good People

Forty Years of Ali: The Making of an Icon   137

The Legacy of Ali's Exile and the Nation of Islam   139

The Prodigal Son Returns   148

King of the World: The Consequences of Monarchy   154

Death of a Salesman   160

Lonnie Ali: The Savior   164

Thomas Hauser: The Literary Rehabilitation of Ali's Legend   167

Olympic Torch: From Literature to Television   175

Beyond Moral Authority: The Apotheosis of Muhammad Ali   182

Culture Meets Commerce: The Muhammad Ali Center,
Naming Rights, and the Price of Moral Authority   186

The Backlash: Exploring Contradictory Meanings of Ali   194

Notes   199

Index   229

Acknowledgments

Muhammad Ali once said in response to the many people who had taken credit for his success, particularly his father, "Who made me is me." There is a part of me that feels similarly in regard to this book, but my wiser self prevails when I think about all of the people who have helped me to arrive at this point.

I would like to thank the Interlibrary Loan Staff at the University of Kansas's Watson Library for tirelessly helping me find the sources that constituted the brunt of the raw material that I shaped into this book. Sonoma State University provided me with a summer research grant that funded a trip to Louisville, and the National Endowment for the Humanities allowed me to participate in a summer seminar that sowed the seeds for this book. The excellent staff at the Filson Historical Society in Louisville also provided key support. Several people took time out of their busy schedules to be interviewed for this book, and I am grateful to them. They are Bob Moses, Julian Bond, John Lewis, Ernie Terrell, Gordon Davidson, Thomas Hauser, and Robert Lipsyte. Thanks also to Thomas Morrissey for sharing a great story about Ali's role in averting a riot in Chicago, and to the tag team of Chris Beckmann and Dave Tegeder for convincing me that the presidency of Dwight Eisenhower rather than that of Rutherford B. Hayes made for the best comparison to the Cassius Clay–Archie Moore bout.

Of the many people affiliated with Temple University Press who worked on this book, three deserve special mention. I thank series editor Amy Bass for her unflinching support of this project. I thank Gary Kramer for his marketing creativity. I thank Nanette Bendyna for her careful copy editing.

I have had many teachers in my life, and some of them stand out for their creativity, hard work, and willingness to devote attention to me when I needed it most. Francis F. Wilson Elementary School in Rockville Centre, New York, has been blessed with many excellent teachers, but I would like to mention three who changed my life. Judy Birnbaum, my first-grade teacher, met my tempestuous personality with kindness and always found ways to challenge my intellect when the curriculum would not suffice. Judy Lewis, my fourth-grade teacher, taught me how to respect learning environments without having to give up my individuality and increased my self-worth tremendously. Charlie Busk ran something called the Learning Center and always opened his door to me, teaching me new ways to learn when the classroom just wasn't working out.

There were two professors during my undergraduate career at Union College in Schenectady, New York, who deserve special thanks for the life-changing lessons they so selflessly bestowed upon me. During my junior year, I found myself forced to take a history seminar in order to meet my major requirements. The only available one was a course in race and historical memory, which at the time seemed more to me like a problem than an opportunity. Despite my closed-mindedness, it wound up being the single most influential intellectual experience I ever had, jump-starting what would become a paradigmatic shift in my awareness of the world. A. T. Miller, thanks for teaching me that the political is personal. I never fancied myself an actor but somehow wound up taking four theater courses with Barry Smith while at Union College. A maverick seemingly able to understand the core of someone's being in a matter of moments, Smith showed me a better way to live and act, how to care about the world beyond myself, and that the personal is political. I thank him for that.

I don't know anyone who has ever said that graduate school was a fun experience. It was an enormous challenge getting a doctorate in American Studies at the University of Kansas, but there was one man who shepherded me through the process, giving me untold support and guidance in myriad ways that are still becoming evident to me every day of my life. This man is David Katzman, my dissertation adviser and mentor. Nobody, with the exception of my parents, has taught me more in my lifetime. I cherish my relationship with him. His selfless dedication is the primary reason I was able to achieve my goal of becoming a college professor, and I will never forget or take for granted all that he has done for me and continues to do for me to this day. David, I love you, and I thank you for everything. Dedicating this book to you is the best way I know how to express my admiration and respect for the example you have set for the world.

Another mentor I've had over the years who deserves special mention is writer extraordinaire Carlo Rotella, who has guided me through my career with generosity and wisdom. I have asked him countless questions, and he has provided countless answers, almost all of them correct. He is one of those people whose graciousness matches his talent. Although a relatively young man, he is old school. I am proud to have benefited from his tutelage.

I must also thank the people who read this manuscript and gave helpful comments and criticisms that made the work better. My father, Joel Ezra, and my sister, Marni Goldberg, did what I would describe as righteous copy editing work on this manuscript. Others were equally generous. Gary Moser went through the draft with a fine-tooth comb and found typos and awkward phrasing that even my father and sister missed. Charles Farrell raised a number of key questions, some of which I could not answer, that made the book tighter, more accurate, and more honest. Kurt Noltimeier contributed several helpful observations and caught a factual error I had made. Sean Malone took time out of his busy senior year to read the manuscript, and his ideas were greatly appreciated.

I would also like to thank my sister Marni Goldberg and my longtime friend Clara Thompson for blazing trails that smoothed my path. Almost everywhere I've been, Marni has gotten there first, and I have benefited greatly from her experience. I've known and admired Clara for nearly thirty years, and her unique perspective has taught me a lot about how the world works.

Now, the most important acknowledgments of all—to my parents and my wife. My mother and father, Maxine and Joel Ezra, have been right by my side every step of the way, providing the kind of generosity and guidance that I only hope I am able to one day give to my children. Words cannot ever capture the gratitude that I feel. Ali may have said, "Who made me is me," but I know better. Those who made me are Maxine and Joel Ezra, and I will never forget that. They are with me every moment of my life, and without them things would have turned out for the worse. I think they know how much I appreciate all they have done for me, and are aware of my undying love for them, but now the world knows, too.

Finally—to my wife, my true love, Kim Lichtenecker. You uprooted your life to become a part of mine. You made sacrifices so that I could achieve my goals. You have endured all of the insanity that has come along with my writing this book. I appreciate your sticking with me, and I only hope I can one day match the kindness, patience, and understanding you have offered throughout this process. I have learned so much from you. I adore you and look forward to spending the rest of my life with you.

Introduction

Why Another Book about Muhammad Ali?

For almost thirty years, Muhammad Ali has held the Guinness World Record as the most written-about person in history. Although John Lennon once claimed that the Beatles had become bigger than Jesus, Ali is the one who really deserves such distinction, at least in a literary sense. Why, then, would anybody have the temerity to think that he could add something to this already overflowing mix? What makes this book worth reading? Though library shelves may buckle under the weight of the Muhammad Ali literature, there is surprisingly little written about key aspects of his life, such as his pre-championship boxing matches, the management of his career, and his current legacy. I concentrate on these three important themes.

Understanding Ali's transformation from a controversial to a revered figure takes knowledge of his entire life in the public spotlight. To comprehend this phenomenon, one must look at Ali's career holistically, from his appearance as an Olympic champion in 1960 to his present incarnation as an iconic international hero. The problem for readers is that so much is already written about Ali, and so much information is at hand, that one must wade through everything to find events and trends that have enough representative clout to get at key meanings without drowning in detail. Although this book spans nearly fifty years, from 1960 to the present, it is hardly a comprehensive account of Ali's life. Instead, *Muhammad Ali: The Making of an Icon* is a distillation of crucial paradigm shifts in how Ali has been perceived by various segments of the public.

At the heart of this book is a study of the relationships between Muhammad Ali's cultural image and its commercial manifestations. The central concept that I use to get at these meanings is what I call moral authority, a term I use throughout this book. My thesis has two parts. First, the most significant way people have made meaning of Muhammad Ali over the years has been through their understanding of him as a moral force, both positive and negative. Second, the crucial way many Americans have arrived at their moral understanding of Ali—his cultural image—has come from their perception of who is making money by associating with him—the commercial manifestations. This book traces the relationships between public perceptions of Ali, the economic entanglements surrounding his career, and the cultural meanings that have emerged from such connections.

The idea that Ali's moral authority is intimately bound to the economic consequences of his public life and career is a new one. The dominant interpretations of Ali usually tie his moral authority to his political or racial symbolism. The generic Ali Story explains his transformation from an oppositional to a mainstream figure as a product, among other things, of his stand against the Vietnam War or his being a member of the Nation of Islam. As these versions go, Ali's moral authority and cultural image crumbled as he took an unpopular political stand in challenging the Vietnam War and turned toward black nationalism by joining the racially separatist Nation of Islam. But over time, the public began to reject the war, Ali renounced the Nation's core tenets, and he became a morally authoritative cultural hero. There is much more to the process, however; namely, the economic aspects of these seemingly racial, political, and moral changes. My argument is that Ali's relationships to the Vietnam War and the Nation of Islam, as barometers of his public moral authority, were important not primarily because of their political and racial content, but because they represented who had economic ownership of him. What brought Ali infamy during the 1960s was not necessarily that he was a politically oppositional force, but that he threatened to generate wealth for the wrong people. The public's sense of Ali's moral authority has always been a function of its perception of who has economic ownership of him.

I have divided this book into three parts, each of them a response to the ever-evolving question "Who owns Cassius Clay/Muhammad Ali?" Part I, "Louisville Sponsoring Group," details Clay's rise as pugilism's biggest box-office draw under the management of the millionaire boys' club known as the Louisville Sponsoring Group. Part II, "Nation of Islam," explores the difficulties he encountered as his cultural image and commercial viability plummeted when the black nationalist religious sect took control of his career. Part

III, "Good People," is a study of the fighter's rebirth as an admired cultural icon representing corporate interests.

Before I begin the narrative, I want to make four points that will help readers understand my perspective and goals. First, you may have noticed that I treat the words *Ali Story* as a proper noun. The reason for the capitalization is that I consider history to be primarily art rather than science. The Ali Story, although certainly based upon fact, is a construct: part fact, part myth, part interpretation. Like all history, my version of the Ali Story leaves out far more than it includes. This book is neither definitive nor comprehensive. Instead, *Muhammad Ali: The Making of an Icon* is a plausible interpretation of how people have made meaning of Muhammad Ali's life and times. The book is truthful but is not the truth. Second, this study bucks the trend of most Ali literature that insists upon making moral judgments about him. I view Ali as neither great nor wicked, but rather a person with both strengths and weaknesses. This book is neither a sentimental celebration of Ali nor an iconoclastic attempt to knock him off his pedestal. What I have tried to do instead is explain how people have come to invest or divest moral authority in the rich and multifaceted cultural symbol known as Muhammad Ali. I will leave the fool's errand of identifying his true and essential nature to others. Third, my protagonist changed his name from Cassius Clay to Muhammad Ali shortly after winning the championship from Sonny Liston in February 1964. When I discuss the pre-championship man I refer to him as Cassius Clay. When I discuss the post-championship man I call him Muhammad Ali. Fourth, this book explores the economics behind the boxing matches of Cassius Clay/ Muhammad Ali. It is often difficult to figure out exactly how much money had been made and by whom. I relied on newspaper reports for the most part to do this work, but such reports are often conflicting and inconsistent. Whenever faced with contradictory information, I have done my best to honestly and accurately follow the money.

I

Louisville Sponsoring Group

Louisville's Favorite Son

The Professional Debut

You've heard the story. A youngster goes into a merchandise fair in his hometown Louisville and parks his new Schwinn bicycle against a nearby wall. When he returns, the bike is missing. The agitated boy finds the nearest policeman and vows to beat up the culprit. The cop offers to teach the lad how to box. The kid becomes one of history's greatest fighters.

Twelve-year-old Cassius Marcellus Clay Jr. took up boxing in 1954, several months after the Supreme Court issued the landmark *Brown v. Board of Education* verdict, which ordered public schools to be desegregated and thus jump-started the civil rights movement. Told and retold by virtually everyone who has chronicled his life as if it were one of its central events, the origin narrative pairing young Clay with policeman Joe Martin, his first amateur trainer, has become one of the seedbeds in which his cultural image has flourished. It is wrong to assume that the genesis of Clay's amateur boxing career would necessarily become a cornerstone of the Ali Story. Its rising to such prominence is an important clue as to how people have made meaning of the legendary figure now known as Muhammad Ali. It is the first tale of the Ali mythology.

Prior to 1960, when Clay won the Olympic gold medal and achieved national recognition, his fame was local. Once he was introduced to a wider audience, interest in Clay's backstory developed. The young fighter's relationship with Martin, and then his business agreement with the Louisville Sponsoring Group (LSG), became the focus of coverage meant to acquaint people with him. Both Martin and the members of the LSG were white. Martin was a cop, a source of great displeasure to Clay's father, who had had his share of minor run-ins with the police. The LSG was made up of old-moneyed aristocrats who used Clay's career for sport and investment. What is critical here is that the earliest presentations of Clay to a national audience featured his ties to Martin and the LSG, and observers made sense of Clay's essential character and standing within American culture based upon the racial composition of these alliances. Early in his public life, Clay's acceptability emanated from his ties to white people.

The civil rights movement was a key reason that these narratives, both in their packaging and consumption, became central to the tradition of telling Cassius Clay's story. By the time Clay made his professional debut, the civil rights movement was changing life in the South. The movement generated support—although its halcyon days of public approval wouldn't come until a few years later—but it also engendered bitterness and resentment. The passion it produced made the black freedom struggle the leading domestic story of the period, and it could be seen and heard all over the cultural landscape.

The sit-in movement and its spawning of the vanguard Student Nonviolent Coordinating Committee (SNCC) were the two most important civil rights developments of 1960, the year Clay first achieved national recognition. Led by teenagers and people in their twenties, particularly college students, the sit-in movement rippled through places that had held fast to segregation. It started in February in North Carolina, when four protesters sat down at the white-only lunch counter at a Woolworth's store in Greensboro. News of their courage spread like wildfire, and by the middle of the month, young people throughout the state, as well as in South Carolina, Tennessee, and Virginia, had taken similar stands.

Most impressive about the sit-in movement was how it marshaled participation by young black people who wanted to be a part of the civil rights struggle. Coordinated by SNCC, sit-ins gripped nearly the entire South by the end of the year, even in places like Alabama, Mississippi, and Louisiana. As these campaigns grew stronger, owners of segregated businesses began to feel the economic pinch. They had to worry about disruptions in day-to-day activity, negative press coverage, and threats of violence against protesters. Targeted storeowners met the dilemma of having to either resist the demonstrators and face legal action or capitulate to them and face the wrath of segregationists. That showdown after showdown was featured in the media only escalated tensions.

White resistance took on many forms, the most spectacular and deadly occurring when people assaulted demonstrators, often with the blessing of local law enforcement. There were those who formalized their resistance and joined organizations like the Ku Klux Klan, blew things up, burned crosses, and shot people. Many others simply showed up at local sit-ins to make life tough for protesters when the opportunity presented itself. Resistance turned sit-ins into mob scenes, and black participants were often at great peril. There were also those white people, constituting the largest group of resisters, who just stayed home and watched television, shaking their heads and questioning why blacks were so angry.

As an eighteen-year-old southern black arriving on the national scene, Cassius Clay faced pressure to understand and articulate himself in relation to the civil rights movement. By the time he turned professional, the black freedom struggle was firmly entrenched in the news and culture and influenced how people understood who he was. In calculating how his public persona would affect his professional life, particularly his ability to make money, Clay and his advisers had to estimate how best to respond to these developments. Such consideration went back to Clay's amateur days, when a Soviet reporter at the Olympics asked him about racial discrimination in the United States, and Clay scored points with his answer: "We got qualified people working on that problem, and I'm not worried about the outcome."[1]

Throughout his amateur and early professional days, Clay developed a knack for coming up with the right answers during troubled times. Some people found him obnoxious, but mostly he was recognized as a good kid. Even at his most controversial, Clay enjoyed a special relationship with his hometown of Louisville, Kentucky, one characterized by mildness. Clay had what could be described as a typical working-class upbringing. He grew up in the predominantly black West End of the city. Less than a quarter mile to the east of the family home lay tracks belonging to the Kentucky and Indiana Terminal Railroad Company. A little farther in the opposite direction ran U.S. Highway 60, which had recently been incorporated into the interstate system. He wasn't necessarily on the wrong side of the tracks, although he was close to them. But there was always something to eat, presents at Christmas, and decent clothes. His mother Odessa worked as a maid, and his father Cassius Sr. made a living as a sign painter and commercial artist. With both parents present, he grew up in a private house, and he finished high school. In comparison to that of other heavyweight champions, Clay's upbringing was comfortable.[2]

There is no doubt that Louisville endorsed Cassius Clay, as there is no doubt that he experienced frustrations growing up in a city that did not desegregate its public accommodations until the middle of 1963. Clay's father was outspoken about the foibles of white people, holding racism responsible for his inability to advance further as an artist and frequently lecturing young Cassius and his little brother Rudy about the pitfalls of growing up black in America. Although in reality it often typified the injustices of a segregated

racial order, in the early days Clay's story would be framed in ways that up-
lifted white Louisville and assuaged its doubts about the civil rights movement. Clay's standing as the city's major-league sports franchise and a municipal representative held fast throughout his first few years as a professional
fighter.[3]

Locals initially took notice of Clay because of his boxing ability. Winning
the gold medal in the light-heavyweight division at the 1960 Rome Olympics
made front-page headlines in his hometown. Clay had lived his entire life in
Louisville, and he was known to many city dwellers, especially sports fans,
prior to the Olympics. He had already won national titles at the two most
important amateur boxing tournaments, the Golden Gloves and the Amateur Athletic Union. But even before that, he was recognizable to many residents as the talkative, spindly kid who had been seen a bunch of times on
the local television program *Tomorrow's Champions*, for which he received
four dollars per appearance. Joe Martin's connections gave Clay access to
the show.[4]

Although he often trained as an amateur with a black man named Fred
Stoner, far more people know about Clay's relationship with Martin. There
are several explanations floating around about the entanglements between
the boxer and his two trainers. One is that Stoner kicked Clay out of his gym
for failing to listen to instruction. Another is that Clay hid his relationship
with Stoner so that Martin would not get upset and ban him from the television show. The most popular version of the story paints a friendly relationship between Clay and Martin while leaving Stoner out altogether. In the
early days of Clay's career, it was critical that people recognized Joe Martin as
his trainer because it produced the governing sentiment that the young man
had to be OK if his mentor was a white cop. This was no small thing in a
southern city during the tense early days of the civil rights movement.[5]

It wasn't what Clay said or didn't say that made him an accessible symbol,
but the way he appeared to approach life. He seemed simple enough: a
clean-living kid who avoided trouble and wanted to become a boxer for the
right reasons, namely to make money. The corniness of local coverage surrounding Clay's Olympic victory testifies to the wholesomeness of his image
at the time. A big story centered on the giant turkey dinner his parents
planned for his return to town, and articles played up, wrongfully, his quiet
and unassuming manner. "I'm the onliest champion in the world that's got
nothing jingling in his jeans," he said. "Just as soon as I can find me a manager with some money, I'm turning pro." Boxing one day would become Clay's
vehicle to historical status beyond what anyone could have expected, but at
the time of his turning professional, it was simply a means to become rich. It
was what he excelled at, and it potentially paid very well.[6]

There was also a sense that Clay didn't really have what it took to shake things up beyond the ring. His academic profile was limited. He withdrew from high school near the end of tenth grade after making horrendous grades but returned the following year. He never fulfilled Central High School's graduation requirements, but the principal insisted that he pass anyway. "One day our greatest claim to fame is going to be that we knew Cassius Clay or taught him," Atwood Wilson told faculty. "Do you think I'm going to be the principal of a school that Cassius Clay didn't finish? Why, in one night, he'll make more money than the principal and all you teachers make in a year." The matter was settled. Clay would be ranked 376th out of 391 graduating seniors, receiving not a diploma but the minimum recognition, a certificate of attendance, for his efforts. Anyone familiar with his story could have easily thought that he was kind of stupid, his quick-witted outbursts notwithstanding.[7]

The icing on Clay's cake of acceptability came in Rome, when he told the Soviet reporter who had grilled him on race relations, "To me the U.S.A. is the best country in the world, including yours." It wasn't just high white society that was pleased. The local black weekly, the *Louisville Defender*, called him "an ambassador of goodwill . . . with his stark honest interpretation of U.S. race conditions." Clay's whole package was one that all of Louisville could appreciate. Amid the torrent of nationwide racial unrest, Clay's friendship with a white cop and lack of scholarly ambition were sources of relief.[8]

Combined with the real achievement of winning a gold medal, these narratives led to an enormous reception for Clay, one that might normally be reserved for a visiting head of state, when he returned to Louisville from the Olympics. First there was the airport reception, as about 200 people, including politicians, cheerleaders, friends, and family packed Standiford Field to meet him, letting out a roar when the plane touched down. Once he got his bearings, there was a television interview alongside Mayor Bruce Hoblitzell, who congratulated the young man on behalf of the city. Then a fifty-car motorcade led Clay down Walnut Street, renamed Muhammad Ali Boulevard some two decades later, toward Central High School, where Louisville's leading citizens joined the rank and file for a celebration.[9]

At the assembly, Congressman Frank W. Burke told the audience that Clay "has brought honor not only to his school but to Louisville and all of Jefferson County. We have great pride in him for his accomplishments. This is only one of several steps that will lead him higher in his field of endeavor." Despite Clay's academic past, a procession of teachers, students, administrators, and principals lauded him. "You just can't beat success," said William Chilton, Louisville's assistant superintendent of schools. "I wish to honor Clay personally for his ability to get to the top. This is a great honor for the entire school system." Around town, people from all walks of life feted young Cassius. Neighborhood improvement groups presented him with certificates. He sang at the Kentucky State Fair. The *Louisville Defender* bought into the image, describing him as "intensely happy," "humble," "unassuming," and "awed." He was Louisville's favorite son, seemingly endorsed by the entire city.[10]

Then came Clay's professional debut, which from a promotional standpoint was different from any other in his career. Because it stands apart from the rest of his bouts, and requires an explanation all its own, there is an utter lack of coverage of the match in the Ali literature. This is disappointing because it is a critical indicator of the young fighter's cultural image at the start of his professional career and of the commercial benefits he stood to reap as a result of it. A slice of Americana wrapped in red, white, and blue bunting, Clay's professional send-off was marked by pageantry and righteousness. Few boxing matches enjoyed the authoritative backing that this one had.

Fueled by a peculiar combination of civic pride, ego, political opportunism, philanthropy, and integrationist belief, a coalition of Louisville elites, spearheaded by Mayor Hoblitzell and consisting of the city's business leaders, politicians, boxing insiders, and community groups, planned Clay's professional debut. Although he had yet to hire a managerial team, Clay had been adopted, if you will, by bigwigs who made it their business to make sure that his career got off on the right foot.

Mayor Hoblitzell and automobile dealer Wood Hannah, with the cooperation of Bill King, the city's leading boxing promoter, hatched a plan to start Clay's career right and "put a little money in the kid's pocket." It would take place October 26 at the State Fairgrounds, and proceeds would benefit the nearby Kosair Crippled Children Hospital. Clay would receive a $2,000 purse, which for a professional debut was outstanding. The *Louisville Courier-Journal* called it "very generous" and a "terrific payday," while the *Defender* referred to it as "quite a chunk of money for a fellow in his first fight."[11]

With the mayor and other powerful citizens behind this benefit for a children's hospital, Clay's debut seemed as much a good deed as a sporting event. It indicated that great spoils went along with being admired. Clay's moral authority, his being the right kind of symbol, stood to benefit him financially. His debut was an early indication of the linkages between cultural image and commercial viability. Nationwide civil rights unrest and a burgeoning student movement intensified the power of this connection.

Not just elites, but large segments of the community got involved. Local media treated the fight as a major event. Half-page newspaper ads, accompanied by a full-body picture of Clay in fighting togs, implored readers to "HELP A CRIPPLED CHILD WALK!" How could you not want to get involved in something like that? Kroger, the grocery chain with seventy-one area stores, sold tickets and provided free parking for the event. An executive for the franchise told *Louisville Courier-Journal* reporter Clarence Royalty that the corporation wanted "to give Clay an excellent start in his pro career and to do something for the Kosair Crippled Children Hospital." Through direct solicitations, business leaders canvassed their friends and sold 1,500 top-priced seats. Wilma Rudolph, three-time Olympic gold medalist and student at nearby Tennessee A&I, was brought in to generate interest. Governor Bert Combs waived the State Fairgrounds rental fee. Two weeks before the bout, *Courier-Journal* sports editor Earl Ruby reported that promoter Bill King had found an opponent "capable of letting Cassius know that he's no longer meeting amateurs." Tunney Hunsaker, the Kentucky native who had become the police chief of Fayetteville, West Virginia, would face the Olympic star in a six-rounder. Hunsaker, who received $250 plus $100 expense money, was experienced and game but little else. He sported a 13-9 record and had taken on contenders like Bert Whitehurst, who twice went the distance with the fearsome Sonny Liston; Tom McNeeley, who had lost a championship match to Floyd Patterson; and a young Chicago prospect named Ernie Terrell, who had beaten him by decision.[12]

About six weeks after returning from Rome, Clay debuted amid what Bob Weston of the *Louisville Times* called "probably the greatest fanfare ever drummed up for a six-round bout." The fight itself was one of both disappointment and promise, of criticism and praise, of failure and success. About 6,000 people paid over $12,000, an extremely impressive amount for such an event, to see a closed-circuit telecast of a welterweight bout from New York, a pair of four-round scraps involving inexperienced local pros, and the main event between Clay and Hunsaker. Such gate receipts portended a potentially huge windfall to whoever won the sweepstakes to manage the Olympic champion. Clay earned a unanimous-decision victory, becoming the first heavyweight champion in nearly thirty-five years (James J. Braddock) not to win by knockout in his first pro bout. Clay took the match decisively, closing Hunsaker's right eye and bloodying his nose. Even so, some fans booed near the end of the contest, and local sportswriters were not impressed. The charity arm of the show was also something of a letdown. Expenses ran higher than expected, the closed-circuit broadcast cost over $2,300 to air, and the Kosair Crippled Children Hospital received only $2,500 from the benefit. "This didn't come close to what we expected," said a spokesperson for the mayor's committee. Despite the imperfections, however, things basically went according to plan. Clay received a nice purse and got some experience. Louisville got a boxing show and a chance to celebrate a local hero. The Children Hospital got a check. Most important, Clay was firmly aligned with Louisville's elite. With their economic clout and perceived moral authority behind him, he was ready to move on to bigger and better things.[13]

Choosing Management

The Courtship of Cassius Clay

Boxing isn't easy. Most people think the physical grind is what makes it so tough, and at the sport's highest levels, this is true. What separates the greats from the almost greats is athletic ability, mental toughness, and most of all, the willingness to train oneself into peak condition, for it is in the gym where matches are won and lost. On championship fight night, the result often boils down to who can most effectively synthesize mind and body in the face of opposition determined to demolish that connection.

Most of the sport, however, takes place at a lower level. For a great many fighters, boxing is a second job, and excellence is impossible to achieve. Commonly boxers work a full shift and then go to the gym. Although many approach their craft honestly, there is only so much they can do. For them, the sport is not necessarily about reaching a physical peak, but about survival. Doing enough to get by and get paid is the primary concern. While they might dream about the improbable series of events that would lead them to a championship, these pugs realize that they are in league with the preponderance of journeymen who lack the resources to make boxing their sole vocation and therefore reach their potential as fighters.

Almost always, management makes the difference between those who are lucky enough to devote themselves full-time to the sport and those who aren't. Boxers who somehow convince backers that their career is worth financing have a reasonable chance to succeed. Those who don't will toil within a dangerous world that offers sporadic pay, no health insurance or benefits of any kind, and no representation. As in Hollywood, boxing is no place to manage oneself.

There are even those who have it all—adequate backing, physical excellence, and mental toughness—but are stifled by boxing's nearly unconquerable elements. Corruption penetrates every level of the sport. Sanctioning bodies, state athletic commissions, managers, trainers, judges, referees, and journalists all have been justifiably accused of imposing their will on destiny and of bending the truth in ways that deny the deserving and benefit the connected. Although success in boxing is sometimes based on merit, boxing has never been a meritocracy. Some of the greatest fighters in history, among them Sam Langford, Eddie Booker, and Charley Burley, never even got title shots.

This was the world that Cassius Clay entered as he began his professional career. Even if it were possible, it would not have been expedient for him to remain a ward of the city of Louisville for the rest of his career. Although he had powerful support, he needed boxing people who understood the sport's unique rules, pecking orders, and codes of conduct that neophytes couldn't hope to master. While Clay's professional debut amounted to a very nice gesture by Louisville's city fathers, his future lay elsewhere.

What, then, were the decisions facing Cassius Clay? Before anything, he needed to put together a team to manage, promote, and train him. Managers in boxing serve functions similar to those in other businesses. They arrange matches and training accommodations, coordinate travel, and do everything day to day that fighters don't. Some managers serve as surrogate parents to boxers, giving advice on everything from dating to nutrition, while others are only minimally involved in the lives of their clients. Managers generally receive about a third of what fighters earn, the maximum legal cut, plus any expense money they have put up or advanced. Promoters put together boxing matches. They arrange the site, pay all people involved, from boxers to referees, and organize the event. Their profits come from ticket sales, ancillaries, and advertising revenues. In an honest deal, the promoter and manager must be independent of each other, because the manager negotiates with the promoter to determine the boxer's purse. A trainer is the fighter's technical adviser. Good trainers teach boxers how to fight better. They generally receive either a salary or about 10 percent of a fighter's earnings.

Although selecting the best people is obviously the simplest formula for assembling such a team, there were other things that Clay had to consider. There were both professional and cultural ramifications accompanying his choices. Clay's decision had symbolic import, in addition to the real dollars that would be at stake. While commercial success in his boxing career depended mostly on the decisions made by his management team, he also had concerns about how the ticket-buying public perceived them. For example, Clay could choose well-connected mobsters to run his career, and they could be powerful within the sport, but at the same time that decision might open him up to public scrutiny that would ultimately cost him money.

Turning professional in 1960 meant that Clay had to consider the state of affairs specifically in boxing and generally in America. Against the backdrop of the massive corruption going on in the sport and the social upheaval brought on by the civil rights movement, it would be silly to think that these things did not have an effect on what would ultimately serve Clay as useful choices.

Clay had two matters to reckon with most seriously as he decided on a managerial team. First, there was the investigation into the underworld control of boxing by the U.S. Senate Antitrust and Monopoly Subcommittee, known as the Kefauver Commission. This investigation began that year and led to the conviction of several gangsters who had previously held the sport in a stranglehold. Second to consider was the burgeoning black freedom struggle, which had rapidly taken hold of the South as students throughout the region began to sit in at segregated public establishments. Any choices that Clay made would be seen by many as symbolic responses to these events. Clay had three options. He could take the most tried-and-true route and employ whites to lead his career, which would serve several key purposes. This option would send an integrationist message to the public, demonstrating that Clay was willing to work with whites, and that although he was a young, black, college-age southerner, he was no militant. Such a choice would be consistent with the patriotic narratives that surrounded his Olympic victory and fueled his professional debut. Finding white managers with legitimate credentials would also free him of any suspicion of having underworld ties. Leading heavyweights like Floyd Patterson, who was managed by anti-mob crusader Cus D'Amato, took this route. And even though Patterson had openly backed the civil rights movement while champion, his mild-mannered persona and willingness to work with whites freed him from much of the public acrimony that those involved with the black freedom struggle were beginning to face.

Clay could also employ a black management team, an option that might send a different kind of message. Although black nationalism was barely on white America's radar screen at the time, and although choosing black managers almost certainly would not be associated with the separatism that Clay would espouse once a member of the Nation of Islam, such a choice was risky. Two of the greatest black fighters, Ray Robinson and Joe Louis, who were cultural heroes at large, not just to blacks, had taken this route. Being managed by blacks wouldn't necessarily brand Clay as a militant but could arouse suspicion among those already threatened by the escalating civil rights movement.

Finally, Clay could have gangsters manage him, as Sonny Liston, the other leading heavyweight of the era, had done. Although the Kefauver Commission had rocked mob control of the sport, organized crime's grip still lingered, and many of boxing's major players still had underworld ties. If Clay wanted to take the fast track to success, such an agreement might have been his best bet. Of course, it also potentially opened him up to the kind of scrutiny that nearly destroyed Liston's career.

Whatever Clay's decision, he had to realize that there was a strong relationship between his choice of management, his cultural image, and his ability to make money. It was not enough to be the best boxer. Clay had to win a degree of public acceptance if he was to become champion and get rich.

Cassius Clay was a bit overwhelmed by planning a professional boxing career. "I'm turning pro," he said shortly after his Olympic victory, "but I don't know exactly how. I want a good contract with a good manager." What he needed to do was assemble a team to coordinate his search. "First thing I do when I get home is to see a lawyer to plan pro connections," he told a local reporter. "I need an old head to help this 18-year-old boy avoid mistakes."[14]

Throughout this process, Clay toed a line that anticipated the seismic shifts in race relations that would occur over the next two decades. He knew that whites controlled the big money in professional boxing, as they did in American life. But he also knew that he was black, and any attempt to transcend that reality would eventually come crashing down. Integration was always a shaky proposition, more a function of the goodwill of a powerful few than an indication of radical changes in the country's fiber. Abandoning blacks on the road to the big-time would ultimately lead to a dead end. Clay needed whites to jump-start his career, but he was never willing to yield full control of it to them.

From the beginning, although he benefited from associations with powerful whites, Clay insisted upon employing blacks in key positions whenever possible. As his career progressed, the proportion of black faces to white ones in his camp increased, especially during his years with the Nation of Islam, but even at the start blacks were Clay's most trusted guides. It would have been counter-productive for him publicly to emphasize this, and the press usually ignored Clay's black advisers to profile his business relationships with high-society whites, but the young fighter's preference for black leadership was clear.

As a first step, Clay hired Alberta Jones as his lawyer and the sole negotiator of his first professional contract. The formidable Jones was only twenty-seven years old, a Howard University graduate who became the first black woman admitted to the Kentucky Bar Association and the first woman in the state to become an assistant district attorney. An unabashed community servant, prior to her 1965 murder (apparently a random act of violence), Jones had formed the Independent Voters Association, which promoted voter registration, and the James "Bucky" Welch Rehabilitation Fund to aid an eight-year-old boy who had lost his hands trying to rescue a dog stuck under a train. After finishing law school, Jones remained a resident of Louisville's West End and was determined to use her standing to uplift the race. She was uniquely suited to drive the kind of bargain that would secure Clay's future.[15]

Although the workings of his professional debut seemed to be white-dominated, both Clay's manager and trainer of record for the Hunsaker fight were black. We should not make too much of this. Fulfilling these slots was designed to be temporary, and it would be wrong to project any particular symbolism on Clay's decision to employ them. However, selecting George King as his manager and Fred Stoner as his trainer emphasized the fact that Clay came from a black world. The people he knew and trusted growing up in segregated Louisville were black. For all of the literature and oral history devoted to reminding us that Clay's introduction to boxing came from white policeman Joe Martin, we must realize that their relationship was aberrant rather than indicative of any particular spirit of brotherhood in the Falls City.[16]

Louisville's small cadre of sportswriters, all of whom knew Clay personally, speculated about who would become his manager and trainer. It seemed that the inside track belonged to William G. "Billy" Reynolds, the millionaire vice-president of the Reynolds Metal Company who had aligned himself with Joe Martin to bag the prized boxing prodigy. Reynolds hoped to use Martin's six-year relationship with Clay as an *entre nous* that would convince the kid that he was the right manager. In exchange, Martin would become trainer.

Although Clay could not sign a contract if he was to maintain his amateur status and compete in the Olympics, Reynolds and Martin began their campaign to woo him during the spring of 1960. The trick was to pay Clay for services unrelated to boxing. Clay had made no bones about his desire to live the good life, and Reynolds tried to use that to his advantage. It started when Martin relayed to Clay a job offer on the majestic Reynolds estate in Bridgeton, a Louisville suburb. "No prizefighter's got a manager like Reynolds," explained Martin. "He'll greet you like his own son." Muhammad Ali's 1975 autobiography, *The Greatest: My Own Story*, a source that has been debunked by critics as more concerned with racial allegory than factual representation, devotes significant space to the episode. Clay took the offer, and although he rarely saw his benefactor, he got the idea that the Reynolds Wrap heir was not his kind of people. The work wasn't anything out of the ordinary: he dusted; he mopped; he took out trash; he worked in the yard; he swept porches. Nothing too hard, nothing too rewarding. When lunchtime came, Clay was asked to eat on the porch instead of in the kitchen. He was accused of theft; he was insulted. None of this came directly from Reynolds, of course, but that didn't really matter. Clay found the experience reprehensible, and if the autobiography is to be believed, it all but killed Reynolds's chances.[17]

Clay, however, was pragmatic. One look at the Reynolds estate indicated that the industrialist was wealthy. Clay was not just going to break off the courtship without first tasting the high life his suitor was promising. And it also wouldn't hurt to hear a formal offer. Clay had nothing to lose by stringing Reynolds along, and when his plane landed in New York following his post-Olympic transcontinental flight, he took advantage of the opportunity to have as big of a time as he ever had, all courtesy of his would-be benefactor. There was a steak dinner (Clay had seconds), a visit to Jack Dempsey's restaurant for the famous cheesecake, a trip to Birdland for some jazz, a shopping spree at Tiffany's (Clay purchased watches for his family), and a suite at the Waldorf-Astoria (next door to the Prince of Wales). Clay could now say that he knew how the other half lived.[18]

And then there was the official offer: ten years guaranteed at a minimum of $3,600 annually, plus a $10,000 signing bonus. If Clay's income eclipsed the original $300 monthly wage, he would split the excess with Reynolds. As part of the package, Martin would become his trainer. If what happened at the estate was not a deal-breaker, then this was. Martin was a rank amateur, like the fighters he trained. No serious professional could make it under his tutelage. The possibility also upset Cassius Clay Sr., who bristled at the idea of a formal association between his son and the white policeman. But Reynolds was obligated to Martin for the introduction to Clay. Although the fighter took all of the gifts, he did not take the offer. Like anyone milking a sugar daddy, he didn't make an outright rejection. Instead, he said he would think about it, since there were several other interested managers, including Cus D'Amato. There was also talk of a syndicate of local businessmen organizing themselves to make an offer. Colleges, anxious to bolster their boxing teams, then an important part of intercollegiate athletics, also made scholarships available.[19]

Throughout September, Louisville's sports pages speculated over Clay's decision. *Louisville Times* sports editor Dean Eagle offered unsolicited advice about what Clay should do, and in retrospect it seems that he was on Reynolds's payroll. One Eagle piece suggested that Clay would probably sign with the aluminum tycoon, "who has an unselfish interest in seeing the Louisville boxer get ahead." Another asserted, "Well, if it were me I would run to the nearest phone and call Reynolds. I'd be afraid he would change his mind."

Eagle also downgraded the competition: "In addition, a syndicate is interested in buying your contract. You can be another General Darby with a Go-For-Broke corporation behind you. Think of 50 owners stampeding the ring to collect after your first fight!" Martin remained close to Clay, accompanying him to the state capitol for a visit with Governor Combs.[20]

By the end of the month, however, it was all over for Reynolds. Alberta Jones delivered without explanation a formal rejection of his offer. Larry Boeck, the *Louisville Courier-Journal* sportswriter closest of all local scribes to Clay, reported that "Reynolds recently bowed out because, he said, he wouldn't have the time to devote to managing Clay's affairs as they should be administered," but it was really a face-saving courtesy. Despite the lavish treatment he had been afforded, Clay never forgot his experience at the Reynolds estate. In his autobiography, he vented that the man being so nice to him "didn't seem to be the real Mr. Reynolds. He seemed more real when I sat on his porch eating with the dogs." Although it didn't make too many waves at the time, the fighter recalled in his autobiography that years later, when Cassius Clay became Muhammad Ali and white Louisville was wondering what went wrong, an editorial in a local paper had pointed to this moment as the beginning of the end:

> Why would any normal Kentucky boy who wanted to get ahead in boxing turn down a millionaire benefactor with the generosity, affluence, and connections of William Reynolds? When he turned down Reynolds we should have realized how twisted and misguided was Black Cassius, this same young man we Kentuckians once loved and respected so much. This was the turning point.[21]

With Reynolds out of the picture, Alberta Jones began to ponder seriously the offer made by the syndicate of ten Kentucky blue bloods, which would come to be known as the Louisville Sponsoring Group. In their politics and social standing, as well as the offer they made, the members of the organization were similar to Reynolds. They were old-moneyed, leading citizens of Louisville whose wealth came from Kentucky's signature industries: bourbon, tobacco, horse racing, and newspaper publishing. Of the ten, seven were millionaires and three stood to inherit family fortunes worth millions. The eleventh man, Bill Faversham, was also impressive. An athletic, Harvard-educated former actor whose father was a legendary Broadway performer and Hollywood matinee idol, Faversham was one of the city's most successful investment counselors, which put him into contact with many of Louisville's richest residents and made him the ideal LSG point man. He would act as its managing partner and spokesperson. The others generally remained in the background, preferring to let their investment work for them.[22]

The terms of the contract guaranteed Clay at least $18,000, and would bring much more if he turned out to be a top contender or champion. In exchange, the Louisville Sponsoring Group gained six years of management rights. After that, Clay could renew, renegotiate, or terminate the contract. Clay received a $10,000 signing bonus up front, and the first two years of the deal were guaranteed at $4,000 each. Afterward, the syndicate would decide on a yearly basis whether they wanted to renew the contract. If they did, Clay's minimum annual salary would rise to $6,000. Against these guarantees, over the first four years Clay and his backers would split his gate receipts evenly. Afterward, Clay's take would increase to 60 percent. If Clay's portion of the earnings eclipsed his guaranteed salary, he would earn that much more. One of the unique advantages of the contract was that the LSG agreed to pay all of Clay's expenses out of their share, a hugely important clause virtually guaranteeing that his backers would not rip him off through phony expense reports, a common tactic employed by unscrupulous managers and promoters. Clay would therefore pocket 50 percent of his gross earnings, a significantly larger portion than most fighters took home. Finally, although Clay didn't like it, the agreement stipulated that 15 percent of his share would go into a trust fund that he could not touch until January 17, 1977, his thirty-fifth birthday. Based on Alberta Jones's recommendation, in the law offices of Lieutenant Governor Wilson Wyatt, flanked by his parents and LSG members, Clay signed the contract on October 26, 1960. Although the signing took place three days before the Hunsaker fight, it was contingent on the LSG's agreement not to interfere with that promotion or take a share of Clay's earnings from it. Afterward, he was all theirs.[23]

With the Kefauver Commission and the civil rights movement making headlines, Clay couldn't have made a better choice. The arrangement shielded him from the gangsters, unscrupulous handlers, and racial animosity that plagued many fighters. Clay's alignment with a powerful conglomerate of socially prominent figures safeguarded him from mobsters, who knew they would risk exposure and punishment if they trifled with the Louisville Sponsoring Group. Professionally, the syndicate had enough money to hire first-rate trainers, sparring partners, and medical providers. Clay could devote himself full-time to boxing without having to earn money on the side. He would eat properly. He would not be hustled into dangerous matches prematurely. Since the syndicate did not rely on Clay's income for their own wealth, there was little incentive for them to steal from him. They would also help him avoid the income tax problems that made Joe Louis's post-retirement years a living nightmare. Additionally, Clay's association with this outstanding bunch lent itself to the perception that he was a good kid, a guy who would not upset power balances or social norms, despite his brash and eccentric personality. It would also insulate him from criticism by the press. An attack on Clay, in effect, was an attack on the Louisville Sponsoring Group. During a sensitive time in which both boxing and race relations were in precarious states, Clay's partnership with the LSG protected him without compromising his chances for success.

The syndicate was well aware of these circumstances, and made early efforts to portray itself as a moral force that existed primarily to help a nice local kid. Its initial press statement stressed this: "Each of the 10 members of the group has admiration for Cassius Clay as a fine young man and confidence in his ability as a boxer. The principal purpose of the group is to provide hometown support for Cassius' professional career and to aid him in realizing the maximum benefits from his efforts." Lingering in the background were questions about Clay's true nature, but even then the Sponsoring Group had answers. "Cassius is a really dedicated boy," said Faversham. "His garrulity is a little rich at times, but we don't discourage him. He has decided to create an image and he works on it."[24]

The press liked it. From the beginning of Clay's career, writers portrayed the LSG as the anchor that would keep him moored in steady waters. "Like the PTA," wrote John Underwood of the *Miami Herald*, "Clay is a community project in Louisville. He is pared up like a pumpkin pie, financed by 10 citizens of the solid, solvent type." Underwood also framed the Louisville Sponsoring Group as a band of white knights riding in search of good through the dark trade of professional prizefighting: "Next to boxing's everyday virtues of avarice and greed, undercover management, and Senatorial heat waves, the deal for Clay is as unique as a coconut palm in a snow bank." Even Dean Eagle had to admit that Clay "couldn't have found ten men with higher aims for his future." The Sponsoring Group made as few waves as possible. Members neither sought nor avoided publicity. When Faversham talked to the press, he discussed future matches and contract details, not race and politics. The LSG's influence on Clay's public persona was like that of a steady rhythm section on the vocals of a charismatic lead singer.[25]

Besides Faversham, the other members of the syndicate rarely spoke to the press, but when they did, it was often to cultivate their image as a bunch of do-gooders, which was advantageous to them and their fighter. The first national story on the Louisville Sponsoring Group, published in *Sports Illustrated* in March 1963, featured the following responses by members who were asked why they got involved with Clay in the first place:

"All we want to do is see that Cassius winds up rich."

"One motive is to do something for boxing at a time the sport needs help. And I think, in our own little way, we've done just that."

"We think we can keep him out of the financial trouble Joe Louis got
into—which made me sick to see."

Not surprisingly, author Huston Horn invested the organization with significant moral authority. Of course, the members were interested in profit,
but they were even more interested in doing the right thing. "Innocent of
prizefighting's bad old ways," as they were described, "these gentlemen hope
by their example to put an end to the exploiting of boxers. They expect Clay
to get rich—and to get a little bit richer themselves." The article revealed the
Louisville Sponsoring Group's perfect understanding of how cultural narratives swayed commercial forces.[26]

Perhaps the greatest evidence of the LSG's savvy in this regard, as well as
of its fair treatment of Clay, is the way the organization's historical legacy has
held up over the past fifty years. Although there has been some dissent about
this point by the fighter himself in his autobiography, Clay's biographers have
unanimously portrayed the Louisville Sponsoring Group as solid citizens who
did nothing but good for their young charge. Thomas Hauser's *Muhammad
Ali: His Life and Times*, the 1991 book that made the *New York Times* best-
seller list and became the foundation for the fighter's reemergence during that
decade as a heroic icon, described the contract as being "fair and generous for
its time." British journalist John Cottrell wrote in 1967, "Clay the unproven
professional was entirely happy to put himself in the hands of these eleven
fairy godfathers, and there was an atmosphere of complete trust." Claude
Lewis, one of Clay's earliest biographers, heaped praise on the syndicate in
his 1965 book:

> There are eleven sponsors in the group, and at a time when the boxing
> world is beclouded by underworld dickering, misappropriated funds,
> government investigation, and a general sorrowful malaise, they pres-
> ent an uplifting sight. . . . Not only does their private wealth insure
> Clay that he will never end up broke through any fault of theirs, but
> they surround him with a substantial moral and ethical environment,
> a rare commodity in boxing these days.

In his autobiography, which was critical of most things white, Ali pointed out,
"Every newspaper account I read described [the Sponsoring Group] in the
holiest light, with ten white angels tending charity in the jungle. Not as the
good, hard common-sense business deal it was." Although he would go on to
describe them, as one author put it, "as a bloody-minded band of white businessmen who regarded their charge as little more than a property to exploit, a
Churchill Downs thoroughbred with strong legs and good teeth," these

charges were overwhelmed by the overall portrait, then and now, of the Louisville Sponsoring Group as a team of beneficent guiding lights that wanted
only the best for their young charge. In the early years, the LSG influenced
public perception of Clay. The syndicate moved people to see him through a
prism of respectability, which was no small distinction for a brash young
black man participating in a sport whose reputation was nearly bankrupt at a
time of great racial upheaval. There is nothing in this book to challenge the
historical assessment of the Louisville Sponsoring Group as a positive force.
It explores the organization's effect on Clay's career, namely how it created
cultural meanings that held economic benefits for him, and ultimately reinforces the portrait of the LSG as beneficial to Clay, despite the paternalistic
stances it sometimes took toward the fighter.[27]

Although *noblesse oblige* was the organization's major motivation, we must
also examine what its members got out of the deal. In an age when southern
states did not have major-league professional sports franchises, the Louisville
Sponsoring Group could use Clay to bring civic pride and national attention
to the city. The more he fought there, the more recognition for Louisville.
Perhaps it would even host a world heavyweight title match one day. If this
happened, it would bring LSG members a kind of prestige that money itself
could not. As shown by Clay's debut, the city's residents wanted to embrace
him. That sentiment grew stronger as Clay's nascent career advanced. In November 1960, for example, The Yearlings Club, a community organization,
honored him with a testimonial dinner for "the fame he has brought to our
city, state, and nation. We consider it an honor to applaud this young man."[28]

There was also the potential windfall that came with investing in a future
world heavyweight champion. Although they were quiet about this, the LSG
members wanted to make money from the arrangement with Clay. All of the
investors, with the exception of Faversham, who paid half, had anted $2,800
each to give the group a nearly $30,000 stake from which to launch Clay's
career. The group was operating in the black by 1963, and Clay hadn't even
fought for the title. Just in case anything went wrong, the LSG took out a
$30,000 life insurance policy and a $300,000 accident policy on the boxer.
Big money was on the line, and the Sponsoring Group knew it. The most honest assessment of it all came from one anonymous investor who admitted the
following:

> Let me give you the official line. We are behind Cassius Clay to
> improve the breed of boxing, to do something nice for a deserving,
> well-behaved Louisville boy and, finally, to save him from the jaws of
> the hoodlum jackals. I think it's 50% true but also 50% hokum. What
> I want to do, like a few others, is to make a bundle of money. Why, do

you know a Clay-Liston [heavyweight title] fight might gross a winner's share of $3 million? Split that up and it comes out to $1.5 million for Cassius and $1.5 million for the syndicate. Best of all, it comes out to $150,000 for me.[29]

With management secured, Clay had to find a trainer. Selecting one meant finding not only the right person, but also the right city. Trainers, then and now, work out of gyms where their stable of fighters is housed. Only the greatest boxers, which Clay wasn't yet, have the power to lure trainers away from these home bases. After all, trainers have to work with a bunch of fighters on a daily basis. Their livelihood depends on being accessible to those fighters. Leaving them takes money out of their pockets. Therefore, if a fighter wanted to work with someone, he would come to the trainer. But that wasn't all. Because choosing a trainer tied a fighter to a particular location, it also limited his choices among promoters. In those days, promoters stuck to their regions and fiercely protected their turf through legal and illegal means. Promoters nationwide tended to honor these arrangements. Those who tried to buck them faced an army of resistance. Therefore, choosing a trainer was tantamount to choosing a promoter. With this in mind, the Louisville Sponsoring Group had to base Clay in a city that had both a top-level trainer and a promoter with an honest reputation.

So who to choose? Clay and his handlers all agreed that Fred Stoner was not a top trainer. He would have to be replaced for Clay to have a chance to win a title. While the organization mulled over its options, Archie Moore cabled the group that he was interested in training Clay. This was something. Moore was a legendary figure in the sport, having boxed professionally for over twenty-five years. He had more than 200 fights, many of them against the sport's best, and had been the reigning light-heavyweight champion of the world for the past seven years. Still awaiting his second professional bout, Clay boarded a train in mid-November to join Moore at his training facility outside San Diego. Although both fighters admired each other, their business partnership quickly went sour. Moore made fighters earn their keep by doing household chores. Clay refused, Moore sent him home, and that was that.[30]

With Moore out of the picture, the LSG turned to one of the hottest trainers in the game, Miami-based Angelo Dundee. Dundee was someone who beat you by making you think that you were smarter than he was. Listening to him speak in interviews, even today, he seems almost simple. By 1960, Dundee had built himself a stable of top-notch fighters, including featherweight Sugar Ramos, welterweight Luis Rodriguez, and light-heavyweight Willie Pastrano. All three would win world championships in 1963. In addition to his reputation for training the best, the LSG was impressed by

Dundee's clean reputation, no small thing at the time. "Angelo undoubtedly is one of the best seconds in the game. He knows boxing, is clean of character and sound," Bill Faversham told the press. Another backer added, "Dundee is the best trainer and free-wheeling psychologist in boxing and he's so clean he's practically antiseptic."[31]

The catch was that Miami's leading promoter was Chris Dundee, Angelo's brother. On the surface, this seemed terrific for Clay and the Louisville Sponsoring Group. Chris Dundee was a boxing insider who would be able to make big matches. He was also based out of the same gym as Angelo, and they worked together closely. At the same time, however, the LSG had to make sure that there would be no funny business between the two brothers. Also, about two weeks before Clay was scheduled to report to Miami, the Kefauver Commission accused Chris Dundee of having underworld ties.

The Kefauver Commission came about as a result of a federal investigation in early 1959 that exposed the sport's leading promotional body, the International Boxing Club (IBC), as a racket. The IBC had promoted almost all of the sport's title fights over the previous decade, but it had been operating as a monopoly, and it used criminal tactics to maintain its grip on the sport. Although a federal court had ordered the organization dissolved, its leading operators merely shuffled things around in an attempt to maintain power. As a result, in September 1960, around the same time Clay was turning professional, Senator Estes Kefauver, chair of the U.S. Senate Antitrust and Monopoly Subcommittee, called together a congressional panel to investigate the role of organized crime in professional boxing. Top IBC officials were subpoenaed in December, and they revealed that mobsters Frankie Carbo and Blinky Palermo were still at the head of a criminal network controlling boxing through the IBC. They used strong-arm tactics, death threats, payoffs and bribes, fixed fights, and rigged ratings to impose their will on the sport and its participants.[32]

Chris Dundee had worked for the IBC in New York during the 1950s, and circumstantial evidence indicated that he did not shed his ties to the organization when he moved to Miami. Dundee's shady connections came under scrutiny when the Kefauver Commission turned its attention to Sonny Liston. Liston was far and away the best heavyweight, but Cus D'Amato, manager of champion Floyd Patterson, who was one of the few top fighters not under the control of the IBC during the 1950s, refused to give him a title shot for fear of the crown slipping into underworld hands (and of his fighter getting demolished by the more talented Liston). Liston's career was controlled by Carbo and Palermo, and from 1958 to 1961, six of his fights took place in Miami under the promotional auspices of Chris Dundee. Odds were that Dundee's mob ties gave him the inside track on these bouts. After he was identified by the Kefauver Commission as a possible mob associate, Dundee downplayed it. "Me and Frankie Carbo?" he asked, "I never been that big." Although he claimed they never worked together, Dundee admitted, "I know him, sure, ever since I was promoting in New York." Although Dundee was never convicted of any wrongdoing, told the press that he fully endorsed the Kefauver Commission, and expressed his hopes that the commission would get to the bottom of any corruption in the sport, his reputation was obviously sullied. The Louisville Sponsoring Group withheld comment on the situation, but its members had to have been concerned.[33]

Having Chris Dundee on board became further problematic once Clay began training in Miami on December 19, 1960. Cus D'Amato wanted Floyd Patterson to fight former champion Ingemar Johansson in the Magic City since he felt that having the match there would produce an excellent gate. However, because of D'Amato's feud with the IBC, he refused to work with Chris Dundee. The problem was that Dundee had an exclusive contract to promote boxing shows at Convention Hall, the area's only venue that would make such a bout financially worthwhile. With a stalemate brewing, Dundee agreed to step aside so that the city would not lose a match that would go on to gross over $3 million. Racetrack and minor-league sports franchise owner Bill MacDonald replaced him as promoter. Although Dundee's willingness to get out of the way won praise from sportswriters, it further clouded his reputation as someone with mob connections. LSG members believed that their association with Chris Dundee was an obstacle to their maintaining the air of respectability surrounding Clay's career.[34]

Years later, Louisville Sponsoring Group attorney Gordon Davidson acknowledged that the group was concerned about its partnership with the Dundees, particularly Chris:

> I'm sure the Dundees, especially Chris, had some dubious acquaintances in those days, but when we went looking for a trainer we knew there was no one that was simon-pure. That was boxing in those days. Compared to everyone else, Angelo Dundee was as good as it gets.

The LSG members badly wanted Angelo Dundee as Clay's trainer, but they also knew that they would have to terminate their alliance with his brother if they were to achieve what they wanted from Clay's career. In the short term, it would be no problem, since Chris Dundee was never convicted of any wrongdoing. Long term, however, the LSG looked for a way to sever its ties. It hired Angelo Dundee at a starting monthly salary of $500 (he turned down a 10 percent share of Clay's earnings for the guaranteed salary, although he would eventually negotiate a percentage deal in 1965) and made him Clay's chief of boxing operations. Everything had to go through Faversham and the LSG, but Dundee would make most of the matchmaking and training decisions. For the time being, Chris Dundee would handle the promotional end of things, and from December 1960 to February 1961, Clay would fight four times in Miami under his banner. To prevent any conflict of interest between the Dundee brothers, the LSG arranged for Chris's pay to come directly from gate receipts. With everything in place, Clay was ready to begin his professional career. Meanwhile, the LSG had to think about how to find a new promoter.[35]

The Early Bouts

1961–1962

S o eager was Cassius Clay to train in Miami that he started on December 19, 1960, instead of waiting out the holidays. He had reason to be confident. Chris Dundee had promotional rights to the city's most meaningful venues, and was a boxing insider who could arrange big fights. Angelo Dundee was a shrewd trainer and matchmaker. The LSG had the money to pay for first-class handling. Clay's professional debut had proven that with the right marketing, the fighter would sell a lot of tickets if his ability held up.

Clay's first three bouts under the Louisville Sponsoring Group and Angelo Dundee were knockouts of weak opposition. It is difficult to gauge Clay's overall effect on the gate receipts because he was not the headliner. He fought as the feature supporting attraction, involved in the last preliminary before the main event. His second professional victory, on December 27, came on the undercard of the Jesse Bowdry–Willie Pastrano match, which attracted 3,000 fans. Clay's fourth win, in January 1961, was the main support for a bout between Bowdry and Harold Johnson, which was for the National Boxing Association (NBA) light-heavyweight championship that the organization had stripped from Archie Moore for violating its mandate to defend the crown more frequently. Four thousand spectators paid $21,000 to see it.[36]

Clay was scheduled to face local heavyweight Willie Gulat, a former professional basketball player with a 12-4-1 record. Angelo Dundee assured sportswriters that it would be a tough fight, and they agreed, but he and his brother knew better. Their savvy backfired here, however, because Gulat, knowing that he was a dead duck, failed to show up. At the eleventh hour,

Chris Dundee convinced Jim Robinson, a light-heavyweight who had been knocked out in his only professional bout and had come to the arena merely as a spectator, to face the prospect who outweighed him by sixteen pounds. The massacre lasted 94 seconds. "If Promoter Chris Dundee had canvassed the women in his audience," said the *Miami News*, "he couldn't have found an easier opponent for Clay."[37]

It is easy to understand why Gulat chickened out. The day before the scheduled match, Clay had sparred with Ingemar Johansson, who was in town to begin training for his rubber match with Floyd Patterson. Fifteen hundred people, each paying a dollar, watched a two-round session in which Clay dominated Johansson. Those who had seen Clay working daily with the great fighter Harold Johnson, who defeated Bowdry for the NBA title, were not surprised. Johnson's manager Pat Olivieri swore "on my word of honor" that Clay "is the best prospect I have ever seen. I have never seen a fighter that big who was that fast." Sensing the promotional opportunity, Clay took center stage afterward, telling the press, "If you stay away from Ingemar's right, he will fan you all night," and saying that it was fun to go "dancin' with Johansson." It was rare for somebody with only three bouts to spar with the likes of Johansson, one of boxing's most recognizable fighters, and even rarer for the youngster to get the better of the action. Most important, perhaps, it seemed that Clay was considered to be on the same promotional level as Johansson. As Dean Eagle put it, "Suddenly, Miami has become the boxing capital of the world and Clay is in the thick of things."[38]

Clay's next bout, in February against Donnie Fleeman, looked to be a tough eight rounder. Fleeman was 35-11-1. He was durable, having never been knocked down despite facing decent competition. Newspapers mistakenly listed Fleeman as the 2–1 favorite, but Clay was, in fact, the betting choice. As he would do before almost all of his protégé's bouts, Angelo Dundee indicated that this would be the strictest test of Clay's career. And as it almost always did, the press took him at his word and built up the fight accordingly. Although Fleeman talked big beforehand, he got whipped so badly that he retired from the sport immediately afterward. Straight-ahead guys like the slow Texan, who rarely took a step backwards or laterally, were made to order for Clay. That the press didn't emphasize this testifies to Dundee's ability to work the media, convincing fans that he was making competitive matches, thus drawing maximum gate receipts and praise for Clay. It looked as if it would be a good bout, and 2,100 fans attended Clay's first main event, paying about $3,600 for the privilege. Clay hurt his hand, meaning that he could not fight on the undercard of the Patterson-Johansson bout the following month. But he had proven here that he could be a main-event fighter capable of drawing fans. With the Chris Dundee situation unresolved, the LSG decided that it would be prudent to bring Clay home, where he had generated a huge crowd for his debut a few months back.[39]

Four out of Clay's next five bouts, through the end of 1961, were held in Louisville. All were main events; two were nationally televised. They reflected Dundee's strengths as a de facto manager, the Louisville Sponsoring Group's wise attitude toward matchmaking and promotion, and Clay's ability to anchor a successful event. He fought Lamar Clark in April. Clark's record was a gaudy 47-2-1, but the 47 wins were against unranked fighters—"nobodies" in boxing lingo—and the two losses were knockouts spread over his last three bouts. Clark was the plodding type that Clay owned and a wild swinger to boot. He became the second fighter in a row to retire following a beating by Clay. In two rounds, his nose had been broken and he had been decked three times. The inevitable result notwithstanding, the *Louisville Courier-Journal* had called Clark "a possibly dangerous opponent for Clay." Dundee told the press afterward that it took him four days to convince Faversham to allow the match. A big crowd of 5,400 paid $12,600 to cheer the local favorite. Bill King, the city's boxing promoter, went to New York the following week to arrange a nationally televised bout. "It looks like he could be the hottest local attraction we've ever had," said King. This was no doubt due to Clay's charisma, but Angelo Dundee also deserves credit for convincing people that his fighter's wins were more significant than they really were.[40]

After a June victory in Las Vegas, Clay returned to Louisville the next month for a bout on the ABC television network against veteran Alonzo Johnson. Although ABC lacked a Louisville affiliate, its executives believed that Clay would generate enough nationwide interest to make the broadcast worthwhile. Johnson's record was 18-7. Several years earlier he had ridden a thirteen-bout win streak into a number-five ranking among heavyweights, but he lost when he stepped up against the best, and was now unranked. Bookmakers made Clay an 8–5 favorite. The *Courier-Journal* sports page headline read, "Clay Gets Stiffest Test against Johnson Tonight." Sensing a competitive fight, over 5,000 fans packed Freedom Hall, paying $13,000 at the gate. This bout was closer than previous ones, but Clay won an easy decision despite re-injuring his hand. It was shortly afterward that the mainstream press began to make Clay into a celebrity. He was featured in leading weekly magazines like *Life, Saturday Evening Post*, and *Sports Illustrated*. At the end of the year he would shoot scenes for a movie appearance. This was very early for a fighter to be getting such attention, and it exemplifies the brilliance of Dundee, the LSG, and Clay in promoting the Olympic champion's early career. All of this excitement notwithstanding, Faversham was cool enough to tell the press, "We haven't lost money and we haven't made money. The group isn't interested in profits or losses now. The main objective is to bring Clay along."[41]

Next there was a nationally televised bout in October against Alex Miteff, a marginal contender who had also defeated Alonzo Johnson. Angelo Dundee told the press that he wanted to nix the match, only to be overruled by Faversham, who felt that local fans and writers needed to be convinced that it was Clay and not up-and-coming middleweight Jimmy Ellis who was Louisville's hottest prospect. It seems far-fetched, but if it kept people thinking that Miteff would be a true test, why not? Almost everyone who wrote about the match said that it would be Clay's toughest to date, even though Miteff was just another plodder, tailor-made for a sharpshooter like Clay. He had lost ten times, despite twenty-four wins, and was cut-prone. Although Miteff had a good trainer, a twenty-pound weight advantage, and experience against the division's best fighters, he was helped by none of these when crumbled by a single right hand in the sixth round, which Clay had predicted. The crowd was smaller than usual, perhaps because Louisville had since acquired an ABC affiliate, but nevertheless 3,500 people paid $12,000 to attend. Clay collected $8,000, his largest purse to date. Clay's farewell hometown fight was a November win against the easy Willi Besmanoff, who fell in the forecasted seventh round. In a bout for which not even Dundee and Faversham could bust out the old toughest-test-yet trick, the main event still drew 4,000 fans and $9,000. Everything was going according to plan. Clay was on the verge of a top-ten ranking. It was time to get him into more important markets than Louisville.[42]

Clay's lone 1961 bout outside Louisville was probably his most important of the year. It received little press coverage, drawing only 2,500 people, and featured a lackluster Clay taking an easy decision from mediocre Duke Sabedong, who had lost seven of his last nine bouts. It was not the fight itself that impacted Clay, but rather his meeting professional wrestler "Gorgeous George" Wagner, whose foppish mannerisms, bombastic tongue, and arrogance toward his opponents had made him his sport's top draw, despite being hated by fans. Three days before his June Las Vegas fight, Clay had seen Wagner headline a show that drew a packed house. Afterward, Wagner invited Clay backstage and explained to him the benefits of being bad: "A lot of people will pay to see someone shut your mouth. So keep on bragging, keep on sassing, and always be outrageous." Clay was impressed and took the advice to heart. Until he joined the Nation of Islam, perhaps nobody had more influence on Clay's public persona than Wagner. In the months to come he would increase his rhetorical focus on his own good looks, his prettiness, and his unmarked face, while his disgust toward his opponents' abilities became more pronounced. Although up to this point the narratives surrounding Clay emphasized his decency, such coverage was not inevitable. Not all of Louisville was enthralled with him. He had been booed during the Johnson fight and during the ring announcements before and after the Miteff fight. Dean Eagle piped up, writing that he knew of many people "hoping to see Cassius Clay get knocked on his white trunks." Although still likable to many, Clay was also beginning to attract a different kind of interest.[43]

The Clay camp had taken strides to ensure their fighter's popularity, and his veering off that course is worth mentioning. It is more prudent to explore a range of reasons why some people were bothered by Cassius Clay than to identify a single cause. Perhaps foremost among Clay's foibles was his cockiness, which violated old-school tenets about sportsmanship. The degree to which this was exacerbated by race generally, and the civil rights movement particularly, although impossible to calculate, is worth thinking about. Readers should also consider that Clay's persona was affected by his involvement in a sport that over the years has been fundamentally distrusted by a large portion of the American public.

By the end of 1961, the civil rights movement was going full throttle. During the previous year, important southern institutions, among them state university campuses, became battlegrounds of desegregation. Even the segregationist's last bastion of hope, the University of Mississippi, was desperately fighting a losing battle in federal court to prevent the inevitable from happening. Sit-ins continued throughout the region, as the Student Nonviolent Coordinating Committee (SNCC) mobilized itself into a grassroots force. The biggest events, of course, were the Freedom Rides launched by the Congress of Racial Equality (CORE) in response to the Supreme Court's ban against segregated interstate travel facilities. The Freedom Riders were met in Alabama by a mob of angry whites, whose beating of the protesters and torching of their buses made national news.

It would be foolish to assert that the relationship between Clay's persona and the civil rights movement was a direct one and that merely by being black Clay reminded white people that the freedom struggle was coming to upset their lives. It is important to recognize that as the civil rights movement spread, white empathy as well as white resistance grew. While there were many whites who supported the attacks on the Freedom Riders, there were also many who found the attacks deplorable. Indeed, some of the most popular African American athletes backed the civil rights movement, and it seemed to make them even more admirable to the public. In February 1962, for example, heavyweight champion Floyd Patterson took a break from his training regimen to appear alongside Jackie Robinson at an NAACP conference in Jackson, Mississippi. Nevertheless, Clay's participation in a sport that aroused suspicion at a time of great racial unrest probably meant that his unorthodoxy sometimes had a negative effect on his cultural image.[44]

By 1962 the New York boxing market was in bad shape. If ten years of televised fights was the terminal disease that put the New York boxing scene in the hospital, then the Kefauver Commission was the rogue orderly that considered snuffing out its life with a pillow to the face. The corporation behind Madison Square Garden, one of the sport's longtime nerve centers, had been a stomping ground for IBC gangsters, and it was now paying the price. The Garden was hit hard by federal indictments. The venue was restricted to promoting only two championship bouts a year and was banned from holding an exclusive contract with any boxer it promoted. Because of the IBC presence, Cus D'Amato, heavyweight champion Floyd Patterson's manager/trainer, refused to do business in New York, although he was a resident. Furthermore, the New York State Athletic Commission (NYSAC) refused to license leading heavyweight contender Sonny Liston because of his connections to the IBC. It wasn't just the Garden that was being squeezed. The Kefauver hearings and subsequent federal indictments hurt boxing clubs around New York.[45]

Things would get much worse before they would get better in New York. Because it was frozen out of top-tier heavyweight boxing, Madison Square Garden's brain trust felt it wise to pursue championship fights in the lower weight divisions. This strategy backfired when welterweight champion Benny Paret died after taking a horrendous beating from challenger Emile Griffith in a nationally televised contest from the Garden. Since the broadcast was the first ever to have slow-motion instant replay, fans at home were able to witness the macabre scene in gruesome detail. Nationwide, but especially in New York, anti-boxing sentiment flourished. The state legislature allocated $20,000 to the formation of a committee to determine whether the sport should be banned. The Gallup Poll reported that almost 40 percent of Americans believed that boxing should be made illegal. These were hard times for the sweet science.[46]

It was into this crumbling landscape that the LSG chose to make Cassius Clay's New York debut in February. Things did not go smoothly. The problems began when the fighter tried to get a license from the now-paranoid NYSAC, which had called in former U.S. Marine Corps Major General Melvin Krulewitch to be chairman. Historically a rubber-stamp organization designed to facilitate the sport, the NYSAC was now enforcing all of its bylaws, including the one that capped a manager's purse share at 33 percent. Clay's contract, which paid the Sponsoring Group half of his earnings, violated this regulation.

The quick resolution of the matter illustrated the importance of having reputable backers like the Louisville Sponsoring Group to clear the political hurdles that popped up as movements to reform boxing mushroomed. Krulewitch called Faversham into his office four days before the scheduled bout between Clay, now ranked in the top ten by *The Ring* magazine, and Sonny Banks, the hard-hitting but raw prospect from Detroit. Faversham explained why the contract was fair, and Krulewitch accepted his position, with one exception. Although he immediately granted Faversham a manager's license, he would not allow him to serve in that role and as the Sponsoring Group's managing partner. Instead, he ordered Faversham to get signatures from all ten syndicate members verifying the contract terms. Once this was done, the bout was approved. Because it was highly organized and had an upstanding reputation, the LSG cleared this hurdle without difficulty. But one should not take for granted its role in doing so. During the previous three years, in the wake of the Kefauver Commission's findings, some of the sport's most important fighters, including Liston, Archie Moore, and middleweight champion Sugar Ray Robinson, had either their licenses or titles stripped from them by the NYSAC.[47]

The bout, both promotionally and professionally, was disappointing. Clay knew he was being groomed as a potential resurrector of Big Apple boxing. "I want to put life back in the fight game," he said, "and when I'm champion, I'll be like Joe Louis and fight everybody." Yet only 2,000 fans showed up at the Garden, and they booed his introduction. As a 5–1 favorite, Clay was expected to win easily, but he was knocked down in the first round by a left hook. Although he won in the predicted fourth round, and controlled most of the bout, it was not what Clay, Dundee, and the Louisville Sponsoring Group were hoping for. Clay had a long way to go if he were to become the next big thing in boxing.[48]

Just two weeks later, in late February, Clay and company returned to Miami. There, it was business as usual: another mediocre opponent, another good crowd, another dominating performance. Over 4,000 fans paid $8,000 to see Clay's fifth-round victory over Don Warner. Chris Dundee commented on Clay's drawing power in the city: "Every time Clay fights for me," he said, "two busloads of fans come from the LaGorce Country Club. They like to see this fellow fight." Clay also understood the importance of selling tickets. Before entering the arena that night, he asked the reporters gathered outside how the crowd looked.[49]

The Louisville Sponsoring Group and Angelo Dundee pondered their next move. They knew that New York was impossible to crack for the time being, but they also believed that their charge had to fight in big cities if he were to become a top contender. Los Angeles, with its increasingly robust fight scene, was the logical choice. Clay was matched with trial horse George Logan for a bout in late April on a card co-promoted by Joe Louis, the former heavyweight champion who was still one of the sport's most renowned names despite having been retired for over a decade.

Clay took to Tinseltown like a fish to water. Although he would appear on the card alongside top-ranked welterweight Ralph Dupas and second-ranked heavyweight Eddie Machen, Clay's bout with the unimpressive and unranked Logan was tabbed the main event. Although Clay was a 6–1 favorite against Logan, who sported a 22-7-1 record against mediocre competition, bled easily, and was molasses-slow, the fight was all reporters seemed to care about.

As Clay garnered major press coverage, the bout was scheduled for closed-circuit television. This was of ultimate importance. Closed-circuit television was the be-all, end-all of boxing promotion. From the 1950s until the early 1990s, when home pay-per-view eclipsed it as a medium, no fight could become a blockbuster without the aid of closed-circuit television. It was the most lucrative aspect of contemporary fight promotion. It was costly to produce, however, because it required special projectors, select venues, and extra advertising. Furthermore, fans had to be convinced to travel to a theater or sports arena and pay to see the fight. Boxing promoters had to weigh carefully the decision to broadcast a bout in this manner and calculate whether it would be a good investment. As seen by Clay's professional debut, a telecast could cut significantly into overall profits. It was a high-risk, high-reward medium. It was tempting because the potential seating capacity of closed-circuit arenas around the country greatly outnumbered those at the site where a fight actually took place. Furthermore, because movie-theater chains and boxing promoters wanted to maximize their control of the sport in various cities, they sometimes boycotted independent operators who wanted to show closed-circuit fights. Putting a bout on closed-circuit television did not guarantee its success but gave it a chance to become a blockbuster. If a bout caught on, it would gross far more across the country than if tickets had only been sold for the live event itself. The decision to put Louis's promotion on closed-circuit was essentially a test of Clay's marketability and drawing power. The card lacked a championship bout, and although Dupas and Machen were competent fighters, they were hardly box-office idols, each lacking the requisite charisma and talent to captivate a nation. It was an experimental telecast. Unlike for the biggest fights, the broadcast would be sold only to a select group of markets nationwide. Whereas hundreds of venues would broadcast major contests, Clay versus Logan would be shown in only twenty-three cities.

The bout was a smashing success. Between the excellent live gate and the modest closed-circuit take, the promotion profited and reinforced Clay's legitimacy as the next big thing in boxing. A closed-circuit company paid $15,000 for the broadcast rights, and the telecast sold out in several places, including Louisville, New Orleans (Ralph Dupas's hometown), and Tucson, where projector failure forced theater owners to issue refunds. Although small-scale, this response foretold wonderful things for bigger Clay fights in the future. In Los Angeles, about 7,500 fans, "most of them blown in by the big wind from Louisville," according to George Main of the *Los Angeles Herald-Examiner*, paid $57,000 at the box office for tickets priced between $2 and $10. Clay earned $8,000, double what any other fighter on the card took home. Entering the ring to the in-house organist's rendition of *Pomp and Circumstance,* which Gorgeous George always used for his ring walk, Clay butchered his opponent over four rounds before Logan's corner threw in the towel. Local sportswriters were critical of Clay's in-ring performance, but it was no matter. He would definitely be back. Hollywood loved Cassius Clay.[50]

Sensing that their fighter had reached a new level of popularity, the Louisville Sponsoring Group brought seventh-ranked Clay back to New York three weeks later for a nationally televised match against prospect Billy Daniels, who had won all sixteen of his fights. Daniels was a smooth boxer, and once again sportswriters warned fans that this would be Clay's toughest bout to date, although the Louisville Lip was a 4–1 favorite. For once, however, they were right.

Clay again failed to impress New Yorkers. Although he predicted a fifth-round knockout, he struggled throughout. He opened a ten-stitch gash over Daniels's eye in the second round, though, and it proved to be the margin of victory. With the scorecards close, the referee was forced to stop the contest in round seven because of the excessive bleeding. The mere 1,650 fans in attendance at the less-than-half-full St. Nicholas Arena booed the decision mercilessly. The gate was a meager $4,300. The press badmouthed Clay.[51]

Cassius Clay was becoming something of an enigma to boxing fans and his handlers. In some fights, he looked spectacular in front of big crowds packed with people who anxiously awaited his next antic. In others he looked mediocre before disinterested, small assemblies. Although his inconsistency was something to be expected from a young fighter, in Clay's case it was magnified by the endless amount of hype that preceded him. As long as Clay talked the way he did, people would hold him to a higher standard than others in his position. On the one hand, Clay's self-promotion was a plus, because it generated interest and separated him from the hordes of young fighters trying to make names for themselves. On the other hand, people took notice when he failed to live up to his billing. The Louisville Sponsoring Group made no effort to quiet Clay, and even if its members had tried to, it is doubtful that they could have. But people were beginning to have serious doubts about whether he was anything more than a big talker. His next few matches would be important in his development as a fighter and box-office draw. Although only thirteen bouts into his career, he was already ranked in the top ten, and whether he would ultimately establish himself as a contender or a champion was something that would soon become apparent, one way or another.

It was back to Los Angeles for Clay, Dundee, and the Louisville Sponsoring Group for a July fight against ranked Alejandro Lavorante. Bookmakers made it an even-money fight, taking into account the Argentine's knockouts over Tunney Hunsaker and Duke Sabedong, who both had gone the distance with Clay, and his major upset of top contender Zora Folley, who would fight for the championship five years later. In his last bout, Lavorante had been demolished by Archie Moore. But Clay, too, had been unimpressive of late, and Lavorante's 19-3 record was good enough to impress bookmakers, sportswriters, and observers into thinking, once again, that this would be Clay's toughest test to date. For the first time in his career, Clay was not the clear betting favorite on fight night.[52]

He should have been. It was a slaughter both in the ring and at the box office. Boldly predicting that he could stop Lavorante in half the time it took Moore, Clay made good on his word by battering the Argentine into semi-consciousness in round five. The referee didn't even bother to count over the stricken Lavorante. It was a devastating victory, and once again the future looked bright for Clay. Over 12,000 people showed up, producing $70,000 at the gate. Clay earned $12,500 plus a share of the box-office receipts. More important, he had steered himself into what potentially could be a big-money contest against Archie Moore, who had been at ringside for the match. Moore and Clay were boxing's two best showmen, and they had the chance to hype their bout into a blockbuster. Clay remained inactive over the next four months while his handlers began negotiations with Moore.[53]

Meanwhile, heavyweight boxing underwent a dramatic change. For four years, Sonny Liston had been toiling as the division's top contender, cleaning out the division with one knockout after another. Liston's victories were total. Durable, talented fighters had left the ring with broken bones in their faces, missing teeth, and far fewer brain cells than before. Floyd Patterson and his manager/trainer Cus D'Amato had avoided Liston like the plague, and they got away with it because Liston's criminal past and mob ties gave them an excuse to refuse the match. But Patterson's time came after President John F. Kennedy watched a closed-circuit doubleheader that featured Liston knocking out a hapless opponent in round one while Patterson struggled to defend his crown against one of the many second-raters he had been taking on since he won the title six years earlier. The press seized upon Kennedy's idle comment that he wanted to see the world's two best heavyweights meet, and Patterson, with his reputation at stake, could run no more. Once the match was made, Kennedy summoned Patterson to the White House and told him to "make sure you keep that championship." The National Association for the Advancement of Colored People (NAACP) also officially backed Patterson, believing Liston to be an unacceptable representative of the race.[54]

In the context of the civil rights movement, it was a classic good guy/bad guy scenario that made for box-office gold. Patterson embodied the liberal integrationist ethos of the times, appearing at civil rights rallies and marches, moving into an all-white neighborhood, and speaking in hopeful terms about loving one's enemy and turning the other cheek. Liston's menacing demeanor, his refusal to stay out of trouble, and his lack of political involvement completely disregarded those who would have the heavyweight champion, or a would-be heavyweight champion, conform to standards of behavior that were acceptable to mainstream America. The contrast made for one of the most highly anticipated bouts in boxing history. It was the subject of an endless stream of newspaper reports and television coverage.

The fight was a bonanza. Nearly 19,000 fans packed Chicago's Comiskey Park to see it, paying over $650,000. The closed-circuit take was $4 million, at the time making the fight the biggest in history. For their money, however, spectators got little, as Liston pummeled Patterson into helplessness two minutes into the first round. That the fight was such an incredible mismatch, yet did such incredible business, reinforced that the promotion of a fight was more important than its competitiveness. Clay and his people realized that if he could build himself into someone whom the public was desperate to see, his in-ring performances would, in some ways, become less important than his persona beyond the ring. The best-case scenario, of course, would be that people took Clay seriously both as a boxer and as a gate attraction, but Clay's inconsistency in the ring seemed to indicate that he might not ever achieve the former. The Louisville Sponsoring Group wanted to cash in on its investment regardless, and hoped to turn the impending bout with Moore into such an opportunity.[55]

Clay vs. Moore

The Seminal Text

C hoosing Cassius Clay's/Muhammad Ali's bout with Archie Moore as his most significant fight is like picking Dwight Eisenhower as the most important American president. Sure, interstate highways were necessary, but haven't far bigger things come out of 1600 Pennsylvania Avenue over the years? While Cassius Clay versus Archie Moore was an interesting contest, it doesn't enjoy even a hint of recognition from boxing connoisseurs or the general public as an essential Ali bout. That honor is usually reserved for his matches with Sonny Liston, Joe Frazier, and George Foreman. These fights have become freighted with near-mythological importance, generating lasting cultural significance and even vocabularies of their own. They have become reference points in sports history and have gained standing as landmark moments of the 1960s and 1970s, the civil rights movement, and the globalization of American popular culture. We know where these bouts took place and what happened: the Thrilla in Manila, the Rumble in the Jungle, the Rope-a-Dope, and the Phantom Punch are recognizable even to those who don't really care about boxing. It seems unlikely that a relatively unknown contest like Clay-Moore could possibly equal in significance such superfights, yet that is exactly what I'm claiming.

It was Clay-Moore, more than any other single fight, that turned a relatively powerless, intriguing-but-unproven boxer named Cassius Clay, whose primary value was as an entertaining sideshow, into the most potent box-office draw to come along in boxing in years. After fighting Moore, he began to be perceived not only as a serious contender for the heavyweight title but also as a special person whose life would ultimately be measured by standards beyond boxing. His name would not become Muhammad Ali until fifteen months later, and all of the sociopolitical import attendant upon his renaming as Ali would not begin to circulate widely in the culture until then, but the Clay-Moore bout was a tour de force that ushered in a new phase of Clay's public meaning. In retrospect, a unique tangle of professional, financial, and cultural significance can already be discerned around Clay's persona at the time he fought Moore, but it wasn't obvious to his contemporaries, which is why this fight is not held in the same regard as his first bout with Liston. Although the latter match was the moment of his being recognized formally as World Heavyweight Champion Muhammad Ali, it is clear in retrospect that the event was merely the public unveiling of a process that had come to fruition a year earlier.

Individually, the elements of Clay's becoming Ali existed before the Moore fight. Their coalescence at that instant, though, is what made the bout extraordinary. Appraisals of Ali's worth as a boxer that fail to consider his cultural significance are incomplete. His meanings as a cultural figure are by-products of their commercial consequences. His boxing career has been the narrative basis of his meaning beyond the ring. You cannot understand one without the other. Alone they meant little; together they produced one of the most important popular cultural figures of the past seventy-five years. The legendary status of Ali's bouts with Liston, Frazier, and Foreman is built upon their making these linkages obvious, but it was the Moore fight where they first came together.

The November 15, 1962, bout with Moore confirmed Clay as the biggest gate attraction in boxing and demonstrated his potential to become one of the sport's all-time generators of revenue. During the early buildup, however, this was not apparent to Clay and the Louisville Sponsoring Group, much less the fight's promoters. As a result, the original contracts excluded any broadcast of the bout. The reasons for this were obvious. The promoters, the fighters, and their managers felt that the best way to protect their investment was to make as many people as possible pay top dollar to see the event live at the Los Angeles Sports Arena. Putting the bout on television or radio would keep people at home, and everyone involved believed that doing so would stifle gate receipts. The bout just wasn't interesting enough, they felt, to justify such a move. They believed that the money earned from television and radio would not compensate for the corresponding loss in ticket sales. It did not appear to be a fight that people wanted to see at all costs. So, they agreed to black out broadcast coverage in order to draw all interested parties to the arena itself, where they would be forced to pay full price if they wished to see the bout. Such caution reveals that everyone involved had no idea how big the match was to become.

But soon it began to generate much more interest than anyone had imagined. Cal and Aileen Eaton, the promoters who ran the Olympic Boxing Club and controlled the fight game in Southern California, started to believe that the bout was worthy of a nationwide closed-circuit-television broadcast. This was a wonderful opportunity for Clay, but also a challenge. If the promotion foundered, he would have little ammunition to justify Sonny Liston's taking his challenges seriously. After all, the champion was in the sport to make money. If the inclusion of Clay became a questionable step in that process, Liston would look elsewhere for opponents. Of course, even if the promotion failed, Clay could have other chances to redeem himself, but in the fast-money world of professional boxing, where a fighter's window of opportunity to make big bucks is often measured in weeks and months, the pressure was on to succeed. If Clay was ever to emerge as Muhammad Ali, he would have to prove to boxing's power brokers that he was a nationwide box-office draw who single-handedly could generate ticket sales and profits.

With the blessing of both boxers and their camps, the Eatons arranged a mid-sized closed-circuit telecast. They contracted fifty-five North American venues with a seating capacity of 200,000 to broadcast their promotion. They told the press that in addition to the potential closed-circuit revenues, they hoped that 15,000 fans would come to the arena, generating about $150,000 in on-site gate receipts. Since an average closed-circuit ticket cost anywhere from one-third to one-half of the average live seat for a given contest, it was safe to estimate that the closed-circuit broadcast stood to generate up to seven times the on-site gate in the extremely unlikely event that the telecast was a complete sellout. In a very short time, the match had gone from local to national.[56]

Financially, the fight exceeded everyone's expectations. Attendance was a sold-out 16,200. It generated on-site receipts over $180,000, which shattered the California state record for an indoor sporting event. After paying about $75,000 to Moore and $40,000 to Clay, $20,000 in taxes, a $10,000 rental fee for the arena, $5,000 for security, advertising and printing expenses, an appearance fee to Sonny Liston, and other miscellaneous costs, the Eatons cleared $30,000 on the live gate alone. This profit was in addition to fees between $3,000 and $5,000, depending on the size of the venue, that they received from each of the fifty-five closed-circuit-television operators that carried the fight. The Eatons weren't the only ones who did well. Profits from closed-circuit showings soared, as people nationwide were turned away from full houses. There were sell-outs in some of the nation's most important markets: New York, San Francisco, Boston, San Diego, Seattle, and Louisville. In total, closed-circuit revenues neared $250,000. The bout was front-page news in several major cities, including New York and San Francisco.[57]

Clay was clearly the biggest thing boxing had seen in many years. His ranking jumped from seventh to fourth, and the victory led to a series of offers: $55,000 to fight Eddie Machen in San Francisco; $10,000 per round to face Cleveland Williams; $25,000 to battle Zora Folley in Denver; an undisclosed amount to take on former champ and number-one contender Floyd Patterson in Madison Square Garden. A title fight seemed imminent, as sportswriters and fans began discussing the possibility of a Liston-Clay match.[58]

Because Clay's standing as a gate attraction became central to his rise to prominence as a cultural figure, we must explore why his bout with Moore caught fire. Understanding why his early bouts succeeded financially is critical to comprehending his transformation from Cassius Clay the entertainer to Muhammad Ali the geo-political figure. Clay's economic significance and cultural significance were intertwined. A rise in one necessarily meant a corresponding increase in the other.

It is also required that we deal with the Clay-Moore bout specifically as a boxing match. All of Clay's appeal as a gate attraction, and ultimately as a world-historical figure, boils down to the perception of him as an all-time great fighter. If he were to have lost his match with Sonny Liston, for example, nobody would care that he went on to change his name to Muhammad Ali. His significance came from his boxing success. The Ali legend beyond the ring directly correlates to and depends upon his accomplishments in the ring, which is why we must scrutinize his boxing matches. They were the cultural texts upon which people would base the remainder of Ali's meaning.

Nearly a half century after it happened, it is still impossible to pinpoint why Clay-Moore was such a blockbuster. It seems ridiculous that people would pay so much to see a forty-five-year-old ex-champion do battle with an upstart only fifteen bouts into his professional career. And although to some it may not have been apparent beforehand, the bout was an utter mismatch. Clay dominated every moment, scoring three knockdowns en route to a TKO win in the predicted fourth round. Overwhelmed by the younger man's speed and power, Moore hardly threw a punch. There was not a second of the fight in which it looked as if he would win. Why would people have expected otherwise?

Sportswriters were certainly skeptical of the bout's viability. Syndicated *New York Times* columnist Arthur Daley predicted that the fight was "unlikely to hit any jackpots." Why would people pay to see an event when its "attractiveness was grossly overestimated" and "its inherent magnetism isn't quite that irresistible"? It would be one thing to show it on home television, "where it would have drawn millions and fascinated viewers," but closed-circuit was another matter altogether. Even though promoters were hopeful, Clay-Moore was never a guaranteed financial success. Its record-breaking gate receipts, however, are not as mystifying as one might think.[59]

Although the degree to which the public will consume the hype generated by those trying to sell it boxing matches is always unknown, fights that satisfy certain criteria have an advantage over those that don't. In the case of Clay-Moore, three elements were critical to its success: (1) its apparent competitiveness as an athletic contest; (2) the remarkable, publicity-generating personalities of the two fighters; and (3) a vague sense that something larger was at stake, that the fight had some kind of sociopolitical importance.

Almost always, the most critical element to the success of an otherwise capably managed promotion is the perceived quality of the main event. In order for a boxing card to succeed, the public has to be convinced that the featured bout will be worth watching. Only on the rarest of occasions will fight fans pay big money when the result of a contest seems predestined. For example, when Mike Tyson returned to the ring in 1995 following a three-year prison sentence, there was not a scintilla of doubt that he would defeat the incompetent Peter McNeeley. The bout still did tremendous pay-per-view business, however, because the unresolved question of how Tyson would respond to his time away from the ring compelled viewers. Overwhelmingly, however, people pay to see competitive bouts, and those selling the promotion must convince them that the show will be worthwhile.

The one-sided outcome of the Clay-Moore fight notwithstanding, it is understandable that fans bought into the idea that it would be competitive. Although Moore was in his mid-forties, and the match would turn out to be the penultimate one of his twenty-eight-year, 220-bout career, his recent performances indicated that he was still hard to handle. Furthermore, Moore's overall record stood as one of the most accomplished in boxing history. Only a select group of perhaps twenty fighters can claim to have matched Archie Moore's lifetime ring accomplishments. If anyone had ever earned the credibility to convince fans that he could pull off one last great fight, it was Moore.

In the thirteen years prior to facing Clay, Moore enjoyed one of the most remarkable runs that any boxer has ever had. Between 1950 and 1962, he went 75-4-3, including wins over International Boxing Hall of Fame (IBHOF) members Jimmy Bivins, Harold Johnson, Joey Maxim, and Bobo Olson. He also beat a number of top heavyweight contenders, including some who outweighed him by over twenty-five pounds. Of his four losses during the period, two were in world heavyweight championship bouts against Rocky Marciano and Floyd Patterson. Another loss was to Johnson. The fourth defeat was on a decision in Rome to Italian fighter Giulio Rinaldi, which Moore convincingly avenged on American soil the following year.

In 1952, approaching his thirty-sixth birthday, with a record of 132-19-9, after battling the sport's best for seventeen years, Moore finally received his first title shot, and won the light-heavyweight crown from Maxim. Of course,

Moore had to pay for the opportunity. In what stands out as perhaps the most unfair purse split in boxing history, Moore received $800 to Maxim's $100,000. The agreement was indicative of what black fighters had to go through if they were to be given the chance to win championships. Going into the bout with Clay, Moore was still the undefeated light-heavyweight champion. Although some sanctioning bodies had stripped him of the title for not defending it as frequently as they mandated, and therefore recognized other fighters as light-heavyweight champion, to most observers Moore would be the division's kingpin until someone defeated him in a title bout or he retired.[60]

Although he had slowed, Moore's bouts in the year leading up to the showdown with Clay were impressive. In one, he decked 1956 Olympic gold medalist Pete Rademacher eight times on his way to a sixth-round TKO victory. In another, he beat third-ranked heavyweight contender Alejandro Lavorante so badly that the Argentine was carried from the ring on a stretcher. Lavorante would die from injuries sustained in a bout six months later, and it seems clear that the frightening amount of punishment he took from Moore had something to do with it. To understand the significance of Moore's win, one should realize that just four months later, Lavorante returned to the ring to take on Cassius Clay, and oddsmakers made it an even-money fight. Lavorante was a well-regarded, credible young heavyweight, and Moore had destroyed him. Immediately prior to meeting Clay, Moore had fought a draw against future IBHOF member and light-heavyweight champion Willie Pastrano. There was nothing on Moore's record that indicated any dramatic slippage.

It is easy, therefore, to see why fans felt that the bout would be worth-while. Moore was one of the sport's all-time greatest fighters, a living legend who had knocked out more opponents than anyone else in boxing history and had come out on top against the best fighters of his era. He was still fighting at a high level. And who was Clay anyhow? He had only fifteen bouts under his belt, hadn't beaten anyone great, had been knocked down by upstart Sonny Banks, struggled with mediocre Billy Daniels, and had a bunch of bad habits that the crafty Moore could exploit. Although it would be difficult for observers to fathom how Moore would cope with Clay's speed, it was also fair for them to assume that he would figure it out, having solved virtually every problem ever presented to him in a boxing ring over the past twenty-five years. Indeed, Clay's shining moment had been his victory over Lavorante, and Moore's win over the Argentine was just as impressive. The betting odds reflected some of the uncertainty surrounding the bout, as Clay was installed as a solid, but not overwhelming, 2–1 favorite. Both the United Press International ("Clay takes the biggest step in his brief boxing career") and the Associated Press ("Cassius Clay . . . faces the toughest test in his brief career tonight") agreed that Moore was Clay's most capable opponent to date.[61]

In addition to the public's acceptance of the bout as a viable athletic contest, we must consider the remarkable, publicity-generating personalities of the two fighters, since they literally talked their way into a record-breaking gate. There are hundreds of evenly matched, tough-to-predict fights a year that don't generate the kind of interest that Clay-Moore did, so it is safe to say that their promotional genius had something to do with it. From a narrative standpoint, the bout was a natural. There were several compelling story lines that the press could have exploited to create interest in the bout, among them the nearly thirty-year age difference between the fighters and the fact that Moore was Clay's ex-trainer.

Moore and Clay were the sport's two most charismatic figures. Moore had been a promotional wizard for years. His heavyweight title shot against Rocky Marciano, for example, had come only after an extensive press campaign in which he wrote letters to hundreds of newspapers accusing the champion of cowardice and daring him to accept the challenge. Clay, too, stepped up his already formidable rhetorical arsenal for the bout, insulting the respected Moore every chance he had. In the past, although Clay sometimes referred contemptuously to his opposition, his focus was usually on his own greatness. But this was different. Clay realized that Moore was an underdog legend trying to pull one last great performance from his aging body. There was no way Clay would be the fan favorite, so he played the villain to the hilt. It worked.

Clay's training site was a madhouse. Fans packed the Main Street Gym daily, paying a dollar each, double the going rate, to heckle Clay. Owner Howie Steindler had to hire police to keep angry fans away, and they ejected several who threatened violence. "From now on," he said, "I'm going to have to have a couple of cops on hand every day to keep order. Clay's a character and he draws my biggest crowds, but we don't want any trouble." Clay knew what was going on, and he encouraged it. "Let them yell," he taunted. "The madder they get the more tickets they buy. It's OK with me. They'll be there to see this loudmouth get a licking. People stop me on the street and tell me to my face they hope I get whipped." And when Clay learned that Moore was becoming irked by his comments, he stepped it up: "You tell him that if he thinks I have been vicious I'm going to get viciouser. If he is sore at me, he is going to be sorer. This is going to be an annihilation. This will be a mismatch. I don't care about his feelings. I'm out to win the world championship." For good measure, Clay predicted that Moore would hit the floor in four. Although this was merely gamesmanship, as he acknowledged afterward, it got to a lot of people, including the usually unflappable Moore. Clay, on the other hand, loved every second. To many, it was not just a boxing match, but also a battle between lifestyles: the old-school ways of Moore, and all they represented, against the new kid on the block who had no regard for the time-honored customs of sportsmanship.[62]

During the week immediately preceding the fight, the following happened: the movie *Requiem for a Heavyweight*, featuring Clay in a cameo role, was released nationally; Moore held public training sessions while backed in-house by the live accompaniment of legendary jazzman Buddy Collette and his band; Sonny Liston, brought into town by the Eatons to add championship legitimacy to the promotion, appeared in nearby Las Vegas to clown onstage with friend Louis Armstrong during Satchmo's local run; and Clay and Moore engaged in a nationally televised "Great Debate." Such gimmicks became irresistible in the hands of masters like Clay and Moore, and they generated massive interest.[63]

The trickiest and least palpable aspect of understanding the appeal of Clay-Moore is determining how people perceived its meaning beyond boxing. Other than the clichés it generated—good versus evil, experience versus youth, cool versus excited—was there anything to it? Although the buildup to the bout was mostly pugilistic, there was a vague sense developing that Clay was something more than an entertainer. Some newspaper reporters began to pick up on the idea that Clay was a moral force, someone with substance outside athletics, and it penetrated their coverage of the match. It was subtle, indeed, and only a select few acknowledged it, but it was there. This feeling went back several months to Clay's previous Los Angeles fight, against George Logan. While the association with a Joe Louis promotion was certainly good for Clay's image, it was on his individual merits that sportswriters drew conclusions about his inner worth.

Longtime *Los Angeles Times* reporter Sid Ziff sat down for a breakfast meeting with young Clay and was puzzled by what he encountered. The kid was dressed in a dark suit, starched white shirt, and bow tie, hardly the patchwork ensemble he was used to seeing from fight people. Clay was probably on his way to prayer services or some other gathering held by the burgeoning Los Angeles branch of the Nation of Islam, although Ziff wouldn't have known this. That he was in the preaching mood became apparent when Ziff ordered some boiled ham, and Clay lectured him on trichinosis and the dangers of eating pork. Ziff found this quite annoying, but it was indicative of someone who answered to a higher authority. Clay capped the interview by quoting from the Bible, adding that "Everyone wants to get to heaven but nobody don't want to die." From there he recited a short poem praising Joe Louis, and just as quickly as he had entered, he was gone. Ziff had no idea what just hit him.[64]

Others were more impressed. A week later, Clay spoke with *Los Angeles Times* sports editor Paul Zimmerman, who thought the young fighter was worth following in the ring and someone worthy of admiration beyond it. "Behind the glib exterior of this smiling, fun-loving, personable young man," he wrote, "is a moral code that demands admiration." A moral code that demands admiration? This was something new in the fight game. If Zimmerman was to be believed, Clay was a God-fearing, red-blooded American boy, clean inside the ring and out. "I've never been locked up," said Clay. "I've never been cautioned in the ring for holdin' or hittin' low nor nothin'. I live by the Bible. My mother and father taught me to live right. No stealin', no drinkin', no smokin'." For good measure, he added, "[H]e who reads the good book will understand to tell the truth." Even Jim Murray, the *Times* syndicated columnist who was no fan of Clay, topped off a piece that week advising readers that if they ever wanted to find young Cassius, they should look for "the one with the halo around his head and the choir singing in the background." With boxing's reputation at a low ebb, it was certainly strange to see this young fighter whose social mores seemed opposed to what was expected of athletes, especially blacks, being feted for morality.[65]

What made Clay odd were the conflicting messages he transmitted. Although cocky, loud, and brash, he also dressed well, listened to his parents, read the Bible, and fought cleanly. He was managed by the right people. He admired the great Joe Louis. It was as if he was willing to play ball with those who would demand certain moral and behavioral standards from him. But lurking beneath the surface was something different, probably undetectable to most. In a sense, Clay was telling everyone that he took his moral cues from blacks, not whites. His outfit and diet were telltale signs that he belonged to the Nation of Islam, although few whites were familiar with the fringe group at the time. It was his parents, not the Louisville Sponsoring Group, whom Clay credited with teaching him right and wrong. Clay didn't make these points explicitly. He couldn't if he wanted a title shot. After all, he was still expendable and could be blackballed if he deviated too far from what people expected. Sonny Liston had to wait and wait and wait for a title shot despite clearly being the world's best heavyweight for almost four years. Discretion was necessary, but those able to read between the lines could tell that something big was brewing, that Clay would be heard not only from within the ring, but also on a larger stage. It was this tension that leaked into public perception of his bout with Moore and subtly drove it into something more than a mere boxing match.

The Most Hated Man in Boxing?

The Early Bouts, 1963

Arctic cold gripped Pittsburgh near the end of January 1963. Temperatures of eighteen below zero, accompanied by snowfall and winds reaching thirty miles per hour, had paralyzed the city. Traffic jams, impenetrable roads, school closings, business shutdowns, frozen and burst pipes, frostbite cases, and other chaos dominated the local scene. You did not want to be outdoors unless you had to.[66]

Despite these frigid and inhumane conditions, however, an undeniable excitement had taken hold of the Steel City, for Cassius Clay was in town for a fight with former gridiron star Charley Powell. Even Clay's workouts had become public spectacles, drawing crowds of over 600. The clamor notwithstanding, ticket sales for the bout were slow. The cold weather had made it difficult to get people out of their homes on a weeknight. With just twenty-four hours remaining before showtime, only 7,000 tickets had been sold.[67]

But on fight night, the Pittsburgh Civic Arena was packed to the rafters. What started as a trickle of walk-up business had turned into a flood. By the time Clay entered the ring, over 11,000 tickets had been sold for a gross of about $56,000, shattering the city's attendance and gate receipt records for a boxing match, and insuring a nearly five-figure profit for promoter Archie Littman. It wasn't just fight fans who showed up. Vast crowds of men, women, and children who had never before gone to a boxing match wanted to be at this one. They came to see whether Clay could fulfill his promise to knock out Powell in round three. They came to boo the Louisville Lip. They came to see greatness. They were not disappointed. Cassius Clay, the fistic Pied Piper, would put on a display not easily forgotten.[68] ·

That evening, fans witnessed a shellacking of the highest magnitude as Clay pounded out a one-sided, two-fisted, three-round decimation of Powell. Although some charged that Clay's successful prognostication indicated a fix, all they had to do was examine Powell in the dressing room to understand how real it was. The former pro footballer had been reduced to a near corpse. An inch-long gash over his left eye required five stitches to close, and he spent an hour after the bout vomiting blood in his dressing room. He was told by the ringside physician to take at least six weeks off from the sport, and he indicated afterward that he was contemplating retirement. It hardly seemed worth the $6,700, before doctor's bills, that Powell had earned. Clay took in nearly $14,500 for doing what was necessary. He had electrified boxing fans and destroyed the opposition. Powell was no great fighter, but he was competent, and the victory was impressive. Having just turned twenty-one years old, Clay was already telling reporters that he wanted a shot at champion Sonny Liston, vowing in the headline of a *Life* magazine profile that he would "chop that big monkey to pieces."[69]

Clay was walking a dangerous line as he seized upon the promotional strategies he had learned from Gorgeous George. His transformation from a popular local boy, an Olympic hero seemingly divorced from civil rights turbulence, into an obnoxious, loudmouthed ring assassin was paying dividends. But for how long would people tolerate this? The Louisville Sponsoring Group was worried, but as long as the fighter avoided things political, he would likely be insulated from official sanction that would compromise his road to the top. The Moore and Powell fights had proven that Clay was both the most hated man in boxing and the sport's biggest attraction in many years. For a fighter not yet perceived by most insiders to be championship material, especially compared to a juggernaut like Sonny Liston, who many contemporary observers swore was the best heavyweight ever, media interest in Clay was virtually unprecedented in boxing history. Record-setting crowds were coming to see him work.

While the phenomenal response he had evoked signaled to the LSG that it was on the cusp of making enormous money on its investment, it also indicated to Clay that he wielded power. He alone was responsible for generating millions of dollars for others. Knowing this gave Clay new confidence in revealing his true identity as a member of the Nation of Islam. If people were bothered that he used his fame as a boxer to discuss politics and race relations, tough luck. Yet Clay's willingness to speak out on such issues scared the Louisville Sponsoring Group. Its members knew what had happened to Sonny Liston, and they didn't want to get squeezed out of the title picture just as they were on the verge of hitting the jackpot. Tensions began to emerge between the fighter and his managers.

For the first time, the LSG allowed itself to be thrust into the national spotlight, agreeing to be profiled for a glowing *Sports Illustrated* feature. Such favorable coverage counterbalanced anxieties about Clay's brashness and checked public inclination that he was a fire burning out of control. And in the next few months, the syndicate would make several public gestures indicating its restraint of the young heavyweight.[70]

Clay Mania, meanwhile, was reaching even greater heights. *Time* magazine's ten million readers found Clay's increasingly familiar visage staring at them from the cover of the March 22 edition, released on the eve of his fight in Madison Square Garden against local heavyweight contender Doug Jones. Although Clay's previous two New York bouts had been disappointing, his revitalized publicity campaign as a villain who was the most hated man in boxing created a colossal public response in the Big Apple. Without question, the Jones fight single-handedly revived a sport that had been comatose in the longtime hub of boxing. Even more incredibly, Clay accomplished all of this while the city was in the midst of a three-month newspaper strike that included all of its major titles, but not the black *New York Amsterdam News*. Clay was nothing short of a national phenomenon, a major celebrity, box-office platinum.

Ticket sales were astonishing. The fight was the first in the arena's thirty-eight-year history to sell out in advance. Even balcony seats, which were always reserved until the day of an event, had to be put on sale early to placate demand. It was Madison Square Garden's first boxing sellout in over six years. Overall, more than 18,000 fans paid about $105,000 at the gate, generating the venue's largest gross receipts in ten years. It was also the first closed-circuit broadcast from Madison Square Garden. Previously, such telecasts were blacked out in cities that hosted the live event. Because New York represented so many potential closed-circuit sales, area promoters rarely hosted matches that would be better served by the city's vast theater capacity. In this case, however, Garden officials felt that the bout was too prestigious to turn down despite the potential loss in closed-circuit-television sales, which nevertheless went well. In total, almost 150,000 fans paid their way into forty venues nationwide, producing over $400,000 in revenues and "a hell of a profit," according to matchmaker Teddy Brenner. None of this, by the way, had to do with Doug Jones, the nearly 3–1 underdog.[71]

There were two interesting developments that transpired as a result of the bout's closed-circuit arrangements. First, it marked the beginning of the relationship between Cassius Clay and Mike Malitz, who would later become a member of Main Bout Inc., the corporation founded by Ali to replace the

Louisville Sponsoring Group. Madison Square Garden's boxing division hired Sports Network Inc., a closed-circuit-television company run by Malitz and his father Lester to produce the broadcast. Sports Network was in charge of selling the program to closed-circuit theaters and making sure those venues received a clear signal on fight night. Second, it foreshadowed problems that Ali would encounter once Main Bout took over his career. Sports Network failed to sell the transmission to theaters in Los Angeles. Clay's three 1962 bouts in the city had proven his drawing power; surely the telecast would sell out in multiple venues if it were shown there. But the city's boxing kingpins Cal and Aileen Eaton felt that it would take away publicity from an upcoming promotion they had planned for later in the month. As a result, they success-fully pressured area closed-circuit operators to pass on the fight. *Los Angeles Times* sports editor Paul Zimmerman wrote that "[T]he Olympic organization [i.e., the Eatons] had Los Angeles blacked out. The big misfortune for Los Angeles boxing fans is that they were deprived the opportunity of seeing the bout on local theater screens." These actions illustrated how rival forces within the industry were willing to forgo short-term profits in an effort to protect their niches.[72]

Clay predicted that he would knock Jones out in the fourth round, al-though the Harlem heavyweight had never been stopped in his twenty-seven-fight career. Ranked third in the world, Jones had done well for himself since turning professional four years earlier, having won twenty-three of his fights, including a knockout of highly ranked Zora Folley. Jones was not a great fighter, but he was skilled and durable and was expected to make it a tough contest. The fight was a close one, with Clay eking out the decision. Fans booed the announcement of the scorecards and heaped abuse on Clay as he celebrated the win. Clay antagonized them, staying in the ring longer than one normally would, urging the crowd to intensify its catcalls. *The Ring* se-lected it as its bout of the year. Clay's performance convinced most observ-ers that he would not be ready for Sonny Liston anytime soon. The champion, who took in the closed-circuit telecast from Miami Beach, quipped, "Clay showed me that I'll get locked up for murder if we're ever matched." For the bout, Clay earned about 30 percent of the net revenues.[73]

Although Clay was now cultivating his role as the most hated man in box-ing, there was some good-natured sport to it all, and it would be a mistake to think that the public regarded him in the same way as Sonny Liston. For one thing, Clay had an air of respectability about him because of his relationship with the Louisville Sponsoring Group. He was also funny. When fans started throwing peanuts at him while he celebrated the victory over Jones, he picked one up, shelled it, and ate it. He disparaged the opposition, but to many it was clear that it was tongue-in-cheek. He was not anti-social, like Liston, who had done hard time, hung around with mobsters, and once broke a police-man's leg. Clay was annoying. Liston was scary. People loved to hate Clay. They were afraid of Liston. Clay was like your friend's little brother who kept bothering you to allow him to hang out. Liston was like your friend's older brother who threatened to kick your ass if you bothered him. Clay was loud and cheesy. Liston was silent and brooding. Clay was a pest. Liston was a scourge, but nobody could deny that Clay lived a clean life. He neither drank nor smoked, and he had never been in any kind of trouble. There was a big difference between each of their claims to be the most hated man in the sport. Perhaps most important, Clay's in-ring difficulties kept people from believing that he was a long-term threat. Almost nobody thought that he was ready to take the championship from Liston, and most people felt that he would be lucky to even survive the first round. Clay may have been the latest big thing, but there was a sense that his staying power was finite.

Nevertheless, in the months surrounding the Jones fight, Clay began to assert himself in ways that trod dangerous new ground, particularly as he began to invoke controversy about race issues. If there was one safe thing about Sonny Liston, it was that he seemed utterly disinterested in the civil rights movement. He was no political symbol, and he knew it. Clay, however, was having a hard time keeping quiet, especially as his entanglements with the Nation of Islam, which were no less real because of their being shielded from the public, intensified. As the civil rights movement ground forward, as Clay grew increasingly aware of his own power, and as the inevitability of his gaining a title shot became clear, he was finding it less prudent to remain si-lent about things he felt were important.

Although the newspaper strike had shut down New York's major white dailies, the black press was out in full force, as were the city's freelancers, and it was to these reporters that Clay began to position himself in relation to the civil rights movement. It started innocuously enough on the day of the Jones bout, with Clay telling a New York Amsterdam News editor, "I will be the first heavyweight champion to fight a benefit for the NAACP." This was obviously nothing to be concerned about. Floyd Patterson had associated himself with the organization in previous years with no ill effect on his popularity. And by the 1960s, the NAACP had taken something of a backseat to groups that were seen as more militant, like SNCC and the Southern Christian Leader-ship Conference (SCLC), led by Dr. Martin Luther King Jr. An endorsement of the NAACP was hardly militant.[74]

Later in the month, however, Clay began to reveal publicly that his views on the black freedom struggle were not in accord with what many people would have liked them to be. In an interview with New York Post writer Pete Hamill, whose newspaper, then the city's most liberal daily, was still on strike, he asserted, "I have no use for the NAACP. I'm a fighter. I believe in the eye for an eye business." Continuing his tirade, Clay disparaged James Meredith, the student who had desegregated the University of Mississippi: "I'm no James Meredith. He's got more guts than I'll ever have. He showed me something. But I don't want to meet him. I don't like people like that." This was something new. Meredith had been hailed as a hero by the civil rights leadership, and a 1966 march would be organized in his honor when he was shot. In Clay's eyes, however, Meredith epitomized what was wrong with the civil rights movement. The focus on black and white brotherhood and cooperation was unrealistic, he thought. "I believe it's human nature to be with your own kind," he said. "I know what restrooms to use, where to eat, and what to say. I don't want people who don't want me. I don't like people who cause trouble. I'm not going out there to rile up a lot of people. No sir, I'm no fool. There's no referee in the street." Finally, he declared, "I'm a fighter. I believe I'm no cheek turner. The NAACP can say, 'Turn the other cheek,' but the NAACP is ignorant. You kill my dog, you better hide your cat."[75]

Such comments raised concern, especially among blacks and white liberals. Hamill called Clay "a young man with a lot of charm who is in danger of becoming a dreadful bore." In all major cities—New York, Chicago, Los Angeles, and San Francisco—and even in Louisville and Miami, where Clay had based his operations, white newspapers passed on the story. It was, however, front-page news in the national edition of the important black newspaper the *Pittsburgh Courier*. "Generally," the *Courier* story began, "the Negro community was shocked by Clay's remarks, and gave him a verbal lashing, often in unprintable terms." At a time when SCLC protesters were being attacked by police dogs and sprayed with high-powered fire hoses in Alabama, and generating national news for their sacrifices, Clay's dogging the civil rights movement was taken by some as treason. For the first time, the black press speculated openly about where Clay's loyalties lay. "When this story first appeared," wrote one reporter, "many Negroes scoffed at Clay's attitude, and insiders said that he might be influenced by the Black Muslims. He has been seen with them on occasion, it was reported." The NAACP also got its public relations head, Henry Lee Moon, to write a letter to the *Courier*'s editor. "If Cassius Marcellus Clay has been quoted correctly," he jabbed, "it is not amiss to suggest that this talkative young man take the time to read and he would learn something." To some people, Clay had declared war on the black freedom struggle, and it was no laughing matter. They felt that the success of the movement depended on black unity and that Clay's comments could undermine such an effort. As a result, the response to him was swift and heavy-handed.[76]

The Louisville Sponsoring Group had reason to be alarmed. Between the difficulties that Clay had in the ring with Doug Jones, and his politicizing the terms upon which his status as the most hated man in boxing rested, the organization may have felt that things were about to come crashing down. Public speculation about Clay's membership in the Nation of Islam was especially alarming, and it appeared that such talk was leaking into the newspapers. In light of this development, coupled with the discomfort caused by the Jones fight, the LSG was becoming increasingly cautious. If it was to turn the narratives surrounding its young charge back to boxing, it had to find Clay an opponent quickly. The group thought it best to return him to Louisville, a smaller, friendlier market that would curtail some of the controversy before it got out of hand.

On the short list of potential opponents was George Chuvalo, who would eventually fight Ali in a 1966 championship bout that is of major importance to this book. The son of Croatian immigrants to Toronto, Chuvalo had the kind of upbringing that often foreshadows ring careers. His father was intense, a "disciplinarian in the strictest sense of the word" and "a very hard man to live with," said George. The older Chuvalo completed only a second-grade education, had a dysfunctional right arm resulting from a childhood injury, and had never mastered English. George Chuvalo likes to tell a story that he feels encapsulates the attributes, namely focus and determination, his father passed on to him. The elder Chuvalo had a job skinning cattle on the killing floor of a slaughterhouse that mandated he take two weeks' vacation per year. Annually, he would spend that fortnight not on holiday, but by going to work and observing the two men needed to replace him. Monday through Friday, eight hours a day, he would pull up a stool and watch them. He even brought lunch. Such was the economic insecurity and paranoia about unemployment that characterized the Chuvalo household. Chuvalo's kindness, which becomes apparent to anyone who meets him, must have come from his mother. She worked plucking chickens for poultry magnate and sports entrepreneur Irving Ungerman, who would become Chuvalo's manager in the mid-1960s. Every day on her break, she would run to young George's school and throw lunch, usually a pomegranate and a bag of chips, over the fence to her son. She would kiss him through the mesh and then run back to work.

Despite this inadequate diet, Chuvalo developed into a massive young man, weighing 200 pounds in high school during an era when even the beefiest of teenagers were rarely that size. He decided that he wanted to become a boxer. Chuvalo had been infatuated with the sport since boyhood, when he picked up a copy of *The Ring* at a newsstand and became spellbound by its contents. He quit school to work days at a meatpacking plant while training at night. Motivated by his father's admonitions that young George would quit the moment his nose was bloodied, in 1956 he entered the novice heavyweight tournament sponsored by former world champion Jack Dempsey, at Toronto's Maple Leaf Gardens. That night, the eighteen-year-old knocked out four opponents to win the $500 first prize.

Although his professional debut was auspicious, Chuvalo's early career was marked by inconsistency. He worked road construction between matches and could not devote enough time to become a first-class fighter. He lost bouts to inferior opponents and had trouble dealing with smooth boxers. Still, he was popular in Toronto. Ten thousand fans saw him beat James J. Parker in the first round to win the Canadian Heavyweight Championship. But by the time he was mentioned as possible competition for Clay, he had lost the title to fellow prospect Bob Cleroux, was disqualified in his next fight, and had been inactive throughout 1962 because of managerial problems.

Clay first made close contact with him in May 1963 when Chuvalo came down to Louisville for a nationally televised main event against Angelo Dundee trainee Mike DeJohn. The contest was exactly the kind that matchmakers got paid to conjure. It pitted against each other stylistic opposites whose intersection would create action-packed theater. And since Cassius Clay had agreed to face the winner, it introduced audiences to the rising heavyweight's next opponent.

Both fighters seemed safe enough competition to be slotted as such. Losers of a combined eighteen bouts, Chuvalo and DeJohn had failed major and minor tests against boxers of variable quality. They had also amassed their share of wins, but both fumbled their most meaningful assignments. Neither had seriously contended for the world championship. They were credible but not great fighters. Either would make a good trial horse for the up-and-coming Clay. Not too easy, but not too difficult, thought Dundee and the Louisville Sponsoring Group.

What they did not yet comprehend, however, was that Chuvalo's spotty record belied an otherworldly ability to take punishment. The oversight was understandable, because at the time he hadn't faced the world-class competition he would later in his career. If boxing matches were still fought the old way, ending only when one man could not continue, George Chuvalo might have become one of history's greatest fighters. During his ninety-three-bout career against the very best fighters of the heavyweight division's very best era, he was never knocked down. He withstood beatings that nobody else could. He was nearly impossible to hurt. He was an iron man.

Chuvalo wasn't just tough; he was rough, too. The most telling sequence of the DeJohn match came in the second round. It started when Chuvalo ripped a vicious right hand to DeJohn's groin, a foot below the belt, lifting him off his feet and allowing Chuvalo to follow up with a left hook to the jaw. Off-balance and hurt, DeJohn reeled to the ropes, where Chuvalo did the extraordinary, folding his six-foot-four opponent backwards over the top strand, like a track coach showing a novice high jumper how to execute the Fosbury Flop.

If boxing had an ethics exam, Chuvalo would be facing a critical question. Break cleanly or smash DeJohn's unprotected face? The first choice adhered to boxing's rule book, the second to the rules of boxing. To a hard man like Chuvalo, this was an easy one. Risking disqualification, he dropped a right-left-right-left series of pile drivers from directly above the helpless DeJohn, finding his chin with all of them. DeJohn crumbled. He rose with great difficulty twenty seconds later, but chaos was erupting at ringside. DeJohn's corner protested the obvious foul and demanded that its fighter be declared the victor. Chuvalo's corner acted as if its man was the knockout winner and cut off his gloves. After a ten-minute delay to sort it all out, the referee ruled that DeJohn would be awarded a two-point round and that the match would continue. But the big man was finished. He would need days, not minutes, to recuperate from such a battering. Chuvalo dominated the last eight rounds, winning a decision. Truly a crossroads, the bout spelled the end of DeJohn's twelve-year career while unlocking a number of opportunities for Chuvalo, the most tantalizing of which seemed to be a fight with the hottest commodity in boxing.

Clay's management did not like what they saw. This was clearly not a guy who would be an easy tune-up for anyone. Clay downplayed Chuvalo's victory, dubbing him "The Washerwoman" in response to the awkward but brutal second-round barrage he had unleashed on DeJohn. To Clay, the trajectory of Chuvalo's punches resembled the downward motion that laundresses employed when scrubbing dirty clothes against washboards. Although Clay's team tried to shrug off their agreement to fight Chuvalo, the Canadian would not let them forget their obligation. He told any reporter who would listen that Clay was afraid to fight him. When Clay appeared on a talk show to discuss his future, Chuvalo crashed the set in drag, talking in a falsetto, and brandishing what he claimed to be a valid contract to fight the Louisville Lip. Surely, he accused, Clay was not afraid to fight a washerwoman. Distinctly uncomfortable with Chuvalo's antics, Clay avoided questions about whether they would meet.[77]

Local boxing people were also miffed by Clay's refusal to fight Chuvalo. After all, he had signed a letter of intent to take on the winner of DeJohn-Chuvalo in a nationally televised November 8 bout in Louisville, and now he was leaving promoter Bill King holding the bag. Clay charged that he was right to renege because "Chuvalo butts and fights inside. I could get an eye injury. Chuvalo is a dirty fighter." Infuriated, King asked Arch Hindman, the executive secretary of the World Boxing Association (WBA), formerly known as the NBA, to do something about it. Hindman warned Clay that he had to stay active if he was to maintain his number-one ranking, but there was little else he could do. But Bill King would remember the slight for a long time. Never again would Clay fight in his hometown.[78]

With his situation more fragile than ever, the Louisville Sponsoring Group did to Clay what its members might have done with their own sons had they been getting too frisky stateside. They sent him to Europe, booking a June bout in London's Wembley Stadium against popular local Henry Cooper, a left-hooker cursed with skin like tissue paper. Cooper was prone to cuts, and three of his eight losses had come as a result of his bleeding too badly to continue. Cooper also had twenty-seven victories, some of them against tough heavyweights, but whenever he had stepped up against the very best he lost by knockout. He was, however, good enough to be the ninth-ranked heavyweight in the world, and a win over the second-ranked Clay would vault him back into title contention.

The LSG would benefit from this scenario in at least three ways. First, it got Clay away from the American press. Clay arrived in England almost three weeks before the fight, which by boxing standards is quite long. But leaving removed the threat of questions about the Nation of Islam or civil rights, since no newspaper based in the United States would pay for a reporter's intercontinental stay of that length to cover a non-title fight. Second, it allowed Clay to repair some of the damage done to his credibility by his shaky performance against Jones and avoidance of Chuvalo. London's bookmakers made Clay the 4–1 favorite, and everyone expected Cooper to be an easy touch. Third, the match would help the syndicate expand Clay's marketability. The cultivation of a European fan base would provide them with insurance. Even if Americans lost interest in him, either because of his big mouth or because of a crushing loss to Sonny Liston, he could potentially make money fighting in Europe. There had not been a world heavyweight title fight outside North America since 1933, and fans abroad were far less likely than Americans to discard boxers who were not the sport's greatest. Henry Cooper was a prime example, being a national hero in Britain despite a less-than-stellar record. It would not be the last time that Clay would escape to Europe when things got too hot to handle in the United States.

Sticking with what he knew best, Clay decided to promote the Cooper match by being as obnoxious as possible to the British fans. In doing so, he emphasized Cooper's popularity and drove people to the box office to see him lose. Only a week after Clay's arrival, Cooper was already saying things like, "Surely by now he knows that everybody in Britain, including me, hates his guts." Peter Wilson of the *London Daily Mirror*, however, sensed the effectiveness of Clay's methods. "There won't be more than a handful of people hop-ing to see him win at Wembley tonight," he wrote, "yet this astonishing young Negro has done more to restore worldwide interest in boxing than any indi-vidual I can remember since the palmiest days of Joe Louis." There had been other black American fighters who had captivated the British public, but "no one, I believe, has become quite such a household word—even if it is a rude one—as CASSIUS MARCELLUS CLAY." On fight night, Clay wore a red velvet crown into the ring, further antagonizing British fans, who responded by boo-ing and throwing things at him. During the bout, he taunted Cooper by drop-ping his hands to his sides and daring the slower, smaller fighter to make a move. The British Broadcasting Corporation's (BBC) television commentator chided, "This is not the way to go about being a top heavyweight con-tender. . . . He's trying to make Cooper look small." On BBC radio, listeners could hear the announcer call Clay "a terrible man." Desmond Hackett of the *London Daily Express* explained that the "British do not love a braggart and a bully who is not anything like as majestic as he proclaims." After the match, when the victorious Clay was leaving the ring, he was attacked by a fan who had broken through his escort of twenty-two bobbies. It also took Clay's party several hours to get out of Wembley's parking lot when their vehicles were surrounded by an angry mob.[79]

Clay's strategy to provoke people into paying to see him fight worked. The 55,000 fans in attendance filled 90 percent of the arena, constituting En-gland's largest crowd for a boxing match since 1935 and producing a gate of about $300,000 despite daylong rains that did not cease until the bout's sec-ond round. Clay received an $85,000 purse, while Cooper got $40,000, by far the largest payday of his career. The fight itself, however, further tarnished Clay's in-ring reputation. Clay had predicted that he would stop Cooper in round five. When the tender skin around Cooper's left eye burst during the third round, Clay eased up in an attempt to realize his five-round forecast. Near the end of the fourth round, Clay's nonchalance turned disastrous when Cooper exploded a left hook on his chin, dropping the young American to the canvas. Although Clay rose at the count of four and was immediately saved by the bell, he was shaken badly. He would come out in the next round to reopen Cooper's wound, producing a horrifying blood flow that forced the referee to intercede in the chosen round five. Nevertheless, it was an unsatisfying re-sult. If Clay could be knocked down by a fringe contender like Henry Coo-per, what would Sonny Liston do to him? Peter Wilson encapsulated the be-liefs of writers and fans everywhere when he asserted that "[A]ny suggestion that Clay—fast though he is, clever at blocking and staying out of range—should be matched with Sonny Liston in the near future should be laughed out of the rings of the world." Nevertheless, it appeared that contest would be the next heavyweight championship match. Liston's representatives were in England to observe the fight and offer Clay a title shot. For Liston's people, it was an easy decision. Clay looked like a true moneymaker and a soft opponent for the champion.[80]

Getting Clay out of the United States, although a temporary fix to its problems, proved once again that the Louisville Sponsoring Group was unable to throttle the fighter completely. While in England, Bill Faversham and attorney Gordon Davidson announced that Clay would no longer speak to the press. "The voice goes into deep freeze as of now. From now on, I will do the talking for Clay," said Davidson. Yeah, right. Clay did a bombastic interview with the *Daily Express* just two days later. For the first time, the LSG, through Faversham, began to criticize its prodigy, implying that he was unable to get along without them. "A big fault is that he is too generous with his money," said Faversham. "Give him $5, $50, or $500—and he'll spend it. And nobody can really say where it goes." Such talk was new for the organization, whose members had never before disparaged the fighter's financial or personal habits. At ringside in London, Faversham made a scene, ordering trainer Angelo Dundee to "make [Clay] stop the funny business." Nearing a huge payoff for the Liston match, and with its perception of the fighter as vulnerable inside and outside the ring reaching a peak, the Louisville Sponsoring Group sought unsuccessfully to tighten its control over Clay.[81]

Of course, the LSG members could not, and when he returned to the United States, Clay continued to discuss race matters with the black press. In town for a July Sugar Ray Robinson fight, Clay told the *Pittsburgh Courier* that he wanted to move to New York because he was "fed up" with the police harassment he was facing in parts of the South. He compared his treatment by police to that of Sonny Liston and was particularly disturbed by "those begrudging little fellows among whom I'm strictly from nowhere. These little guys simply cannot take it." Clay was referring to the repeated traffic stops, which he suggested were usually for imagined offenses, that he had experienced while driving his Cadillac. He even had the car repainted in an attempt to reduce the harassment.[82]

Having begun negotiations with Sonny Liston's camp for an early 1964 title match, the Louisville Sponsoring Group was desperate to keep Clay under wraps just a little bit longer. Although the Group members hoped he would win the fight, it is doubtful that they were confident. Liston was an absolute terror, and while Clay had shown flashes of brilliance, he had also struggled time and again against mediocre opposition. None of the experts took Clay's chances seriously. But even if the bout exposed Clay as just another contender, the gate receipts would dwarf anything that he and the

Sponsoring Group had earned in the three years they had been partners. All the LSG had to do was prevent him from messing it up by making sure that the cultural narratives surrounding his career did not intersect with the resulting financial consequences. It would prove to be a difficult task.

Damage Control through
Moral Authority

The Louisville Sponsoring Group's Specialty

By steering Cassius Clay through boxing's rough waters and landing on a title shot with Sonny Liston, the Louisville Sponsoring Group had essentially done its job. Certainly the members did not expect him to win, so all that was left for them to do was try their best to ensure that the gate receipts for the match were massive. After that, presumably, they and their fighter would sail off into the sunset carrying bags of money. There was no guarantee, however, that the bout would draw well. Clay's obnoxiousness had gone bad. Once fresh, it now threatened to stink up the sport. Rumors that Clay had joined the Nation of Islam didn't help. A fight that needed a good guy to foil the despised Liston had lost its protagonist. It was under these circumstances that the Louisville Sponsoring Group would pull off its greatest feat by helping salvage the gate for a fight that was poorly promoted from the beginning.

To the overwhelming majority of the public, it was a question not of whether Sonny Liston would defeat Cassius Clay, but of what round Clay would be pounded into insensibility. Only three of the forty-six sportswriters sent to Miami to cover the fight predicted that the challenger would win. Bookmakers installed Liston as a 7–1 favorite, huge odds for a boxing match and a reminder that many considered the champion to be the greatest heavyweight in history. The challenger, on the other hand, had struggled in his last two bouts, winning unimpressively against Doug Jones and then being knocked down by Henry Cooper. The morning of the title match, the physician assigned to examine the fighters diagnosed Clay as terrified to the point of being unable to compete, citing his rapid heartbeat, elevated blood pressure, and hysterical ravings. Many observers felt that this was going to be Cassius Clay's last fight as a serious contender, if not altogether. His winning or losing wasn't the issue; his health was.

Although initial projections indicated that the bout was going to produce the biggest gross in boxing history, Clay-Liston was a potential box-office bust for several reasons. The first was that people saw the encounter as a probable slaughter, that Clay would have no chance against the fearsome Liston, and that the fight would not be worth watching. While there were those who would go to fights to see somebody get hurt, most boxing fans would not be lured to closed-circuit theaters unless they felt that the featured match was going to be worthwhile. While mismatches were somewhat tolerable in person because fight clubs had special ambiance and because main events were backed by an undercard, nobody liked to pay five dollars to see two minutes of action on a screen. There was also Clay's big mouth to reckon with. It was one thing when he had targeted opponents and kept things lighthearted, but now the Louisville Lip was turning political. His disparaging remarks about the civil rights movement and his increasing indiscretion about his association with the Nation of Islam threatened everything. A subtle shift was occurring. People who once believed that Clay acted like a jerk were starting to think that he really was one. Normally, this would not cut into gate receipts, because as the first Patterson-Liston fight proved, and as Gorgeous George had emphasized to young Clay, a good guy/bad guy pairing was the most lucrative one. But Liston was one of the most hated champions in history, thought of as a menace to society, and if Clay kept this up, there would simply be nobody to root for in this match. Fans usually did not come to see two fighters they didn't like. Despite these issues, the fight did very well at the box office. Its doing so was an indication of Cassius Clay's ability to generate interest in his fights and of the Louisville Sponsoring Group's calming influence on a public that was growing increasingly distrustful of both Clay's ability and his character.

From the beginning, the LSG did right by its fighter. Clay's representatives worked out a deal with the champion's camp in which the Louisville fighter would earn a 22.5 percent cut of the total revenues, at the time the largest share ever earned by a heavyweight title challenger in the closed-circuit era. Bill MacDonald, the local who in Chris Dundee's stead had promoted the third Patterson-Johansson fight, which set an all-time indoor gate record, announced that he would pay the fighters $625,000 from the live gate. He hoped to sell 16,000 tickets, and had to take in about $850,000 to break even. Clay got a $225,000 guarantee from MacDonald, while Liston would receive $400,000. Although MacDonald was usually billed as the bout's promoter, he was in fact a partner of Chris Dundee, who remained in the background. Shut out from the Patterson-Johansson fight, Dundee would finally have the chance for a windfall.[83]

The signing and hyping of the bout coincided with a series of major civil rights campaigns that dominated the period's news coverage and popular ideology, and both fighters responded to them in ways that alienated the press. Although Liston had earned a reputation for being apolitical, the surge in civil rights activity, and the increase in violent resistance to it, moved him to comment on the state of the nation. He told reporters that he was "ashamed to be in America," and their criticism of him quickly followed. From a public relations standpoint, Clay wasn't doing much better. His brashness was getting to reporters, and he increasingly brought up race in ways that bothered them. At the contract signings, he had infuriated strait-laced writers with his shenanigans, which was nothing new. What was unique, however, was Clay's defense of his actions. His act was not simply about getting rich, but about doing so in a racist society. "Where do you think I would be next week if I didn't know how to shout and holler and make the public sit up and take notice?" he asked. "I would be poor for one thing, and I would probably be down in Louisville, KY, my hometown, washing windows or running an elevator and saying 'Yes, suh' and 'No, suh' and knowing my place." For some people, especially those who reveled in Martin Luther King Jr.'s "I Have a Dream" speech at that summer's March on Washington, such comments touched a nerve and reminded them that things were not as rosy as they may have hoped.[84]

The most difficult narrative for the Louisville Sponsoring Group to contain, and the one that stood most to affect Clay's development as a public figure and the gate to his upcoming title fight, was his rumored affiliation with the Nation of Islam (NOI), also known as the Black Muslims. The Nation of Islam was a religious organization loosely based on Islam but customized to appeal to black Americans. Led by Elijah Muhammad, it preached that blacks and whites would never be able to live together peacefully because whites were fundamentally evil. It was the philosophical opposite of the contemporary civil rights organizations that preached brotherly love and integration as the way to solve race problems, it scared a lot of people, and it was unpopular among large numbers of blacks and whites. Despite this fear and loathing of the NOI, it is important to recognize that the organization was not simply a hate group built upon antipathy for whites. The NOI's philosophy of economic nationalism drew from longstanding African American self-help traditions previously embraced by leaders like Booker T. Washington and Marcus Garvey. However, few whites regarded the organization in this manner, and therefore, even if it could not reckon directly with Clay's increasing association with the Nation of Islam, the LSG had to assert its moral authority in ways that counteracted the potential effect of Clay's Muslim connections on the gate.[85]

The main source of concern was Clay's association with Malcolm X. Although his relationship with the organization had deteriorated by the time Clay and Liston came to terms, Malcolm X had been the longtime face and voice of the Nation of Islam, by far its most famous member. He and Clay had struck up a close friendship in the months preceding the title bout, and the press took notice. Clay, under advisement by the LSG, refused to confirm or deny whether he was a member of the organization. Angelo Dundee, however, who was always in close contact with the syndicate, did damage control. Although Dundee had a policy to never discuss a fighter's personal life, he explained, "The Black Muslim stuff is hokum. That's a hate group. Cassius likes people. The only group that Cassius belongs to is the Cassius Clay group." Some reporters, however, were skeptical. Dean Eagle claimed that the fighter's religious and political ties threatened his career: "The Clay image has deteriorated. Clay could have been the good guy in this 'battle of the Palm Beaches,' but instead he will be the bad guy because of his association with the Black Muslims. Promoter Chris Dundee says that stigma has hurt the gate."[86]

But there were also many people who did not get overly alarmed about Clay's possible membership in the NOI. They thought he was going to get smashed by Liston and therefore fade into insignificance anyway. Furthermore, Clay was still carrying on with his own unique and goofy promotional style, the one that got him a title shot in the first place. Whereas leaders like Malcolm X and Elijah Muhammad appeared to be menacing demagogues, serious all the time and a threat to whites, Clay still seemed to be a mischievous, fun-loving kid. It also didn't hurt that he finally shut his mouth, at the behest of the Louisville Sponsoring Group, about race and civil rights issues. In Miami, as the bout approached, it was business as usual, and the fighter seemed to be back to his old self. Refusing to comment after being questioned about his relationship with the Nation of Islam, he tried to crash Liston's training camp. At the nearby Surfside Auditorium, where Liston was sparring, Clay and nine members of his entourage attracted a crowd of over 500 when they gathered outside.

What was strange about the episode was that Clay was being associated with a group that framed the civil rights movement as anathema, yet he had been greatly affected by the movement and its methods. When the local police chief refused Clay—whose getup included a black tuxedo, ruffle shirt, and elaborately carved cane—and his entourage admission into the training facility, the fighter invoked the language and tactics of the movement. "I'm ready to go to jail if I'm breaking the law, but I'm not doing a thing," Clay said. "This is a public place and I have a right to pay to go inside." When the chief refused to back down and told the fighter to stop blocking the sidewalk and keep his voice down or risk being jailed, Clay and his group marched to city hall to seek a permit to picket Liston's training camp. The city council agreed to hold a hearing on his request. For all of the sentiment distancing Clay from the contemporary freedom struggle, he was clearly influenced by it and employed its signature methods and rhetoric. About a week before the bout, Clay and company again made a ruckus when they pulled up outside Liston's gym. Traffic stopped on a busy street and the police chief had to hustle Clay into a nearby parking lot in order to ease the congestion. These kinds of headlines took some people's minds off Clay's possible association with the Nation of Islam.[87]

The Louisville Sponsoring Group further mitigated the damage by standing alongside its fighter, thus abandoning the tactic it had tried in London when it briefly distanced itself from him. Bill Faversham pleaded with reporters to understand things from Clay's perspective. "People sometimes tell me that Clay is a braggart, a showoff," he said. "I reply that he is no different than any other youngster would be who is making a half-million dollars a year." Although privately the organization was running out of patience with him, it publicly stood by Clay, lending its considerable moral authority to someone badly in need of it.[88]

On fight night, February 25, 1964, boxing fans saw one of the greatest upsets in the sport's history. All of the talk that Clay wasn't ready for Liston turned out to be poppycock. From the pre-fight stare-down, when it suddenly became apparent to everyone that Clay was the larger of the two men, the challenger dominated the affair. He was too strong and too fast for Liston. Only in the fifth round, after a last-ditch effort by the champion's corner to blind the challenger by pouring a caustic liniment on its man's gloves, did Liston show any spark at all. He was completely outclassed, and when the bell rang to start the eighth round, he spat out his mouthpiece and refused to rise, claiming that he had hurt his left shoulder. Clay had done the impossible, and it made front-page news. The fight produced an excellent gate, but it would also represent one of the final triumphs of the Louisville Sponsoring Group. Its ability to contain the narratives surrounding its fighter was slipping away. Almost immediately following the bout, rumors surfaced that Clay would use his championship earnings to fund Malcolm X's political career outside the Nation of Islam.[89]

The Relationship between Cassius Clay and the Louisville Sponsoring Group

A Summary

Muhammad Ali's biographers have made much of the relationship between him and the Louisville Sponsoring Group, overwhelmingly praising the organization for treating him fairly within a milieu characterized by managerial abuse of clients. But what did the Louisville Sponsoring Group do for Cassius Clay/Muhammad Ali other than pay him what he deserved? What was the actual nature of their relationship? Does the syndicate really deserve the high regard that biographers have afforded it? Does its square dealing with Clay/Ali excuse its paternalism toward him? These questions will always be a matter of speculation, but as new sources become available to scholars, they become more transparent than before. Recently, the private papers of George Barry Bingham, whose family owned the major media outlets in Louisville, including WHAS television and radio, the *Louisville Times*, and the *Louisville Courier-Journal*, were donated to his hometown's Filson Historical Society. Within those documents are the papers of Worth Bingham, his eldest son who worked as the editor of the *Courier-Journal* and was also a member of the Louisville Sponsoring Group. It is this collection of correspondence that for the first time gives us an inside look at the nature of the relationship between Clay/Ali and his benefactors. The material leads me to agree with the conclusion made by previous biographers that the LSG was an enormously positive influence on the fighter's career and deserves to be recognized as such.

Any study of the relationship between Clay/Ali and the LSG must keep in mind two fundamental points: (1) the LSG wanted to make money from its association with the fighter; (2) the LSG quickly realized that it was enormously difficult to do so because of the massive expenses that its young protégé routinely racked up. Despite their financial acumen, LSG members got few riches from their investment. Gordon Davidson said years later, "There's no way to view the whole experience as a financial killing, or even a financial venture. These were millionaires who ended up investing, over six years, more than ten thousand dollars each—and a lot of that was deductible—and came out with twenty-five thousand, in dribs and drabs." Although several in the syndicate believed that the investment was going to result in a massive windfall, the failure of such a sharp group to turn much of a profit despite owning the most valuable commodity in sports indicates a number of possibilities. The most interesting are that it was either exceedingly hard for novices to turn much of a profit from boxing—no matter how formidable their business sense and talented their clients—or that it was exceedingly hard for honest people who treated their client appropriately to do so.[90]

In the early years, while the organization was in the red, managing partner Bill Faversham, attorney Gordon Davidson, and treasurer James Todd had to frequently remind LSG members that their investment in Clay was a long-term one and that it was unrealistic to believe that the group would show immediate profits. The impatience of several members indicates that there was a strong economic motivation behind the LSG's partnership with Clay. One memo, for example, tells the syndicate that all of the expenses associated with managing, promoting, and training the young fighter were tax-deductible. After a $300 assessment was levied on members to pay for Clay's larger-than-expected expenses, an accompanying note explained that the problem was not Clay's profligacy, but that the LSG was having a difficult time finding ranked contenders to take him on. At times, group members had to be reminded to be patient. Faversham wrote them to explain that bringing along a fighter the right way took time. "We have not got a heavyweight champion today, or the next day, but we have a marvelous prospect for a couple of years from now, and, as your representative, I am not going to allow promoters to push us into fights that I think are too much for the boy at this time." Some, like Worth Bingham, wanted to leave the group because they felt that the return on their investment was not coming quickly enough, but Faversham convinced them not to withdraw. The LSG was carefully constructed with each member having a specific role, and Clay would become upset by any change in management. Bingham decided to stay after Faversham assured him that profits were not far away. Faversham even had to make promises about the future in order to keep certain members interested. In May 1962, he made the following claim, "At the moment I am working on another fight for July which would be, by far, the biggest purse we have ever received. . . . I can say to you, however, that if the terms for the July fight are as I expect, we will be definitely in the black for this year, and might even look forward to making back some of the original investment." When the entire group got impatient that summer about the slow pace, Faversham told them, "I feel sure this year will be considerably in the black although the original investment will not be made up. However, if all continues to go well, the latter should take place next year." The frequent correspondence in which LSG members had to be assured that their investment was a wise one indicates that for some of them the interest in Clay was mostly financial. But as will also be seen, many of the members remained loyal to Clay long after it was apparent that the partnership would not produce the expected bonanza.[91]

The Louisville Sponsoring Group provided Clay with security and protection that regular boxing managers could not. At times, the organization used its formidable political contacts to put Clay into advantaged situations. LSG attorneys Gordon Davidson and Arthur Grafton both worked in a law firm whose partners included former Louisville mayor and then lieutenant governor Wilson Wyatt. But the LSG's connections went far beyond the local scene. One of the most remarkable episodes of LSG altruism toward Clay took place in mid-1963, when he was next in line to face Sonny Liston. Knowing that their fighter was going to be pushed into the highest tax bracket and have a huge portion of his purse share taken away as a result of the massive lump sum he would receive for fighting Liston, LSG members lobbied federal officeholders to change tax laws so that Clay could take advantage of his making the financial big time. William Cutchins, a syndicate member and president of the Brown and Williamson Tobacco Corporation, wrote a letter to Wilbur D. Mills, chair of the U.S. House of Representatives Ways and Means Committee, urging the prompt passage of a proposed revenue measure that would permit citizens to average earnings over a period of several years. The new law would thus prevent Clay from having his share from the Liston fight taxed all at once. "We were astounded and shocked to examine at first hand the extremely unfair results which our tax laws impose upon a young man such as Clay," he wrote, "who has suddenly reached a peak of earning power in a few short years which will of necessity be followed by an extreme decline as his physical powers decline and eliminate him from boxing." If the bill passed, according to Cutchins, Clay would retain almost twice the income he would under the existing laws. Faversham also did his part, making arrangements to see Senator Robert Byrd and members of the Treasury Department and White House staff who were also handling the measure. The bill passed in time for Clay to reap its benefits. While it is impossible to know just how much influence the LSG actually had, or if its members would also have benefited from such an arrangement, it is clear that Clay's backers were willing to go out of their way to help their young pugilistic charge.[92]

Although early in his career Clay had insisted that he would not become another Joe Louis beset by tax problems, there were times when his spending threatened to put him in such a spot. During these occasions, however, the LSG would use its political contacts and sterling reputation to keep him out of trouble. When the new champion improperly handled some income that led to his owing the Internal Revenue Service (IRS) for back taxes, the LSG responded by scheduling a meeting between him and the IRS district director in Louisville, which he promptly skipped. An alarmed Bill Faversham told the syndicate that the move had "jeopardized all of the work that Gordon Davidson had done in keeping Cassius clean with the federal government." Luckily for the fighter, however, the Sponsoring Group intervened, rescheduled the meeting, and took care of the problem. It is doubtful that the Louisville Lip even realized what the LSG had done for him in this situation, despite its importance.[93]

Even the members of the group who felt the most antipathy toward their young charge, like advertising executive Archibald Foster, were earnest in their attempts to help him earn and save as much money as he possibly could, even after the fighter had won the title and made it clear that his loyalties were to the black nationalist Nation of Islam and not the LSG. Foster's simultaneous contempt and concern for the champion came through in a memo he wrote to Arthur Grafton:

> One of the problems most deeply involving Cassius is obviously taxes. The only way his unsophisticated mind can explore [tax deductions] is the giving away of his money to a church. This is commendable, of course, but I feel that if we could devise a way of giving him a tax avoidance program which would throw profit to him in later years, we might not only wean him from the Muslims, but also wed him eternally to us as an amenable, grateful fellow. . . . . It is clear that the champ's focus is on beating taxes. I believe we can muster enough experience in this business to cause his eyes to bulge. I ask us all to remember that Herbert Muhammad [son of Nation of Islam leader Elijah Muhammad], toward the end of our meeting, asked us to forget the giving program to the Mosque because it was not yet qualified as a tax-exempt foundation. I have told Madison Square Garden that there is practically no chance of a[nother] 1965 fight because the Champ is in a tax bind and doesn't want to involve himself until next year.

The memo is a remarkable one because it shows that the LSG did not sit idly by while Ali shifted his loyalties to the NOI. But rather than simply exercise its legal authority as his rightful manager in an attempt to block that relationship, the LSG battled to show the champion that it was the organization best able to represent him because it would provide him the most benefit.[94]

Another thing that the LSG did expertly was pace Clay's career in a way that allowed him to create maximum impression from his fights while remaining in the public eye through endorsements and appearances. Although boxing was new to the LSG, its trust in Angelo Dundee combined with its business expertise to create minimum risk and maximum reward for Clay. When Clay stole the show at the second Patterson-Liston bout in July 1963 by jumping into the ring both before and after the contest, the LSG realized that the public would shell out big money to see him fight Liston. It also understood, however, that delaying the bout was the wisest economic choice it could make for the fighter. As negotiations moved forward for a September bout between Clay and Liston, Gordon Davidson claimed to be "sick about having the fight this year." He felt that Clay would earn $100,000 through exhibitions and public appearances through the end of the year and then make big money fighting Liston from an advantaged tax position in 1964.[95]

During this period there were plenty of opportunities to keep Clay in the public eye without risking his undefeated record. Jack Benny offered the fighter his top price of $7,500 for Clay to be featured on the September season opener of his highly rated television show and was willing to rewrite the existing script to center on Clay. The sponsors of Mister Ed also offered a full half-hour script written completely around the fighter's appearance. While the LSG had no intention of taking that offer ("We don't want to compromise Clay"), Davidson believed "that for the sake of the boy's national image and ability to remain a money making personality if Liston should beat him, that perhaps the Benny show is still worth consideration in fairness to Cassius, since it would give him an excellent debut as an entertainment personality and hopefully a comic star." To this end, Davidson assured the LSG that he and Faversham were "working feverishly on some interesting angles to gain a postponement" of the Clay-Liston bout. Once he won the title, the LSG continued trying to make money for him through such deals. For example, Foster used his connections within the advertising industry to link Ali with the prestigious William Morris Agency in an attempt to maximize the champion's possibilities as an endorser. Another deal that the LSG engineered by exploiting its longstanding contacts, in this case with Lester and Mike Malitz, made Ali a closed-circuit commentator for the January 1965 bout between Floyd Patterson and George Chuvalo. For talking between rounds, publicizing the bout, and visiting the camps of the two fighters, Ali received nearly $10,000.[96]

It is important to remember that the Louisville Sponsoring Group was doing all of this for Ali long after its members realized that the endeavor was never going to be as profitable as some of them had originally thought it might be. From an earnings standpoint, the organization's big problem was that it had to pay Ali's expenses from its share of the revenues, and the fighter ran up large bills. In the first four months, the organization operated $14,800 in the red. In 1961, its first full year, despite grossing nearly $20,000 in revenues from Clay's fights, the LSG lost nearly $10,000. In 1962, it took in nearly $90,000, showing a $20,000 profit. The organization's accounting logs from 1963 illustrate just how hard it was to make money in the sport, especially when taking care of the big-spending Clay. That year, its total income was about $165,000. Almost all of the money came from three sources: Clay's fights ($128,000), an album Clay made with Columbia Records ($20,000), and Clay's personal appearances ($16,500). Despite this, the organization came away with a net income of $24,000. Training expenses were nearly $21,000. Clay was paid $81,000. About half of the money generated by Clay's personal appearances ($7,000) was offset by expenses, and the album also cost the LSG $5,000 to make. In addition, the group had to bear over $16,000 in miscellaneous costs, not to mention nearly $11,000 in insurance policies it had taken out on the fighter. The year 1963 was a huge one for Clay. His fights with Powell, Cooper, and Jones were all record setters, and he was at an all-time peak of popularity and public interest. Yet for all of their group's work, each of the LSG members took home only $2,400. Some were obviously tempted by the prospects of the payoff from a title fight with Liston, of course, but even after that bout, the LSG's total balance was only around $56,000. For three-and-a-half years of work, each member showed a taxable profit of about $5,600. In a private document sent to a journalist, Worth Bingham estimated that the investment had garnered him a net gain of $12,500 between 1960 and 1965. For millionaires, as almost all of the LSG members were, this was peanuts. We must recognize that there was more than a little charity in the LSG's handling of Clay/Ali. By the time of the Liston bout, all the members must have realized that as an investment, the partnership would not produce large returns. Yet they continued to work hard to ensure the viability of Ali's career and future. The organization deserves praise and credit for not abandoning the fighter. Their paternalism notwithstanding, its members were clearly motivated by more than greed.[97]

The LSG did its best to manage the fighter's out-of-control spending habits, but that was almost impossible to do. The various battles over such matters were draining and repetitive. It wasn't that the LSG simply paid him a fair percentage of his purses, not to mention his expenses, but the organization even went so far as to loan him money regularly without charging him interest. By January 1965, he had amassed nearly $45,000 in debt to the organization. While such loans were tolerable when LSG members felt that they were one big fight away from being deeply into the black, by this time most of them suspected that they would never see repayment of these moneys, unless they wanted to take Ali to court. Furthermore, the LSG had lost all of the profit it had made, and had gone into debt itself, when Ali suffered a hernia that forced the postponement of what was to be a late-1964 rematch with Liston. The LSG had to eat all of the considerable training expenses it had fronted, and saw no remuneration. Also faced with Ali's free-falling public image, the group, it seemed, would never recoup its losses, although relatively strong gates from the Ali-Liston rematch and Ali's title defense against Floyd Patterson put the LSG back into the black by 1966. It continued to loan Ali money, but by this time the latest $5,000 installment included a letter from the Sponsoring Group urging the fighter "not to incur any additional indebtedness during this period of time between now and the next fight."[98]

During this time, the LSG was forced to contend with unnecessary expenses and battles resulting from Ali's spending, the latest being Drew "Bundini" Brown's addition to the weekly payroll at a rate of $100. Half mystic, half court jester, Brown had hooked up with Clay during 1963 and had remained a constant presence in his training camp, although what he did was not really tangible or quantifiable. If you wanted to be generous, you could call him Ali's spiritual adviser.

The Sponsoring Group saw him as one of the many unnecessary accessories employed by the champ that had broken its bank account. Davidson had written Brown a letter in November 1964, addressed to Brown's room at the luxury Biltmore Hotel in Miami, explaining that the LSG had lost $60,000 as a result of the cancellation of the second Liston bout and would no longer pay any of Brown's expenses except when he appeared in Ali's training camp. With Ali laid up from hernia surgery, and not even in the same city as Brown, it seemed ridiculous to pay Bundini, yet the following week he was put on the payroll. Things like this made it almost impossible for Ali to accumulate wealth from his more-than-generous share of the fight revenues and frustrated the LSG. That much was obvious from a February 1965 letter from Davidson to Brown, which contained a salary advance of $200 and a note telling him, "Get to Chicago and do your job."[99]

Ali must have been aware of the care that the LSG members put into handling his career, but it is doubtful that he realized just how much money they had to shell out for his expenses, since they came directly out of the LSG's end. In July 1964, with no scheduled fights upcoming, the LSG decided that it would be best to finance Ali's expenses through bank loans, which it would pay back once Ali fought again. By March 1965, the LSG owed $65,000, which it told the bank it would repay once it got the proceeds from the now-scheduled Liston rematch. Ten-thousand-dollar loans in March and April jacked up the bill to $85,000. The loan eventually peaked in June

1965 at $125,000, and it would continue to accrue interest until the LSG finally collected in September a $350,000 share of the money it was owed from the second Ali-Liston fight.[100]

All of this financial support was part of a larger attempt by the LSG to make the fighter feel protected. For all of his bravado, Clay was still a young man, and the LSG members provided him needed moral support and the feeling that they cared about him and his career. LSG members attended all of Clay's Louisville fights, and Faversham implored them to come to his out-of-town bouts whenever possible. Although the match with Duke Sabedong was in Las Vegas, the managing partner urged that "some of us should make the trip as, at no time, do we want our trainer, Angelo Dundee, and Cassius to think we are not keeping tight reins on the situation." Similarly, Faversham urged LSG members to turn out for the Louisville bout between George Chuvalo and Mike DeJohn in order to scope out Clay's probable next opponent and indicate their interest in his career. "I know Angelo would appreciate it greatly if you would take in the fight as he would love to see the Group who he has not seen in a long time."[101]

These messages also indicate that the LSG was keeping a close eye, or at least the appearance thereof, on its fighter and trainer. There were times when the LSG used its executive muscle to convince Clay to go along with things that it felt were in his best interest. When in 1963 the fighter became convinced that he wanted to start training in New York instead of Miami, the group told him that it was not possible. Clay acquiesced when Faversham called his mother on the telephone to urge her to convince her son to train in Miami. Promoter Bill King, who was trying to put together a fight between Clay and the winner of the DeJohn-Chuvalo bout, at the request of the LSG, also made an announcement that he would not promote it unless Clay trained in Miami. According to William Cutchins, "This seemed to have convinced Cassius that we meant business, and I thanked Bill King on behalf of the group for his help." Although the bout never took place because Dundee realized it was unwise to match Clay with someone as rough as Chuvalo, the episode indicated the group's active hand in steering its charge's career.[102]

But the relationship between the LSG and Cassius Clay/Muhammad Ali was far more amicable than the fighter let on. He appreciated what the LSG, particularly Faversham, had done for him. When the LSG's managing partner suffered a heart attack in December 1964, Ali drove 300 miles from Chicago to Louisville through the night to visit him in the hospital. Although the attendant staff prevented the champ from seeing Faversham, who was in no condition to receive visitors, Ali offered to stand by and lend a hand. With Faversham out of commission, the syndicate appointed Angelo Dundee as

Ali's manager of record. Dundee was ordered by the Sponsoring Group's executive committee—which included Cutchins, Bingham, and Davidson—to "take no action of major implications without being in touch with us." Dundee's weekly pay rose to $300 and he would also receive a 10 percent share of the gross receipts of Ali's fights from the Louisville Sponsoring Group's share. The LSG also agreed to pay the premium on a life insurance policy for Dundee.[103]

Despite his public disregard for the LSG, especially as he became more involved with the Nation of Islam, Ali tried to prevent any of its members from selling interests in the syndicate to outsiders. When poor health moved one of them to try to unload his shares, Ali became resentful, refusing to go along with the deal until he spoke to the men who were interested in buying into the LSG. He believed the sale was a personal affront indicating that at least one of the members had lost confidence in him and that the group as a whole, since it seemed unwilling to buy the share, had felt similarly. This logic was questionable but was also an indication that Ali cared about what the LSG thought of him. Davidson was confident that "Cassius' position is not one of antagonism but is more one of failure to understand the transaction or the reason for it. . . . When dealing with Cassius one can never be prepared for what may occur. As stated previously, his position is not one of trying to cause additional trouble, but is, I believe, based upon the fact that he fails to understand why new people are coming into the Group at this time." Ali eventually wound up approving the sale after about a month of resistance.[104]

But even the LSG had its limits, and some of its members began to wonder whether it was worthwhile to remain involved with Ali. Although Ali had said shortly after the Liston rematch, "I'll sign with them again, but I'll want more money," the organization was somewhat unsure. Faversham believed that they had done right by Ali and was confident that the fighter wanted the partnership to continue. "Our contract with Clay expires October 1966. We don't have an option on renewal, but we have right of first refusal. We wouldn't want to hold him, but he's been pretty happy with us." Yet Sponsoring Group members were having serious doubts. "The more I think about the situation, the more I want to be quit of my association with the champion," wrote Archibald Foster:

All of our long-term purposes have been frustrated. We had hoped to be completely free of underworld connections, but we seem to have new ones in Chicago [a reference to a proposed match between Ali and Ernie Terrell, who was reputed to be a mob fighter]. Certainly we don't like the anti-American philosophy which attaches to us by association [a reference to Ali's recent stand against the Vietnam War]. Finally, the money rewards are so little that I can't believe any of us are interested in those. What I'd like to do is give Cassius back his contract. I would like to do this publicly before the press.

Although Foster's position was representative, that his advice was not followed is an illustration of the loyalty the group showed the fighter, even when that loyalty was not reciprocated by Ali.[105]

The Sponsoring Group also handled changes in Ali's personnel smoothly, especially as the champion allowed the Nation of Islam to take a larger role in running his career. When Elijah Muhammad's lawyer Chauncey Eskridge took over as Ali's primary counsel in early 1965, the Sponsoring Group did its best to ensure a smooth transition and to inform Ali's new legal team about the particulars and peculiarities of handling the champion. In February, Davidson sent a terse and strident note to Eskridge after a Chicago newspaper reported that Ali was scheduled to fight a ten-round exhibition match. Because a longer bout might jeopardize his upcoming rematch with Liston by taking too much of a physical toll on him, the LSG had made an agreement with Liston's handlers that no Ali exhibition would eclipse four rounds. Davidson instructed Eskridge to make sure that the rule was followed. The following month, Davidson wrote the attorney again, reminding him to pay Ali's auto insurance, which the LSG had been doing since he was under its auspices. And when the champion requested that a $500 check be sent to his mother, it was Gordon Davidson who did it. In May, it was also the Sponsoring Group that sent Clay a $12,000 income tax return check with instructions that he must endorse it as "Cassius M. Clay Jr." Ali had repeatedly signed his Muslim name on official documents, and it was causing considerable problems that the group then had to fix. The LSG wanted to make sure that did not happen in this instance, since Ali needed the money. Even as Ali marginalized the organization, it still looked out for him.[106]

The LSG also showed incredible patience when Ali unilaterally tried to install a Nation of Islam–led corporation called Main Bout Inc. as his ancillary promoter. LSG Executive Committee member J.D.S. Coleman was extremely disturbed that Ali would make such a move without first contacting the group, and he claimed that he wanted no part of any organization that did business with the Nation of Islam. Yet despite Coleman's ultimatum, the LSG chose to press on with an upcoming title fight between Ernie Terrell and Ali in Chicago under Main Bout's auspices. Arthur Grafton explained to the group, "We further did not like the flavor of the fight in Chicago, Terrell being reputedly owned by the mob and Clay obviously now being completely dominated by the Muslims. We furthermore lacked confidence in the capac-

ity of Main Bout Inc. to do even a creditable job of selling the closed circuit."
Despite these fears, however, the LSG knew that Ali would not be moved,
and rather than jeopardize its partnership with him, it acquiesced. "Clay,
however, was completely adamant about Main Bout and insisted that unless
it had the ancillary contract, he would not fight at all," reported Grafton.
While the LSG deplored the situation, all but Coleman agreed to go along
with it.[107]

The Sponsoring Group also refused to make a bad situation worse by resisting pressure to publicly criticize Ali for challenging his draft status, even
though it troubled them to see him jeopardizing his future, which they had
worked so hard to safeguard. "As far as his draft status is concerned," wrote
Grafton, "we have taken the position on behalf of the Group that this is an
entirely personal matter to Clay, that we have neither the right nor the responsibility to take any action on his behalf, and that all questions concerning his draft status should be directed to him or to his personal lawyers." Even
after the partnership was finished, LSG members still cared about Ali. Although he admitted feeling "very sorry Cassius has taken this stand," Bill
Faversham added, "I do feel that a man has the right to make such a decision.
But I only hope that this is his decision and not one that was forced on him. I
feel that it is rather tragic that he felt that he had to go this far."[108]

By far, the most important thing that the LSG did for Ali during this period was aggressively try to rehabilitate his image and preserve his moral authority. Due to his cockiness, association with the Nation of Islam, and draft
resistance, as well as the fishy outcomes of both of his bouts with Liston [the
rematch saw Liston knocked out in the first round by a punch that didn't look
very formidable], Ali's moral authority was almost non-existent in the eyes of
a public already disgusted with boxing and escalating racial tensions. One
way the LSG tried to improve Ali's image was by cultivating good press for
him. In December 1964, the LSG paid $100 to take out a full-page ad in a
journal that was being released in honor of the annual Boxing Writers Association of America dinner. Davidson told group members, "I presume most of
the leading fighters will have some ad in the journal, and my personal inclination would be that it is a necessary and worthwhile expense since this is one
group we do not want to snub, or rather, cannot afford to snub." Although
Davidson believed that Ali, rather than light-heavyweight Willie Pastrano,
should have received the fighter of the year award, he also felt that Ali's being
denied the honor was an indication of his tenuous relationship with the press,
which Davidson suspected the LSG's advertisement would help mitigate. Ali
won the award the following year.[109]

The LSG did similar work with the World Boxing Association (WBA), a
sanctioning body that partnered with state athletic commissions to rank

fighters and regulate titles. The WBA had stopped recognizing Ali as the champion, which limited the number of sites where Ali could defend his title. Realizing that cooperation from the WBA was vital, the LSG tried to wine and dine its members. For example, it paid for Bob Evans, Louisville's WBA representative and also the chair of the Kentucky State Athletic Commission, to attend the November 1965 Ali-Patterson bout in Las Vegas. Although the plan failed, in part because of earlier comments by Ali such as, "I hope the WBA won't act like a coward and take my title away from me just because they have the power. If they do, I'll win it right back," the LSG did its best to stave off the opposition. Evans had told the press earlier, "I don't see how we can help it if Clay wants to be a Black Muslim. That's a man's belief and religion. I think Clay was a model of deportment while he was here after winning the heavyweight title."[110]

The LSG knew that the commercial success of Ali's fights was linked to his moral authority and cultural image, and it tried to counter public concerns about corruption in boxing by stressing its own sterling reputation. When brokering a deal with an ancillary company called Sportsvision to promote the Ali-Patterson bout, for example, the LSG learned that Sportsvision's president and vice-president once had indirect associations with corrupt figures. It vetted Sportsvision, demanding a guarantee that the organization was a clean one. Only then would it go through with any agreement. When similar accusations arose against Inter-Continental Promotions (ICP), Sonny Liston's ancillary promoter, which the LSG had no choice but to deal with in order to get its fighter a title shot, the LSG considered getting Ali out of the closed-circuit-television business altogether, although it was the most lucrative aspect of professional boxing. Faversham suggested, "I feel strongly that Home TV is the answer for the public at this time and a much cleaner setup for the L.S.G. . . . There has been a feeling among some members of the Group and some members of the Press that the L.S.G. should try to restore the public's confidence in heavyweight boxing even if we had to do Home TV for free." What was incredible about all of this was that even the mob-connected ICP realized that its association with a reputable organization like the LSG would offer it a degree of protection. ICP attorney Garland Cherry urged LSG members to attend the first Clay-Liston fight because its officers "felt that it would aid the promotion a great deal if all the members of the Louisville Sponsoring Group were present at ringside. . . . [O]ur group felt that from a publicity point of view it would be a lot easier to sell tickets if people knew that the wealthy members of your group were going to be present. I would appreciate your urging them to make every effort to be at ringside on Tuesday, February 25, 1964. By helping the live gate they are helping themselves." Such was the pristine image of the LSG. Even when it worked with the corrupt ICP, or essentially resorted to bribing boxing writers and members of the WBA, it was viewed as more reputable than its peers. There was no greater evidence of how important this moral authority was than the commercial success of the first Clay-Liston fight. Although Clay's cultural image had been in a free fall for quite some time, public disdain for him was tempered by regard for the Louisville Sponsoring Group. Despite being promoted poorly, the Clay-Liston bout turned out to be a big moneymaker. More than a little responsibility for that belongs to the LSG.[111]

The Commercial Elements
of Clay-Liston I

Classic Muhammad Ali texts indicate that the first Clay-Liston bout was a financial disaster because of the disappointing live turnout in Miami Beach. This inaccuracy notwithstanding, it is worth exploring why things went so badly for promoter Bill MacDonald. One explanation, expressed by David Remnick in his best-selling *King of the World: Muhammad Ali and the Rise of an American Hero*, is that Clay's association with Malcolm X offended Miamians, creating enmity toward the challenger and leaving the promotion without a protagonist. If this were entirely true, however, the closed-circuit telecast would have bombed as well, since Miami's residents were assumedly not that much different from other Americans. A second explanation, offered by MacDonald, was that the huge rainstorm that drenched the city hours before the fight prevented what would have been a sizable walk-up business from happening. The problem with this scenario is that ticket sales had been dreadful from the beginning, and it was highly unlikely that traffic the day of the contest would have increased enough to make it profitable.[112]

Another theory is that since the bout seemed to be a mismatch, people did not want to pay big money to see it. This is the most worthy idea, although it also has its flaws, since the most expensive tickets that night, in the $250 section, sold briskly. Furthermore, Ali's November 1965 bout with Floyd Patterson would set an indoor, on-site gate record for a boxing match in Nevada, despite the champion's being a heavy 3–1 favorite. On the other hand, it is fair to say that the perceived lack of competitiveness affected the live gate.

The first Liston-Patterson bout, which bookmakers and the betting public felt would be competitive, as evidenced by the 3–2 odds in favor of Liston, was seen on closed-circuit television by 530,000 fans. Yet only 250,000 paid to watch the rematch, when Liston was the 4–1 favorite. Although Patterson-Ali was record setting, it was a classic good guy/bad guy match, which bolstered sales. Additionally, Patterson was box-office gold. His popularity made him perhaps the most bankable fighter in heavyweight history other than Jack Dempsey, Muhammad Ali, and Mike Tyson. At the time of the first Liston-Clay fight, Patterson had participated in six of the ten biggest-grossing bouts of all time. Of course, this also had something to do with the fact that he was the longest-reigning champion of the closed-circuit era, which had existed for only about a decade.[113]

Was the weak gate in Miami Beach an ominous sign of things to come for Clay and the Louisville Sponsoring Group, or was it idiosyncratic and specific to that particular promotion? MacDonald thought enough of the contest to pay ICP $625,000 for the on-site promotional rights, and by the time he was done advertising and paying other expenses, it needed to gross an unprecedented $800,000 just to break even. A capacity crowd of 16,448 would have brought in $1.2 million, but Convention Hall was only half full, with just 8,300 fans paying $400,000. This added up to a huge loss for MacDonald. So what went wrong? Ironically, there were some people, like Joe Louis, who blamed Clay's antics for the disaster. "I think it got out of hand the minute Sonny got in town. I think Cassius overdid it all the way," said the former heavyweight champ. "I think the public might have gone for it more if Clay had kept his mouth shut from the minute he signed his contract. I definitely think it would have done better." This was an exaggeration, as evidenced by the huge closed-circuit gross and that it was Clay's talking that had previously produced record-setting gates all around the country.[114]

Although hardly considered by contemporary reporters or Ali scholars, the most logical explanation for the problems in Miami Beach was promoter error, namely, MacDonald's overly ambitious scaling of the arena. MacDonald paid $400,000 to promote the 1961 rubber match between Ingemar Johansson and Floyd Patterson. Although the highest-priced ticket was $100, the contemporary standard for ringside seats to big-time matches, the bout attracted nearly 14,000 fans, took in $550,000, and broke the indoor, on-site gate record for boxing. Premium tickets, along with the cheap seats, always had the most demand. Boxing appeals to an element of high society that travels first class and must have the best of everything, regardless of cost. Premium tickets were a status symbol, a chance to see and be seen. In this regard, MacDonald was smart to charge $250 instead of the usual $100 to see the Liston-Clay fight. He probably could have charged $500 and sold out the

720-seat "Golden Circle." As it was, he made approximately $180,000 from these tickets. The 6,160 cheap seats at $20 each also sold well, because they were affordable for regular people who wanted to be at an important sporting event like a world heavyweight title fight. They brought in about $120,000. These two categories of tickets accounted for approximately three-quarters of the live gate.

The problem was that the approximately 10,000 other available tickets were scaled in a way that made it extremely unlikely that people would buy them. There were seventy-two tickets available at $200, nearly 1,000 at $150, 4,100 at $100, and 4,500 at $50. Why would anybody pay $100 per ticket, a price that would normally put them within spitting distance of the fighters, for a seat fifty yards away from the action? High rollers weren't interested in such seats, which would have little more status than those in the nosebleed section, and working people could not afford them. As a result, MacDonald literally threw away $400,000 in sales. The same held true for the $200 and $150 tickets. It was an insult to expect people to pay that much and not be close to the action, and as a result, very few of these tickets sold. For all of the talk that rain, Clay's friendship with Malcolm X, or Liston's menacing personality ruined the gate, the most logical explanation seems to be that MacDonald simply misjudged the buying public's tastes and desires.[115]

Despite the failure in Miami Beach, the fight was a nationwide hit. If newspaper estimates were correct, the final take was over $5 million, with nearly 90 percent of the revenues coming from television sales. Whereas 530,000 fans in 263 venues with a seating capacity of 700,000 paid $3.2 million to watch the first Patterson-Liston fight on closed-circuit, Theater Network Television Inc. (TNT), the corporation that purchased the live television rights for Clay-Liston from ICP, estimated that 700,000 fans in 271 venues with a seating capacity of 1.1 million paid around $4.5 million for the bout. To put that number into perspective, the combined Major League Baseball television rights for all twenty teams for the entire season that year was $13.6 million and for both the National and American Football Leagues it was a combined $15.2 million. Nate Halpern, TNT president, reported: "We have undoubtedly created an all-time record in attendance and gross receipts. It will take a few days before we know the actual figures but from all reports our attendance last night exceeds all others. TNT is very happy the fans received their money's worth."[116]

There were other revenue sources besides closed-circuit television, and they served as a reminder that the heavyweight championship of the world was the most lucrative prize in sports. WABC network paid $115,000 for the live radio broadcast rights, and international radio sales brought even more than that. There was a $50,000 guarantee for the rights to a motion picture based on the bout, $125,000 from those who advertised in the fight program, and an undisclosed amount of money that came in from the 250,000 people in community antenna (now known as cable TV) markets that allowed for live home viewing of the bout.[117]

The biggest financial winner, or so it seemed, was Sonny Liston, who took in over $1.3 million. Cassius Clay took in about $650,000, which he split with the Louisville Sponsoring Group. Closed-circuit theater operators received nearly half of their gate receipts, about $2 million. The remainder of the money went to TNT. As part of their contracts, closed-circuit operators split their receipts up to $20,000 evenly with TNT. The corporation took 55 percent of all gate revenues, after taxes, above that figure.[118]

In addition to the actual facts and figures surrounding the fight, there were four developments that would germinate during its buildup and have a significant impact, both immediate and long-term, on the political and commercial aspects of the new champion's life and career. They were the participation of major movie theater chains in the closed-circuit telecast; the bout's international appeal; Clay's diminishing professional relationship with the Louisville Sponsoring Group and his growing ties to the Nation of Islam; and the intertwining of the civil rights movement with the commercial elements of the telecast. While some of the impact was not clear right away, over the next couple of years it would become apparent.

If you wanted your closed-circuit telecast to succeed, you almost had to have the cooperation of movie theater concerns like Radio-Keith-Orpheum (RKO), Loew's, Balaban and Katz (B&K), and Warner. Their venues were already geared to show closed-circuit bouts and did not have to be outfitted with expensive new projection equipment that cut deeply into profits. They were also located in major cities, near large concentrations of potential customers. Along with sports arenas and concert halls, they were the backbone of the closed-circuit boxing market. The Liston-Clay fight proved no exception. RKO theaters, for example, were responsible for fifteen sellouts and showed the bout in nine major cities from Boston to San Francisco, while Loew's theaters in New York City alone accounted for 5 percent of the telecast's nationwide seating capacity. Without the cooperation of these companies, closed-circuit-television sales would have dropped dramatically.[119]

Bolstered by theater chains, the telecast was a big success in major cities. Ironically, two states that refused to grant Sonny Liston a boxing license, New York and California, produced the largest viewing audiences. Of the 90,000 tickets available in thirty-one New York metropolitan area venues, about 85,000 were sold. Three thousand patrons filled the Paramount Theater. A similar number witnessed the telecast at the Armory in Teaneck, New Jersey. RKO sold out all seven of its area theaters, as 18,500 people paid $120,000.

"Business is very brisk and RKO is happy with the venture," said company official Thomas Crehan. In Brooklyn, Loew's King Theater was packed to the rafters when someone pulled a fire alarm shortly before the main event, causing the building's evacuation and allowing scores of freeloaders to make their way inside.[120]

In Los Angeles, the number one market for the fight, about 105,000 of the available 120,000 tickets sold in twenty-eight area venues, including the Warner chain of movie houses. Metropolitan Theaters, another franchise, reported a 70 percent buy rate at its five area sites. Over 90 percent of the 10,500 seats at the Los Angeles Sports Arena were sold; more people saw the fight there than in Miami Beach. Grauman's Chinese Theater also reported a 90 percent buy rate. The Long Beach Auditorium sold 3,400 of its 4,000 tickets. The Olympic Auditorium reported an attendance of 9,000. In Palm Springs, Frank Sinatra attended a closed-circuit party at the Riviera Hotel Auditorium. The craziest scene of all was at the Orange Drive-In Theater. Amazingly, 15,000 people packed into 1,400 cars to see the fight. The chaos quickly spilled over, as one of the worst traffic jams in area history—no small feat in L.A.—occurred when motorists began parking on the shoulders of an adjacent highway to pirate the broadcast. After those spaces filled up, cars began stopping in traffic lanes, and about 5,000 people gate-crashed the drive-in. It took a combination of seventy-five California Highway Patrol officers, sheriff's deputies, and police to break up the congestion, which had caused half-mile backups in all directions. Sergeant Pete Hurst of the Orange Police Department said, "It was a major disturbance—next door to a riot. We got it just in time, or it could have been just that."[121]

Chicago's eight area venues were packed, producing a total audience of about 26,000, with seven reporting sellouts. The eighth venue, the Harlem Outdoor Theater, which had parking space for 1,800 cars and was expected to draw 10,000 customers, missed a sellout when a snowstorm blanketed the area and limited attendance to a hardy group of 6,000 fans, who crowded into 1,000 cars. Perhaps the greatest example of Clay's drawing power, his ability to resurrect the fight game where people had left it for dead, took place on the west side of the city, at the soon-to-be-demolished B&K Marbro Theater. Although the venue had been out of operation for nearly five months, almost 5,000 viewers attended a special screening of the bout there.[122]

It should not be taken for granted that movie theater chains decided to host the Clay-Liston telecast. Although they were crucial to the success of such ventures, and certainly profited from them, theater companies were not beholden to boxing promoters. For the time being, cooperation between the two entities led to a record-setting closed-circuit take. But if movie theater chains had felt that it was in their best interest to boycott such events, they would have had no problem doing so, to the great detriment of those trying to profit from the fight game.

Although it was clear from Cassius Clay's bout with Henry Cooper in England the previous summer that the young fighter was making waves abroad, it was the Liston fight that made evident the massive scope of his global appeal. Already the biggest draw in the United States, Clay would benefit from technological advances that made it possible to market him to people who had previously lacked access to big-time American boxing. The cultivation of these audiences was significant. They generated revenue and gave Clay and his handlers leverage. If the American boxing market were to somehow dry up, or if Clay were to alienate the ticket-buying public to the point that it refused to pay to see him fight, these new sites potentially would serve as alternatives. Part of the reason the Louisville Sponsoring Group arranged the Cooper fight in England was that its members were worried that Clay's speaking out on race matters would jeopardize his standing among American fight fans. The success of that promotion gave them hope that even if their charge took things too far, his momentum as the biggest moneymaker in boxing would not grind to a halt.

The technical advances that brought boxing to new markets were not developed for that purpose, but it is fair to say that Clay was the catalyst that made them applicable to the sport. His international appeal, and the profits that accompanied it, was strong enough motivation to widen their function. The best example of this was the European television broadcast of the bout, which was the first American sports program to be shown abroad in its entirety within two hours of its taking place. Approximately 165 million people in eleven countries—including Yugoslavia, Finland, Norway, Czechoslovakia, Ireland, Spain, and Sweden—places that never got the chance to see live title fights, watched the bout on Eurovision. The process by which they did so was fascinating. Although the National Aeronautics and Space Administration (NASA) had a policy that its satellites were not to be used for commercial purposes, TNT paid the organization an undisclosed amount (Halpern claimed it was well worth the considerable expense because of the publicity his corporation received) to facilitate a one-time exception. TNT's cameras in Miami Beach took in the action, and the broadcast was transmitted onto videotape via kinescope. The videotape delay was then piped by TNT to NASA's earth station in Andover, Maine. From there, NASA positioned its intercontinental relay satellite to receive the signal from Andover and bounce it to a receiving station in Brittany, England, where Eurovision picked up the feed and transmitted it across the continent. There were also radio broadcasts of the bout to new markets across Asia and South America, but it was the Eurovision telecast that signaled the beginning of a new era in international sports broadcasting, one that would benefit Clay significantly.[123]

Although the Louisville Sponsoring Group still had two years left on its contract with Clay, its direct influence on him was greatly diminished by the time he defeated Liston. Nevertheless, the LSG members were still his managers, and the public recognized them as such. One of the key points of this book is that Clay's box-office power was directly related to his moral authority. When people saw him as a bad person, the revenue surrounding his fights shrunk. When people saw him a good person, the revenue surrounding his fights rose. For the first four years of his career, Clay's partnership with the organization was central to the perception that he was a decent sort. Without it, it was likely that his over-the-top personality would have adversely affected him financially. Although Clay's act was responsible for generating unprecedented interest in him, it was the moderating influence of the LSG that made his antics acceptable to many people who purchased tickets for his fights.

The nationwide backlash against Clay in the aftermath of his surprise victory over Liston began almost immediately as a result of the new champion's conduct. It started when he went out of his way to humiliate sportswriters who had predicted his demise, and it escalated when he announced that he was a member of the Nation of Islam and was changing his name to Cassius X. Column space that normally would have been dedicated to hailing the new champion was instead devoted to asking what was wrong with him. People who once found the fighter entertaining, or at least tolerable, were turning against him with a vengeance. But to understand how strong the mitigating influence of the LSG members was on public perception of the erstwhile Clay, we should turn to their hometown, where the nationwide backlash had not yet descended and never really would. More than anywhere else, Louisville was a place where an attack on the new champion was tantamount to an attack on his managers.

Clay fever gripped the city the night of his victory, as two area venues broadcast the bout to record crowds. There were 5,000 at the Convention Center and another 8,000 at the Kentucky Fair and Exposition Center's Freedom Hall, producing $65,000 in gate receipts. "It was by far the biggest and most enthusiastic crowd we have had for television here," said Kentucky Expo executive Jim Browitt. Unlike in other cities, Louisville's newspapers praised the new champion, albeit cautiously. A *Louisville Times* editorial, "Hail Cassius, The New King," gave "congratulations to the young man from Louisville," although it also asked, "[I]s it too much to hope that he will wear his crown with a bit more dignity than he displayed toward the end of his road to the throne?" Nevertheless, the piece looked back fondly on Clay's march to the championship and bombastic self-promotion, claiming, "His blatant boasting, his fresh face (not to mention fresh manners) added a bit of gaiety to the dingy world of prizefighting." Dean Eagle, one of the sportswriters Clay went out of his way to humiliate, thought that his predicting a Liston victory had earned him some grief. "As I said," he wrote, "a man has to take his medicine at a time like this." He also explained that coverage of the new champion in his hometown was different from that of "the howling displeased mob of newsmen who aren't from Louisville." He even told Clay, "You are the greatest."[124]

More so than in other areas, there was the sense in Louisville that the Sponsoring Group was greatly responsible for the young fighter's success, and that as long as its members were on the scene in any capacity, there was really nothing to worry about. Although the LSG had been outwardly ambivalent toward Clay in the months before the Liston bout, the surprise victory led to a change in tactics. Faversham suddenly had nothing but praise for the new champion. "Clay showed great courage in surviving the fifth round when he couldn't see. If he had wanted to quit, he could have done it gracefully then," he said. This was a wise move, because it made it seem that the two camps were closer than they really were. Cassius Clay Sr. told Faversham, "You are the one who deserves the most credit. You helped make my boy champion." Turning to his son, the hard-drinking father asked where the party was to celebrate the victory. But young Cassius would have none of it. "Who wants to celebrate?" he asked. "How can you celebrate more than being heavyweight champion of the world and making these sports writers eat their words?" Despite this vitriol, there was still the sense that Clay was able to be handled, that all of the hype, even the Muslim stuff, was just an act. Joe Martin enjoyed his newfound status as Clay's discoverer. Sure, Clay would still boast, he told reporters. "He'll still be a promoter. It's his personality." But the boy knew his limits. "That's Cassius Clay. He was like that as an amateur, but I managed to keep him under control." Even years later, some people believed that as long as Clay was under contract to the LSG, he would bear its mark. As Joe Frazier, who succeeded him as champion, would say in 1971 about the Louisville Lip, "What does he know about hard times? He had it easy in boxing. A white man in his corner, those rich plantation owners to back him." Even as Cassius X turned toward the Nation of Islam, people did not simply forget his association with the Louisville Sponsoring Group.[125]

Perhaps there was something to the bond between the fighter and his managers. For all of the signs that they had grown apart, Clay seemed to handle himself differently in Louisville than elsewhere. While this is also attributable to his relationships with family and friends, it is possible that the LSG had a hand in it. The day after winning the crown, Clay told the press that he was a member of the Nation of Islam and should be called Cassius X.

About two weeks later, on March 6, Elijah Muhammad announced during a radio address that he was giving the new champion the Muslim name Muhammad Ali, effective immediately. Ali accepted it right away and insisted that he be called by his new moniker. A few members of the press and broadcast media did so, but most referred to him as Cassius Clay, and it became a pet peeve of the young fighter. While a spectator at a boxing show in Madison Square Garden, for example, he walked out when management refused to introduce him by his new name during its customary roll call of celebrity attendees. He would correct anyone, except his parents, who refused to call him Muhammad Ali. The ugly pre-fight hype for Ali's future bouts with Floyd Patterson and Ernie Terrell would center on the champion's insistence that the challengers call him by his Muslim name or suffer a terrible beating as punishment. Yet on March 11, five days after his renaming, while taking phone calls from the listening audience in Louisville during a radio interview on local WHAS, when a young fan got through and asked for the champion by his old name, he replied, "Cassius speaking." In Louisville, at least for the time being, you could still call him Cassius.[126]

The civil rights movement was never far from the era's newsworthy events, and the Clay-Liston fight gate was no different. For all of the talk that he didn't care about such things, Sonny Liston did his best to ensure that the arenas showing the closed-circuit telecast of his title defenses were not segregated. Using his power as champion, he forced TNT to insert a provision into all of its contracts with individual venues that would ban race-based seating arrangements. When reports surfaced that two out of the three scheduled New Orleans theaters were not in compliance, the venues were refused access to the broadcast feed. Nate Halpern told reporters, "Liston suggested it, and we believe in it too. As far as I know, it's the first time such a clause has been demanded. We can't actually police it, but we do have the papers they signed, and in practice, local people who are concerned will probably call our attention to violations. I imagine that's what happened in New Orleans." Liston's manager echoed this position. "There is a report that this is not being observed in New Orleans, and it is now being investigated," he said. "If it is not straightened out, remedial action will be taken. [We will] pull the plug. We simply won't show it." He also felt that the champion should get credit for his stand and told reporters, "I'd like to add that this provision was put in at Liston's insistence. That ought to be on the record." Because of a federal court decision that called for local venues to desegregate for entertainment events in defiance of city law, and because of Liston's insistence, a crowd of 3,000 people at the Municipal Auditorium became the first racially mixed audience since the nineteenth century to gather in New Orleans for such a purpose. They viewed the bout without incident. In a number of other southern cities that had always segregated such events, including Jacksonville, At-lanta, and Knoxville, desegregation efforts went similarly well. And those cit-ies that refused to comply, including Waco, Jackson, and Montgomery, were not allowed to carry the telecast.[127]

In a sense, it was the ultimate show of concern by Liston, since it cost him money to take such a stand. James Farmer, national director of the Congress of Racial Equality (CORE), wired congratulations to Liston "for your morally excellent stand in regard to the exclusion of the fight from segregated theaters in the south. You reflect in this decision the highest of standards of conduct, which we urge for all public figures." Liston responded as usual, telling re-porters simply, "I feel the color of my people's money is the same as anyone else's. They should get the same seats. If not, I don't want those places to have the fight." Disappointed patrons in New Orleans were hardly comforted by the explanation afforded by the two banned theaters, which released the fol-lowing statement: "In view of Sonny Liston's feelings, as set forth in his week-end statement, and the law of Louisiana, which we are advised are incompat-ible, we regret that the closed-circuit telecast has been cancelled. Refunds will be made at the box office." For a fleeting moment, a handful of Ameri-cans viewed Liston as a hero. The episode was a reminder of the critical rela-tionships between a fighter's cultural appeal and the commercial narratives surrounding his career. Muhammad Ali would soon learn how true this was when he decided to replace the Louisville Sponsoring Group with the Nation of Islam, and his once-profitable boxing career would go into a financial tailspin.[128]

II

Nation of Islam

Main Bout Inc.

How Commerce Affects Culture

At a press conference in January 1966, Muhammad Ali announced that he had formed Main Bout Inc., a new corporation that would manage the ancillary promotional rights to his fights, including all live and delayed broadcasts, starting with a multi-million-dollar March 29 match, hopefully in Chicago, against top contender Ernie Terrell. "I am vitally interested in the company," he said, "and in seeing that it will be one in which Negroes are not used as fronts, but as stockholders, officers, and production and promotion agents." Although racially integrated, Main Bout was controlled by the Nation of Islam (NOI) and built upon its philosophy of economic nationalism. The NOI's command of the most lucrative prize in boxing, the world heavyweight championship, sent shock waves throughout the sport that quickly marshaled into a fierce resistance against Ali.[1]

From the beginning, the corporation faced criticism, initially from white sportswriters. But about a month after Main Bout's formation, Ali's draft status changed to 1-A, meaning that he had become eligible for military service, possibly in Vietnam. Ali responded by publicly opposing the war, and politicians nationwide joined the press in attacking Main Bout. The political controversy surrounding Ali made it easier for Main Bout's competitors within boxing—rival promoters, closed-circuit-television theater chains, and organized crime—to run the organization out of business. Money and politics underpinned opposition to Main Bout, but we must also consider the organization's symbolic value and the moral implications of its success or failure.

Ali's boxing career was financially viable prior to 1966. Although his bouts against Sonny Liston and Floyd Patterson did not achieve their full economic potential, they produced solid gates that indicated Ali's popularity among certain segments of society, as well as the willingness of his detractors to pay to see him lose. The cultural antipathy resulting from Ali's bombast and membership in the NOI had an effect on his moneymaking ability, but not a dramatic one. Under the banner of the Louisville Sponsoring Group (LSG), against two of the biggest stars of the era, Ali parlayed bad-guy status into box-office success. Many people despised Ali, but they did not boycott him.

Ali's three previous bouts, the first of his championship career, had all been lucrative. His last match before forming Main Bout, against Patterson in November 1965, grossed approximately $3.5 million, most of which came from the 210 closed-circuit-television venues screening the match. Nearly 260 locations, with a seating capacity of over a million, had broadcast the May 1965 Ali-Liston rematch, producing a gate of over $4 million. Similar totals resulted from the first Ali-Liston contest. Ali's purses reflected these promotional successes. He earned about $750,000 against Patterson and about $600,000 for each of the matches against Liston. He may have been disliked, but he was still the biggest draw in the sport.[2]

The combination of Main Bout's takeover of the ancillary rights to his matches and the champion's subsequent opposition to the Vietnam War, however, nearly halted his boxing career. Already unpopular, Ali was unable to withstand these twin assaults on his cultural image and the commercial intrigue surrounding his fights. They resulted in a determined backlash that led to a boycott of the Terrell bout and prevented him from boxing in the United States for almost a year. The reaction illustrated the relationship between Ali's economic power as the world heavyweight champion and his symbolic significance as a race man; he demonstrated unprecedented professional, political, and personal autonomy for a black athlete by forming Main Bout and challenging the draft. While Ali's bravado and association with the NOI had not previously crippled him at the box office, his forming Main Bout and coming out against the war were a different story.

Ali's draft resistance was at the heart of the tidal wave of hostility toward him during this period, but it is also crucial to consider the significance of Main Bout in this development. Ali's disassociation with the LSG and the corresponding fear that his boxing matches would produce millions of dollars for the NOI were factors that accelerated and intensified the breakdown of his cultural image and commercial viability. Ali's outcries against the Vietnam War caused his levee of moral authority, previously girded by his clean lifestyle and association with the LSG, to come crashing down, but it was his formation of Main Bout that produced the storms that generated the threat.

The boycott hurt Ali economically, but there were also positive outcomes. Forced to fight abroad, Ali became a true world champion, carving out new markets for his bouts that wound up producing major revenues once Ali shook his draft problems. The fact that he was prevented from making a living despite not having been convicted of any crime also deepened the belief that he was unjustly persecuted. The notion of Ali as a citizen of the world who stood up in the face of injustice would one day become the basis of widespread admiration toward him. The episode also legitimized Ali's status as a race man and rejuvenated his moral authority. Whereas some leaders had previously portrayed him as unreasonably picking a fight with white America, they eventually came to see him as a part of the black freedom struggle and as a target of discrimination from the same forces that had held down rank-and-file African Americans.

Main Bout had five stockholders. Herbert Muhammad, son of NOI leader Elijah Muhammad, was its president. John Ali, the NOI's national secretary who oversaw the religious sect's day-to-day operations, was Main Bout's treasurer. Together, they controlled 50 percent of its stock and half of its board's six votes. The closed-circuit-television operator Michael Malitz and his attorney Bob Arum were Main Bout's vice-president and secretary, each holding 20 percent of Main Bout's stock and one vote. Jim Brown, the professional football player and Main Bout's vice-president in charge of public relations, controlled one vote and 10 percent of the company. Malitz and Arum were Main Bout's sole white members. They came up with the idea for the enterprise while promoting a 1965 fight between Terrell and Canadian heavyweight George Chuvalo in which Jim Brown served as their broadcaster. Malitz and Arum asked Brown to carry to the champion a proposal for a company that would give Ali more control over the finances for his fights and potentially increase black participation in their production. Brown passed the idea to Ali, who had to ask Elijah Muhammad's permission. Despite his frequent pronouncements about the evils of sport, the NOI leader realized the potential windfall for his organization and approved the measure, thus making Main Bout a reality. Furthermore, according to historian Taylor Branch, Muhammad had asked his lawyer Chauncey Eskridge, the Chicago attorney who had represented Martin Luther King Jr. and later would be Ali's lead defender during his draft trial, as early as September 1964 about the possibility of creating an organization to replace the LSG as the champion's management.[3]

Ali announced that Main Bout would become his ancillary promoter even though the move hadn't been approved by the LSG, which had the contractual rights to broker such deals. During the press conference announcing Main Bout's formation, Ali warned the LSG not to interfere with the move. "I am aware that various influences may be exerted upon some of the members of the Louisville Sponsoring Group to make arrangements with companies previously involved in the handling of these fights, but in my opinion such arrangements are outdated and detrimental." Dropping its interest in Ali altogether was a tempting proposition for the LSG. The members certainly didn't need the money, and the investment, even with Ali winning the title, hadn't yielded nearly as much as they thought it would. How long could these aristocrats continue to put their names beside someone as obnoxious and anti-establishment as Muhammad Ali had become? The syndicate refused to be strong-armed by the NOI and had a valid contract with the champion, but Ali had threatened to stop boxing altogether if the organization did not award Main Bout the ancillary rights to his fights. Under the advice of its attorney Gordon Davidson, the LSG agreed to sell the ancillary rights to Ali's fights to Main Bout in exchange for a percentage of their revenues. Years later, Davidson claimed that the deal was similar to others that the group had cut with previous closed-circuit-television companies and that Main Bout's offer was a fair one, but at the time Arthur Grafton, another LSG attorney, told *Sports Illustrated* that "the Main Bout deal was nowhere near as good as the deal we already had."[4]

Jim Brown was the driving force behind Main Bout's potential as a vehicle for black economic empowerment. He told a reporter, "Our goal is to use the money that we make—and hope to make in future ventures—to support the founding of business by Negroes. At first, we'll have to count basically on small businesses." A few months later, Brown retired from professional football and formed the Negro Industrial and Economic Union (NIEU), a nationwide organization that created over 400 businesses in Cleveland ghettos alone, spurring a meeting between Brown and President Lyndon Johnson. Brown's political wherewithal was also evidenced by his relationship with Carl Stokes, who served as the organization's attorney and would become the mayor of Cleveland in 1967. Although Main Bout was not formally connected to the NIEU, Brown believed that the organizations would dovetail. He shared the NOI's belief that economic power was crucial to black freedom. "One of the concepts that we had," he said, "was to be able to show these fights via closed circuit and for the first time in history black promoters could show the fights and have black Americans understand that only through economic development and self-determination could we ever be free." In response to this vision, Ali donated $10,000 to the NIEU in early 1967.[5]

White newspapermen constituted the first wave of opposition to Main Bout, as a number of reporters expressed fear over the NOI's ascent to power within professional boxing. Perhaps these reporters, like their contemporaries in the civil rights movement, understood that expanded economic power often brought with it influence in other areas of American life. Most were concerned about a black takeover of the sport, but others saw the Nation's rise within boxing as a portent of racial violence. Reminding readers that Elijah Muhammad's organization was "the group which advocates violence as the major weapon of racial war," syndicated *New York Daily News* columnist and virulent Ali critic Gene Ward argued that the development of Main Bout could destroy professional boxing. "Any way one sizes up this take-over of the heavyweight title by the Black Muslims," he claimed, "the fight game is going to be the worse for it. This could be the death blow." A longtime Ali nemesis, the eminent sportswriter Jimmy Cannon wrote in his syndicated column that Main Bout's rise had symbolic value that put power into the hands of evildo- ers. "The fight racket has been turned into a crusade by the Muslims. Their great trophy is Clay," shrieked Cannon. Assessing Main Bout's initial promo- tional venture, he insisted, "Herbert Muhammad, who is Elijah's kid, is the president of the firm that controls the Clay-Ernie Terrell promotion in Chi- cago. It is more than a fight. This is a fete to celebrate a religion that throws hate at people." Jack Olsen, the *Sports Illustrated* writer, called the creation of Main Bout "an antiwhite step [fueled] either by Black Muslims or by such defiant antiwhites as Cleveland Brown Fullback Jim Brown." Other reporters less specifically described their fears. Nevertheless, their columns revealed their nervousness over the new order in professional boxing. Doug Gilbert, the *Chicago's American* boxing writer, believed "that if the Muslims own Clay, and also own the television rights to all of his fights, they have what amounts to a hammerlock on all that's lucrative in boxing." Syndicated *New York Herald-Tribune* writer Red Smith complained, "Except insofar as the Black Muslim leadership has a stake in the promotion, there is no good rea- son at present why the [Ali versus Terrell] match should not be accepted." Even the editorial boards of two Chicago newspapers, the *Daily News* and the *Tribune*, got into the act, urging Illinois Governor Otto Kerner to ban the upcoming bout.[6]

Although Main Bout had critics within the black press, a number of writ- ers welcomed its creation. Cal Jacox, the *Norfolk Journal and Guide* sports editor and syndicated columnist, challenged the white press to cover Main Bout fairly. According to Jacox, "Boxing is in an uproar. It seems that pro foot- ball star Jim Brown has joined a group that will promote Cassius 'Muham- mad Ali' Clay's title bout with Ernie Terrell and includes members of the Black Muslim sect among its officers; now, because of this alliance, the alarmist[s] are crying all over the place." Jacox assessed the fears of some white sportswriters. "They are saying that the Muslim philosophy will domi- nate Main Bout, Inc., and with this domination, they contend will come—via Cassius as the heavyweight champion—complete control of boxing." But to Jacox, this was not the issue. Main Bout's significance went beyond sport.

"Jim Brown, in rebuttal, explained that the sole purpose of the new organization is to use its profits to generate capital for Negro businessmen," he continued, "and that explanation is good enough for this corner. And, from here, it
should probably be sufficient for the critics, who are way off base in castigat-
ing the project before they've given it a chance to reveal its program to the
public." Two articles in the *Pittsburgh Courier* voiced similar support for Main
Bout, adding that the organization was a necessary alternative to white rule of
professional boxing, which had resulted in corruption and mob control of the
sport.[7]

In February 1966, less than a month after Main Bout's formation, the
United States Selective Service reclassified Muhammad Ali as draft-eligible.
In 1960, at age eighteen, he had registered with Selective Service Local Board
47 in Louisville and in 1962 was classified as draft-eligible (1-A). In 1964,
however, Ali failed the mental aptitude section of the induction exam. When
asked to retest in front of Army psychologists, Ali again flunked. He was then
reclassified as unqualified to serve (1-Y). In need of more soldiers for the Vietnam War, however, the Army lowered its mental aptitude requirement in
early 1966, and Ali's score became a passing one. With members of Congress
calling for his reclassification, Ali's local draft board reviewed his case in
February. After the fighter's request for an appeal hearing was denied, he was
again declared draft-eligible.[8]

Reporters sought Ali for comment, and he expressed his opposition to the
war. He told Tom Fitzpatrick of the *Chicago Daily News* that he had seen
"lots of whites burning their draft cards on television. If they are against the
war, and even some congressmen are against the war," Ali asked, "why should
we Muslims be for it?" Ali felt that the war violated the principles of the NOI.
"Let me tell you, we Muslims are taught to defend ourselves when we are attacked," he said. "Those Vietcongs are not attacking me. All I know is that
they are considered Asiatic black people and I don't have no fight with black
people." Ali warned that his reclassification would incite the worldwide Muslim community: "I don't want to scare anybody about it, but there are millions
of Muslims around the world watching what's happening to me." The *Chicago
Tribune* reported Ali's assertion that he had been singled out for unfair treatment: "I can't understand why, out of all the baseball players, all of the football players, all of the basketball players—they seek out me, who's the world's
only heavyweight champion?"[9]

Ali's stand against the war resulted in a vicious backlash against him
within the press and professional boxing. White reporters nationwide framed
Ali's stance as based neither on principle nor religious devotion, but rather as
the result of fear and ignorance. Some military people gravitated toward the
NOI, and not all of its members refused to fight in the war. Elijah Muham-

mad, however, had done four years in prison during World War II for violating the Selective Service Act, and he had always instructed members of the organization not to serve in secular wars, including Vietnam. Ali's draft resistance conformed to this tradition. Some of the most important sportswriters in the country, however, refused to acknowledge the possibility that Ali's stand was principled. Dick Young, the syndicated *New York Daily News* columnist and one of Ali's staunchest critics, asserted that there was "no evidence that [the Nation of Islam] is a pacifist organization, or that Cassius Clay is devoted to a policy of non-violence." *New York World-Telegram and Sun* scribe Jack Clary and syndicated columnist Red Smith claimed that Ali was stupid. "It's easy to see why Cassius (1-A) Clay flunked his Army mental," wrote Clary. Smith added, "It has been established to the satisfaction of most that Cassius Marcellus Clay is not a deep thinker." Other reporters felt that Ali was desperately afraid of combat duty. According to Gene Ward, "Cassius Clay is scared. There is a patina of panic glazing his eyes, as he talks compulsively in bursts of words." Arthur Daley of the *New York Times*, who ten years earlier had become the first sportswriter to win the Pulitzer Prize, wrote that "[Ali is] panic-stricken at the thought of military service." None of these writers would even consider that Ali was sincere.[10]

Another common supposition was that the NOI manufactured Ali's draft resistance to save the upcoming fight with Terrell. After that, claimed several reporters, Ali would drop his shenanigans and join the Army. "The Black Muslims will shut up Clay" to save their profits, assured Jimmy Cannon. The editorial boards of Chicago newspapers again aired their disgust with Ali and the NOI. *Chicago's American* claimed to be "sorry for Cassius Clay. . . . [H]e is as innocent as a puppet compared to the gang of fanatics that now owns and operates him. In fact, he is a puppet." The *Chicago Tribune* asserted, "The Black Muslims have ordered [Ali] to appeal as a conscientious objector." They all disputed the sincerity of Ali's position and his understanding of the issues surrounding it.[11]

Ali's draft resistance and an escalating distrust of Main Bout unleashed furious attacks by Chicago newspapers and politicians calling for the Terrell fight to be banned. Editorials in two local dailies urging its termination cited Ali's anti-Vietnam stance and his new promotional scheme. *Chicago's American* analyzed Ali's reasons for disputing the draft and concluded that "none of them [are] particularly convincing." The *Chicago Tribune* found it "deplorable that so many Chicagoans are unwittingly encouraging [Ali] by their interest in a fight whose profits will go largely to the Black Muslims." Twenty state newspaper executives released a joint proclamation criticizing Governor Otto Kerner and the Illinois State Athletic Commission (ISAC) for allowing the bout to be sanctioned. For several days, the front page of the *Tribune* became a forum for those who opposed the fight, including American soldiers in Vietnam. The local branch of the Veterans of Foreign Wars, representing 14,500 former soldiers, passed a resolution urging Mayor Richard Daley and Governor Kerner to "intercede" and cancel the match. Politicians and government appointees also registered their displeasure. State Representatives Clyde Choate and Arthur Gottschalk threatened to investigate the ISAC for approving the contest. State Senator Arthur Swanson called for Kerner to remove the match from Chicago. Charles Siragusa, the Illinois Crime Investigating Commission's executive director, felt that "it is an insult to the people of this state to permit a man like Clay who swears allegiance to an admitted cult of violence to reap a harvest of cash from the very citizens he has insulted with his whining attempts to avoid the draft." Even State Auditor Michael J. Howlett expressed hopes that the fight would be banned. Police Superintendent Orlando Wilson offered critical opposition, telling reporters, "My main concern is with the possibility of disorder arising from the bout, but I am also disturbed by the unpatriotic statements attributed to Clay." Wilson's resistance was especially interesting because he had been known by the city's black community as a progressive. The *Chicago Defender* called him "the brightest star in Chicago's galaxy of government" for establishing an antidiscrimination policy for a department long known for racial bias. But this kind of intersection between professional duties and personal beliefs characterized official resistance to Ali. Meanwhile, Daley leaned on the ISAC to "reconsider" the bout, claiming that Chicago "could well do without this fight." Kerner called Ali's comments "disgusting and unpatriotic." Aided by the local press, city and state politicians, all of them white, formed a nearly united front against the match within a matter of days.[12]

Local boxing promoters Ben Bentley and Irving Schoenwald, who stood to lose the on-site gate receipts, worked to save the bout, concocting a plan in which Ali would apologize for his anti-war statements in exchange for permission to fight in Chicago. Although the ISAC, the state agency in charge of regulating boxing, had the power to stop the match, it agreed to this compromise. This decision made sense because the ISAC would not simply cancel a fight it had already sanctioned. Nothing new had happened regarding the fight's promotion that would give it legal reason to do so. Governor Kerner also had a lot to lose were he to intervene and bar the match. Such action might be seen as racial discrimination. Bentley circulated rumors of a telephone call he had with Ali during which the fighter rescinded his anti-war statements. Taking advantage of public sentiment that Ali was a dupe, Bentley told reporters that, "since he [Ali] doesn't understand politics he's not going to discuss them any further, and he promised he's going to stick to fighting." Bentley also claimed that Ali had admitted that he "went off half-cocked and didn't know what [he] was saying." ISAC Chairman Joe Triner explained to the Associated Press, "Governor Kerner told me that he would be satisfied with an apology from Clay. So as of now, the fight hasn't been disapproved and it remains status quo." The United Press International quoted Ali: "If I knew everything I had said on politics would have been taken that seriously. . . . I never would have opened my mouth." Another newspaper article detailed Ali's "newly-discovered humility" and reported the champion's assertion, "I ain't no authority on Vietnam. I ain't no leader and no preacher." With this narrative established, the ISAC announced that it would reconvene to hear Ali's apology for his "unpatriotic remarks."[13]

This scheme reflected the overriding feeling that Ali's draft resistance was either insincere or uninformed, and it offered him the chance to verify such speculation. If he were to go back on his beliefs, he could pursue his career without censure. White sportswriters, many of whom had already declared the folly of Ali's position, predicted that he would apologize to save the fight. They assumed that boxing and the paydays that accompanied it were more important to the champion than his anti-war stand. They wrote that he would withdraw from political matters in the future and that he had learned his lesson. These reporters also claimed that Ali would skip the NOI's Savior's Day Convention, the organization's annual celebration of founder W. D. Fard's birthday, to showcase this transformation. Such predictions, however, ignored a *Miami Herald* interview with the champion. Ali told the newspaper that such conjecture was "not true. I'll be there. I've got to be there, I've got to. I'm going." Unlike the white press, the NOI's official newspaper *Muhammad Speaks* reported that Ali had come to Chicago to attend the ISAC hearing and to appear at the gathering, announcing that the champion "made preparations to fly into Chicago for a two-purpose visit, one of which included a meeting with the Illinois [State] Athletic Commission, the other with his leader and teacher, the Honorable Elijah Muhammad, during Savior's Day Convention." These statements notwithstanding, Ali refused further comment about the war until the hearing. He flew from his training camp in Miami to Chicago, where promoter Bentley greeted the champion at the airport and plastered a piece of tape across his lips. Ali went along with the gag, responding to questions by mumbling and pointing to his mouth.[14]

At the moment of truth, however, Ali refused to apologize. The hearing was a national event; fifty reporters, twenty-five lawyers, six state troopers, and several government officials packed the ISAC's Chicago office to hear Ali testify. The commission asked him if he was sorry for his anti-war comments. Ali answered, "I'm not apologizing for any remarks that were in the newspapers. I will take that up with government officials and officials of the draft board at the proper time." Ali expressed regrets, but not for his beliefs. He instead apologized "to the people who may be hurt financially. I am sorry I put the commission and Governor Kerner on the spot with my remarks. I did not mean to hurt the children and the sons of persons who are dying in Vietnam." Stunned, Triner asked Ali, "I want to know if you are apologizing to the people of the state of Illinois for the unpatriotic remarks you made." Ali insisted, "I'm not apologizing for anything like that because I don't have to." To make himself clear, he added, "I'm not here to make a showdown plea. I'm not here to apologize in any way that the press has predicted I would apologize." Flabbergasted by Ali's defiance, the ISAC halted the meeting and contemplated its next move.[15]

About a half hour after the hearing, Illinois Attorney General William Clark declared the match illegal. Citing possible inconsistencies in the licensing procedures for Ali and Terrell and a widely ignored rule that any corporation promoting a boxing or wrestling event had to have at least fifty people in it, Clark advised the ISAC to "adjourn their meeting and to so advise the participants" that their promotion was finished in Chicago. While Clark's legal opinion was legitimate, such rules had always been loosely enforced, if not ignored. Almost certainly, Ali's draft resistance and ties to Main Bout brought increased scrutiny over the licensing and promotion of his fight with Terrell. Mayor Daley backed the decision: "The attorney general has issued an opinion holding the fight illegal. All state officials are bound by the opinion of the attorney general. It seems to me the commission has no other choice but to follow the opinion." The ISAC acquiesced and canceled the match. The *Chicago Tribune* praised Daley, Kerner, and Clark for intervening.[16]

Ali's refusal to apologize reinforced his defiance and engendered nationwide opposition to his upcoming title fight with Terrell. Unwelcome in Chicago, Main Bout shopped the contest around the United States with little success. In each city, local boxing people greeted Main Bout with interest, but state and municipal government officials rejected it. As Bob Arum explained, "I got calls from promoters all over the country wanting to hold the fight, even from Huron, S.D." However, "the day after a promoter would call me, the governor of his state or the mayor would announce there'd be no Clay fight in his town or state." Promoters in Louisville, for example, completed negotiations with Main Bout and the Kentucky State Athletic Commission agreed to sanction the bout. Influenced by local veterans' groups, however, members of the Kentucky State Senate announced the next day that they would block the fight. The Senate also passed a resolution urging Ali to join the Army, and State Senator William L. Sullivan demanded that Ali "abandon his reprehensible efforts to avoid duty in the country which afforded him the opportunity to achieve eminence." In Pittsburgh, promoters inquired about hosting the match. The next day, Pennsylvania legislators moved to bar it. After local promoters and the Maine State Athletic Commission announced their interest in sponsoring the contest, Governor John Reed rebuffed them, urging that the champion "be held in utter contempt by every patriotic American." Promoters in Rhode Island, Oklahoma, and Missouri also asked about holding the bout in their states but were blocked. The pattern was clear: as soon as the news broke that area boxing people were interested in the fight, local or state officials opposed them. With the contest less than a month away, Main Bout had yet to secure a site.[17]

At the Savior's Day Convention, which the champion attended, Elijah Muhammad blasted the government's war policy and deemed the singling out of Ali to be racist; but sportswriters denied that prejudice had anything to do with their criticism of Ali. Before 4,000 people, Muhammad asserted that whites only wanted Ali for service after "he entered the army of the Lord [the Nation of Islam]." He also claimed that white politicians had enforced an official policy that "[t]he Negro should go to Vietnam and kill other Negroes while our sons stay home and go to colleges and universities." David Condon of the *Chicago Tribune* denied that racial or religious discrimination had anything to do with Ali's reclassification. Furthermore, he was appalled that "some of Champion Cassius Clay's admirers have bleated that the opposition to this fight is because it involves a great colored title holder. These admirers holler 'hate' and 'prejudice.'" To Condon, it was almost impossible for sportswriters to be racist. "A person would have to be naive, indeed, to believe that sports writers were becoming prejudiced at such a late date," he claimed. "No man of prejudice can be a sports writer today. The majority of the great athletes are colored men, and the sports writers associate with them daily."[18]

Main Bout decided to shop the match around Canada, which was a risky move because it assumed that Ali would receive permission to leave the country. Fortunately for Main Bout, the Louisville Draft Board voted unanimously to let Ali fight in Canada because of its proximity to the United States and because the champion promised that his stay there would be brief. It ordered Ali to return to the United States by April 7 or face desertion charges.[19]

The same pattern occurred in Canada as in the United States. Promoters in several cities, including Montreal and Edmonton, talked with Main Bout, but politicians opposed the fight in response to Ali's anti-war stance. Finally, after a long negotiation featuring a debate on the floor of the provincial parliament, the Ontario Ministry of Labour allowed the contest. Even in Toronto, however, the fight stirred controversy. The management of Maple Leaf Gardens, where the bout would be held, became embroiled in a bitter struggle. In protest, hockey legend Conn Smythe, the founder of the Toronto Maple Leafs franchise, resigned his position as the arena's director. He never again set foot in the building he had made famous.[20]

Almost immediately after Toronto approved the contest, Ernie Terrell withdrew citing financial considerations and forced Main Bout to find a substitute opponent, who would turn out to be George Chuvalo. Chuvalo had pursued a bout against Ali for several years, going back to their aborted 1963 match, when the LSG and Dundee decided that he was too risky an opponent for their young charge. Following the rebuff, Chuvalo had kept after his prospective rival. Once he had interrupted a talk show appearance by the Louisville Lip—in drag no less, a response to the accusation that he punched like a washerwoman—waving what he claimed was a valid contract to meet him. Chuvalo also jumped into the ring and got into a mock argument with the champion following Ali's rematch with Liston. Finally he was getting his chance. With only seventeen days' warning before his title shot, Chuvalo crammed 100 rounds of sparring into that brief period. Although a 6–1 underdog, the eternally optimistic Chuvalo looked forward to the opportunity with his usual glass-half-full perspective. This outlook on life would serve Chuvalo well when later he would have to withstand the death of two of his sons, who succumbed to drug addiction, and the suicide of his grief-stricken wife. One of the toughest men to ever box professionally, he once said, "The best thing I have going for myself is my attitude. I have a hard time quitting on something. I have a hard time walking away from something. I'll be the last guy to quit on somebody." It was former heavyweight champion Rocky Marciano who best summarized Chuvalo's mental and physical strength when he quipped, "If all fights were a hundred rounds, George Chuvalo would be unbeaten in any era."[21]

Although determined, Chuvalo had had a spotty ring career, sometimes showing great promise but almost always failing to win the big one. In the most important match of his career, he had come up on the short end of a unanimous decision in a November 1965 fifteen-rounder against Terrell in Toronto. The result still embitters Chuvalo because he believes that Terrell's alleged connections to organized crime, rather than the in-ring action that night, caused him to lose. He said years later, "I know I beat Ernie Terrell but Ernie Terrell was with the right people. . . . He was with the mob and they had too much muscle. They scared the living daylights out of everybody involved in the fight game in this town." In another interview, Chuvalo claimed that referee Sammy Luftspring told him that "they [the mob] were going to kill me if I didn't vote for Terrell." Chuvalo's manager Irving Ungerman echoed this sentiment, reporting that Terrell's connections threatened to murder him if Chuvalo won. Although the bout was a difficult one to score, and seemed to be closely contested, Terrell won a lopsided decision.[22]

Chuvalo was not the first to accuse Terrell of being controlled by the underworld. Prior to the fiasco in Chicago, his proposed bout with Ali had been beset by rumors that he was a mob fighter. Terrell had been unable to get a boxing license in a number of key states because of these supposed criminal ties. In November 1965, a few days before Ali's championship fight with Floyd Patterson, California State Athletic Commissioner Dan Kilroy urged all jurisdictions to refrain from permitting Terrell to box until he was free from "undesirable influences." Particularly, Kilroy questioned boxing manager Bernie Glickman's purchase of Terrell's contract. A federal investigation several years earlier had identified Glickman as an associate of Chicago mob boss Tony Accardo, and most observers believed that he was still connected. Terrell encountered similar opposition in New York, which also refused to license him. Terrell, of course, denies his involvement in any such entanglements.[23]

Because of Chuvalo's losses to Terrell and others, sportswriters unfairly labeled the bout a mismatch, which further hurt Main Bout's cause. Chuvalo was not as attractive an opponent as Terrell from a boxing standpoint. After all, he had dropped his previous bout to an unranked fighter, while Terrell hadn't lost in three years, racking up a series of victories against several top heavyweights, including Cleveland Williams, Zora Folley, and Eddie Machen. Even if people felt that this contest would be less competitive than Ali versus Terrell, however, it is unlikely that the substitution of Chuvalo, per se, even in a potential mismatch, would make the promotion unprofitable. First, the popular Chuvalo's fighting in his hometown for the championship would boost the live gate and Canadian closed-circuit-television sales. Chuvalo had fought twenty-one of his first twenty-two bouts in Toronto and was Maple Leaf Gardens' house fighter. He was bankable there. Five years earlier, his match against Alex Miteff drew 10,000 fans to the arena. Second, Chuvalo's whiteness was probably attractive to customers, black and white, who saw boxing as racial theater. Third, Chuvalo had previously fought in matches that had done well financially. His February 1965 bout with Floyd Patterson at Madison Square Garden drew 19,000 fans paying $165,000 and was the first sellout at the arena since Cassius Clay's fight with Doug Jones two years earlier. A record-setting 290 applications for press credentials were reported. Sixty-four closed-circuit-television venues with a seating capacity of 300,000 had screened the telecast, which was produced by Mike Malitz. In one of the best heavyweight bouts in years, Chuvalo lost a narrow decision. Fourth, even though Chuvalo had opened as a 6–1 underdog against Ali, the betting odds on the Ali-Terrell bout, before it was canceled, were 5–1. Although Terrell was a better fighter than Chuvalo, it was not by that much. The results would prove this, since Chuvalo wound up doing far better against Ali than Terrell would when he fought the champion eleven months later. All of these factors indicate that Chuvalo's presence alone would not account for a poor showing at the box office.[24]

Those who predicted a mismatch were wrong. Ali-Chuvalo turned out to be an entertaining fight that saw the champion take a competitive yet decisive fifteen-round unanimous decision. Although he never had Ali in trouble, Chuvalo made determined advances that ensured a fast pace and plenty of action. Jim Brown, who curiously referred to the champion as "Clay" throughout his commentary for the closed-circuit telecast, told fans before the fight, "I'm not in the ring, but I'm as nervous as I can be, you know, something about it, I don't know what it is." It was Ali's longest fight to date, and Chuvalo's legal and illegal assaults on his hips, ribs, kidneys, buttocks, and groin left the champion urinating blood for several days afterward. The positive crowd response to the brisk back-and-forth, and the disproving of media predictions of a mismatch, moved veteran play-by-play announcer Don Dunphy to comment, "There was a lot of criticism about this match, and a lot of people saying it never should be held, that it was some kind of social injustice being foisted on the customer, they sound rather happy don't they?"[25]

Its eventual aesthetic success notwithstanding, with only a few weeks to go the promotion was in danger of going bust. A month earlier, the Associated Press had predicted gross receipts of over $4 million and a minimum purse of $450,000 for Ali. This was an excellent guarantee for a title defense against an opponent like Terrell, who was not as well known as Floyd Patterson or Sonny Liston. If sales were better than expected, Ali's share would have been larger. The day after Main Bout announced that it had signed Chuvalo, however, the Associated Press estimated that the fight's gross take would be approximately $500,000. Although there had been radio broadcasts of all of Ali's previous title matches, only a handful of the fight's forty-two sponsors agreed to support the bout, and the radio broadcast had to be canceled.[26]

Despite being in deep trouble, Ali and Main Bout could not quit. If they ever wished to get their venture off the ground, they had to go through with the fight, even if it meant losing money. Jim Brown summarized what was at stake: "This particular situation was very important not just because of the event itself, but what it would represent from the standpoint of other ventures not only in sports because it was like making history, economic history." Bob Arum added that it was a now-or-never, do-or-die, make-or-break situation for the organization: "If we had folded our tents and gone away we would have been dead. Dead ducks. I think it was very very important for Ali and for all of us [that] a fight did take place." Arum nevertheless suspected that the champion was "a dead piece of merchandise . . . as far as big-money closed-circuit is concerned."[27]

Critics of Main Bout, Ali, and the NOI proposed a boycott of the closed-circuit broadcast. In Miami, a 2,700-member American Legion branch vowed that it would picket any theater that showed the fight, asking people to "join in condemnation of this unpatriotic, loudmouthed, bombastic individual." The threat worked, because the Biscayne Dog Track canceled its scheduled screening, and no other Miami sites would broadcast Ali versus Chuvalo. *Sports Illustrated* predicted that "few theaters in the U.S. [would be] foolhardy—or courageous—enough to sign up with Main Bout, Inc., the theater-TV promoter that includes Black Muslims." But other than a pair of demonstrators in Fort Worth and an unfounded bomb scare in Cleveland, the nationwide protest campaign against venues showing the match did not materialize. Some sportswriters encouraged readers to boycott. Eddie Muller, the *San Francisco Examiner*'s boxing writer, chastised any theater operators who "might take it upon themselves to accept the TV firm's promotion and make a quick dollar." Referring to a local embargo on the fight, Muller commented, "If every state follows California's action perhaps it'll be a complete nationwide blackout, which is as it should be." Even Congress got involved, as a number of representatives called for people to stay home. Frank Clark, a Pennsylvania Democrat, proclaimed, "The heavyweight champion has become a complete and total disgrace. I urge the citizens of the nation as a whole to boycott any of his performances. To leave these theater seats empty would be the finest tribute possible to that boy whose hearse may pass by the open doors of the theater on Main Street, USA." Although a threatened boycott of the closed-circuit telecast of Ali's rematch with Sonny Liston had minimal impact on that fight's sales, the opposition to Ali during the brief buildup to his fight with Chuvalo seemed to be fiercer and more determined than before. The possibility of action that would wipe out the gate receipts seemed real this time.[28]

The most crippling blow to the promotion, by far, was its abandonment by closed-circuit-television theater chains. Main Bout had contracted 280 North American venues to broadcast the Terrell fight, but only thirty-two wound up showing the match against Chuvalo. Several cities that normally hosted Ali title fights in at least one local venue, including Miami, Cincinnati, Milwaukee, Kansas City, Minneapolis–St. Paul, Boston, and San Antonio, did not screen the bout. California's two biggest boxing promoters, Don Chargin and Aileen Eaton, met on March 6 and agreed to engineer a statewide blackout. They announced that they would meet with theater owners in an effort to make sure that no venues in California showed the March 29 contest, "in deference to the many families that have loved ones fighting and dying in Vietnam." When Main Bout approached Ray Syufy, the owner of twenty-one drive-in theaters in Northern California, to televise the match, it was turned down, even though Syufy admitted that the company had made him a "lucrative offer." In total, the fight was shown in only two California venues, both of them independent theaters. By contrast, Ali's previous bout against Floyd

Patterson had been shown in thirteen Los Angeles–area theaters alone. In New York, seven Loew's theaters withdrew 13,000 seats from the closed-circuit pool. Ernie Emerling, the firm's vice-president for public relations claimed, "Too much shilly-shallying over the site didn't leave us enough time to print tickets and advertise; we should have had six to eight weeks." Later, New York's Radio-Keith-Orpheum (RKO) theater chain canceled its offer to show the fight in ten area movie houses. While twenty-five New York City venues with a seating capacity of 80,000 had broadcast Ali versus Patterson, only five Big Apple theaters with a seating capacity of 11,000 hosted Ali versus Chuvalo. In Chicago, a representative of the Balaban and Katz (B&K) chain of theaters named Ed Seguin reported that his firm would not show the fight "because of all the uncertainty over where, and whether, it was coming off." Both the B&K and Warner theater chains canceled their nationwide arrangements with Main Bout.[29]

Main Bout needed these organizations' cooperation because most of the theaters equipped to show fights belonged to chains like Loew's and RKO. Few independent operators could stage a profitable closed-circuit telecast because it was too expensive for them to do so. When two locals promoted a Jacksonville broadcast of Ali's first fight with Sonny Liston, for example, their fees and costs were difficult to overcome. The Jacksonville Coliseum had about 9,000 seats. The half-full arena generated $17,300 in ticket sales, but after $1,000 of federal and state taxes were levied on the venture, 55 percent of the remainder ($9,000) went straight to ancillary promoter Theater Network Television (TNT). Although the venue was equipped with a $675 RCA projector, TNT insisted that the promoters rent (for $2,600) a state-of-the-art Eidophor projector to show the bout. TNT, of course, owned the American rights to the Eidophor. Rental of the arena cost another $1,600. The promoters had to install a phone loop that connected the fight's broadcast signal to the theater ($550). They also had to hire security, printers, ushers, a sound engineer, and ticket takers ($1,000). Insurance cost $300 and advertising was $750. In total, the Jacksonville promoters netted less than $500 from their enterprise. TNT probably made more than ten times that amount. As Ali's new ancillary promoter, Main Bout wanted to do as well, and Jim Brown hoped that the organization would eventually facilitate the telecasting of Ali's fights by independent, black-owned theaters, perhaps by lowering its percentage of the take. For the time being, however, Main Bout's success was dependent upon cooperation from the large chains that owned properly equipped theaters.[30]

The promotion was a financial disaster. The closed-circuit telecast sold about 46,000 tickets for $110,000. This gross take was twenty to forty times below closed-circuit revenues from each of Ali's three previous championship fights. The $150,000 on-site live gate was also lower than that for each of Ali's previous title bouts, although the 13,540 fans in attendance set a Canadian gate record. Furthermore, Ali's $65,000 purse was five to ten times smaller than those for each of his three previous bouts and at least three times less than for any fight he ever had from 1964 through the end of his career. The Associated Press summarized, "Theater-television of last night's Cassius Clay-George Chuvalo heavyweight title fight proved a resounding dud, as expected." Eddie Muller crowed, "Forming the Main Bout, Inc. organization was a costly mistake. Whoever put money into the firm must wind up broke. There's no way, as far as we can see, of the organization recouping." Mike Malitz disputed this claim at the time, telling reporters that Main Bout "made enough to pay the bills" and break even, although he felt that the company was "grossly underpaid for the time and effort." Years later, however, Malitz admitted, "We lost money." The fiasco illustrated Main Bout's lack of control over the terms of Ali's fights. The organization would have to weigh its next move carefully if it and Ali's career were going to survive.[31]

Several white sportswriters and at least one black reporter blamed Main Bout's incompetence for the promotion's collapse. Eddie Muller called Main Bout a "fly-by-night enterprise which now louse[s] up the horizon." The syndicated *Los Angeles Times* reporter Jim Murray claimed, "Clay's corporation, . . . ironically, calls itself 'Main Bout, Inc.' and is run by a football player and a couple of guys whose sole qualification is they once subscribed to the Police Gazette." Bob Stewart of the *New York World-Telegram and Sun* poked fun at Main Bout. "It all seemed so simple. You just formed a quickie corporation and put on a title fight." One of Ali's few consistent critics within the black press, A. S. "Doc" Young of the *New York Amsterdam News*, insisted, "It was the stupidest sort of publicity for the Black Muslims to publicize their association with Main Bout, Inc." Others compared Main Bout unfavorably to the LSG.[32]

But there was a great racial divide in media perception of Main Bout, with most black observers believing that racism and a possible criminal conspiracy were the real reasons for the financial failure of the Ali-Chuvalo fight. "There are some reports of possible court action or civil rights agencies may be looking into the cancellations of the closed circuit television showings to ascertain if there was any overt racial discrimination involved," according to Clarence Matthews of the *Louisville Defender*. "What columnists have tried to do is thwart the Black Muslims through castigation of Clay," wrote Marion Jackson of the *Atlanta Daily World*. "It seems as though the Black Muslims for the first time ha[ve] projected a Negro group—Main Bout, Inc., in control of a nationwide closed circuit telecast." *Muhammad Speaks* accused white reporters of trying to obscure their racism through so-called patriotic attacks on Ali. "Outbursts over [Ali's] military draft status were [a] means of killing two birds with one red, white, and blue stone" and an "attempt to smear" Main Bout, according to the newspaper. The most strident response came from Moses Newson of the *Baltimore Afro-American*. Newson, who had covered the civil rights beat for years, had been thrashed by a white mob while reporting the 1957 Little Rock school integration crisis, and was on board the Freedom Ride bus that had been firebombed in Alabama in 1961, congratulated Main Bout for surviving "in face of the most vicious and concentrated 'kill them off' campaign ever joined in by the press, the Mafia, and politicians." He asserted that white "reporters, broadcasters, and others who tried to kill the fight scribbled and spouted bitter reams to a degree that they actually need to offer something more lest they themselves might be thought part of an unholy alliance that includes racists, hypocrites, and mobsters." Alongside New York Congressman Adam Clayton Powell at a press conference on Capitol Hill, Jim Brown contended, "The ostensible reason [for the boycott] is because of Clay's so-called unpatriotic remarks about the draft, but that's just an excuse." Powell added, "They just don't want to see Negroes cutting up this three-million-dollar melon," and vowed to have the U.S. Department of Justice and the Equal Employment Opportunity Commission investigate the situation.[33]

Main Bout had suspected for months that the mob was sabotaging its promotion, but white sportswriters dismissed their concerns. Even Robert Lipsyte of the *New York Times*, perhaps Ali's strongest press supporter, called the assertion "imaginative" because it suggested "an improbable plot of enormous complexity." Another reporter declared that such a scheme was "not evident here. There's only one difficulty in this whole affair and the name is Cassius Clay. He brought it all on himself." Jimmy Cannon admitted that organized crime resented Main Bout's entry into boxing but denied that racism fueled attacks on the company. "The fight mob detests Clay. Their revulsion isn't instigated by race," wrote Cannon in his syndicated column. "They want Chuvalo to beat him because Clay has made the greatest prize in sports worthless. This isn't temporary. He is in trouble for a long while."[34]

Clearly, these sportswriters weren't reporting the whole story, because the Federal Bureau of Investigation (FBI) launched an inquiry into the failed promotion. It suspected that Terrell withdrew not only because of financial concerns, but also because of death threats to him and Bernie Glickman by Chicago Mafia figures who would no longer profit if the bout were moved to Canada. But the legal action, detailed in the note corresponding to this paragraph, proved inconclusive when investigators were unable to link the boycott to the mob, and no further federal examination of the fight took place. The *Pittsburgh Courier* sighed, "as usual, the casting of light on supported underworld control of boxing still remains unfulfilled."[35]

In response to the FBI investigation, some members of the white press acknowledged the likelihood of Main Bout's charge that a conspiracy had foiled its Toronto promotion. The difficulties surrounding the company's initial closed-circuit venture were "apparently an outgrowth of boxing's current scramble for position in a future made uncertain by the troubles of Cassius Clay," wrote Robert Lipsyte. "To the underworld, the new organization meant only that 'a rival gang' had moved in and was in a position to 'ace them out' by not dealing with 'trusted' closed circuit television operators or exhibitors as well as the other businessmen who normally get pay days from a title fight." A United Press International (UPI) writer added, "New York Mafia interests were enraged at the attempt of the Muslims to take over closed circuit television rights and other revenues from professional boxing through Main Bout, Inc."[36]

Realizing that he would not be able to fight under Main Bout at home, Ali considered matches outside the United States, but he feared that his career might be over if he didn't change promoters. "They want to stop me from fighting. They done run me out of the country. . . . This [the Chuvalo match] could be my last fight," he told Phil Pepe of the *New York World-Telegram and Sun*. At first he balked at the possibility of having to leave the country to make a living. "I don't want to go," he said. "I want to defend my title here somewhere or even in a phone booth or in a barge at sea." Bolstered by his international appeal, however, Ali quickly reconciled his doubts. "I'm not fighting for money," he said to the *New York Post*'s Milton Gross, "but for the freedom of American black people to speak their minds." He admitted to a Louisville reporter that he would like to fight in the United States, "[b]ut they can put it in England, Nigeria, France, or Rome if they want to. I don't care about the money. It's a world title I got, not a U.S.A. title, and it can be defended anywhere in the world." During an interview with Larry Merchant of the *Philadelphia Daily News*, he fanned himself with a replica passport and insisted that he would fight wherever he could. Ali's most eloquent expression of this outlook was recorded by Robert Lipsyte: "Boxing is nothing, just satisfying some bloodthirsty people. I'm no longer Cassius Clay, a Negro from Kentucky. I belong to the world, the black world. I'll always have a home in Pakistan, in Algeria, in Ethiopia. This is more than money," he said. "I'm not disturbed and nervous. Why should I be? In a few hours I could fly to another country, in the East, in Africa, where people love me. Millions, all over the world want to see me. Why should I worry about losing a few dollars." The champion concluded, "I'm not going to sell my manhood for a few dollars, or a smile. I'd rather be poor and free than rich and a slave." Ali's comments foreshadowed his and Main Bout's decision to take his next three matches to Europe, where there had not been a world heavyweight championship contest in more than thirty years.[37]

The three European fights earned Ali purses far more lucrative than the one he had received for the match in Canada with Chuvalo, reestablished him as the top drawing power in boxing, and proved that he would not bow to pressure to rearrange his promotional scheme. Ali fought in May against Britain's Henry Cooper for a $350,000 purse, the first world heavyweight title fight in England since 1908. The American Broadcasting Company (ABC) paid Main Bout $75,000 for the U.S. television rights. Beamed over the recently launched Early Bird satellite, it was the first transatlantic sporting event to be shown on live television in the United States. Mexican and Canadian stations that picked up the signal also paid Main Bout a fee. Although smaller than successful American closed-circuit broadcasts, this sum was comparable to the $110,000 grossed by the Ali-Chuvalo telecast. Equally important, the deal gave Main Bout and Ali increased independence from oppositional forces in the United States. It also primed other markets to host future Ali bouts and introduced him to a whole new group of admirers. Primarily through a huge on-site crowd and a successful British closed-circuit telecast, the Cooper fight raked in money. About 46,000 fans packed Arsenal Stadium. The $560,000 live gate was almost four times greater than that of the Chuvalo fight and set a British boxing record. Sixteen English closed-circuit theaters generated approximately 40,000 ticket sales and $280,000 in revenues. After foreign sales and other ancillary deals, the fight grossed nearly $1.5 million. It also began a long and profitable relationship between the champion and the television network. Over the next fifteen years, he would appear on ABC over sixty times, earning the network its two highest audience ratings ever for boxing, participating in the first million-dollar fight on free TV, receiving badly needed income for appearing on the network while he was exiled from boxing between 1967 and 1970, and even getting it to pay the plaintiff's six-figure legal bill when Ali was sued for slandering referee Tony Perez following comments on a 1975 *Wide World of Sports* telecast. Ali and Main Bout had turned a difficult situation into one that signaled their autonomy from those in the United States who wanted to shut them down.[38]

Ten weeks later, Ali returned to Britain and took home a $300,000 purse for his match against Brian London. Main Bout sold the U.S. television rights to ABC for $200,000 and received additional fees from European and worldwide television stations that broadcast the match. Ten thousand people paid $150,000 on-site to see the London fight. British closed-circuit returns neared $165,000. Even as they refused to call him by his chosen name, even as they reported that the fight was a financial bomb, and even as they called upon the British Boxing Board of Control to ban the match, Ali's most virulent critics within the press like Gene Ward still had to admit, "In both of these European ventures, Clay will earn more than he ever could have in the

United States, where his opposition to the draft has left him an unpopular figure."[39]

Ali crossed the ocean one last time in September for a $300,000 payday to take on southpaw Karl Mildenberger in Germany, where there never before had been a world heavyweight title fight. ABC paid Main Bout $200,000 for the U.S. television rights, and 40,000 fans paid $500,000 to see it in person. Although there was no closed-circuit-television broadcast, other ancillary revenues brought in an additional $250,000, and the fight grossed just short of $1 million.[40]

Ali's three European matches during the summer of 1966 were financial victories that broke down the embargo against Ali's fighting in the United States. Ali and Main Bout had appeared to be down for the count, but they rallied back with renewed bargaining power within a hostile and corrupt American boxing establishment that had been thoroughly resistant to their existence. Ali would fight in the United States three times between late 1966 and early 1967, becoming the most active heavyweight champion since Joe Louis, and earning big purses without Main Bout having to relinquish control of the closed-circuit rights. The move also cultivated new markets that added to Ali's ever-increasing international fan base, as closed-circuit television in Europe and radio broadcasts and fight films in Africa, the Middle East, and Asia primed the world to host Ali bouts. At home, the easy access to Ali on free television, where he could represent himself as a boxer rather than being represented by the press as a political radical, eased some of the controversy that had erupted around his draft resistance. People were reminded that he was a fighter first, and a brilliant one at that. Ali's measured comments during post-fight interviews only made things better. Against mediocre competition, Ali had made good money, maintained his autonomy, cultivated new fan bases, and paved the way for his return to the United States closed-circuit market. The European mini-tour was a dramatic success for Ali and Main Bout, a great move amid a difficult situation.

One can only speculate why closed-circuit operators in the United States blinked first and allowed Ali and Main Bout to return on their own terms, but the most likely explanation is twofold. They expected Ali's career eventually to be stalled by his draft resistance and in the meantime wanted to make some money by working with him. After all, the fight game was all but dead without Ali, and its meteoric rise in recent years could be attributed directly to him. There was no shortage of great fighters during the era that immediately preceded Cassius Clay, but a series of scandals had plunged gate receipts dramatically low. Boxing's total revenues in the United States began to rise in accordance with the onset of Clay's career and doubled the year he won the title. A *Sports Illustrated* article estimated that boxing's total gates for

1965 were about $9 million, the vast majority from Ali's fights with Liston and Patterson. Simply put, Muhammad Ali was responsible for most of the money that the sport generated during the early 1960s. Without him, the fight game was not nearly as lucrative. Closed-circuit operators and their promotional cronies realized that they had better get on the Ali gravy train before his draft resistance got him permanently banned. While they were loathe to yield such control to an upstart like Main Bout, the alternative was equally bleak, especially since the organization would probably have to fold once the government had its way with the draft-resisting Ali.[41]

Upon his return to the United States, Ali chose not to renew his contract with the LSG, which expired in October 1966. Ali's decision was probably a relief to many LSG members. Their profits were relatively small and would possibly dwindle even further because the champion was asking for a renegotiated package that would bring him a larger share of his purses. In addition, their patience with Ali had been exhausted. As late as May, there were reports of Ali's saying, "[W]hen the contract runs out in October, we'll probably work out something where we can sign again. We been getting along so good. I feel friendly towards the Group." Even had he chosen to remain with the group, however, it was hardly guaranteed that the LSG would extend the agreement. One member certainly was tired of it all, telling a reporter, "Clay has turned rancid. It's no fun anymore. And there was never much money in it, by the time we paid those fancy expenses of his." Herbert Muhammad, who eighteen months earlier had told Malcolm X that he was running Clay's operations and who had already been receiving a $300 weekly salary as his business manager, officially took over the managerial reins. "We're not trying to be permanent people in the fistical world," said Elijah Muhammad. "We know it's a crooked business, but we want Muhammad to get justice out of it." Herbert resigned as president of Main Bout and was replaced by John Ali. Bob Arum's law firm took over as the champion's primary legal counsel in return for 5 percent of his fight receipts. The LSG contract was amended to pay Ali two-thirds of his purses, but his expenses were now paid off the top, instead of out of the manager's share. Considering Ali's spending habits, that was a bad development for him.[42]

Although a total mismatch, Muhammad Ali's homecoming bout with Cleveland Williams in November 1966 was a big event, as the champion's popularity among blacks drove a successful closed-circuit broadcast. Thirty-five thousand fans watched the contest in person at the Houston Astrodome, paying $460,000 and breaking the American indoor attendance record for boxing. One hundred twenty-five U.S. closed-circuit-television venues with a total seating capacity of 500,000 showed the match, including many sites belonging to theater chains in large cities that had boycotted Ali-Chuvalo.

Pricing tickets between five and ten dollars, twenty-four New York closed-circuit locations with a seating capacity of 68,000, most of them owned by the Loew's and RKO franchises, brokered deals with Main Bout to host the telecast. In New Jersey, three previously uncooperative Warner's theaters also screened it. Although only two venues statewide had broadcast Ali-Chuvalo, six Northern California venues showed the Ali-Williams fight, with one San Francisco theater filling 2,000 of its 2,600 available seats. Jack Fiske of the *San Francisco Chronicle* reported the strong black presence: "The theater audience was at least one-fourth Negro, perhaps the largest turnout for any Clay fight I recall." Another fourteen Los Angeles–area venues screened Ali-Williams. Chicago's B&K movie theater chain, which had also declined to telecast Ali-Chuvalo, showed a feature movie to patrons before broadcasting the title fight. In total, seven Chicago-area venues hosted the match. Downtown theater manager Leo Brown said, "It wasn't a full house, but a good house," and a *Chicago Tribune* reporter noted, "[A]n unusually large number of Negro fans paid $7.50 for reserved seats." Total closed-circuit receipts are unknown, but they probably topped $1 million. Main Bout also arranged for telecasts and films to be shown in forty-two countries around the world. It sold live television rights to Mexican and Canadian stations and delayed-TV privileges to ABC. There was also a live U.S. radio broadcast of the match, which brought in an additional $100,000. Main Bout pocketed 32.5 percent of the ancillaries, and Ali's purse probably exceeded $500,000. What a difference eight months had made.[43]

Ali's long-awaited match with Ernie Terrell took place in February 1967 and also did well at the box office, with 37,000 fans breaking the attendance record set by Ali-Williams and paying $400,000 to see it in person at the Astrodome. The 178 North American closed-circuit venues generated approximately $1 million in revenues, with Main Bout taking home 30 percent and Ali's purse reaching the high six figures. Once again, Main Bout agreed to terms with previously uncooperative closed-circuit chains in large cities like New York, where eleven venues showed the bout. Despite inclement weather, 5,500 of Madison Square Garden's 10,000 seats were filled, with fans paying nearly ten dollars per ticket. In total, the New York metropolitan area boasted twenty-five venues with a seating capacity of 95,000. Newark's Branford Theater, one of eight New Jersey venues, reported a sellout. There was also a series of cable television hookups in nearby cities such as Hartford. Twelve Los Angeles–area venues hosted the bout, and there was also a live U.S. radio broadcast. For Jim Brown, the highlight of the closed-circuit promotion was the inclusion of black promoters and of independent, black-owned theaters. Walter "Dootsie" Williams, the music publisher, independent record label head, and proprietor of the Dooto Music Center in Los Angeles, became the first such person to put on such a telecast. Paul Jones, an African American promoter and longtime friend of Chris Dundee, screened the bout at Atlanta's City Auditorium, which he did not own. It was significant, however, that Georgia's only showing of the bout was at the hands of a black promoter connected to the Ali camp. Jones added that he was planning to meet with Dundee to discuss the possibility of a Clay fight in Atlanta. These were exactly the kinds of operations that Main Bout hoped to encourage.[44]

Ali's March 1967 contest with Zora Folley was not as big as the other two matches, but it yielded a solid $265,000 purse for Ali. The match was Madison Square Garden's first world heavyweight title bout in over fifteen years, but terrible weather in New York limited the crowd to 14,000. They paid $244,000, an arena record, to see it in person. RKO Pictures purchased the worldwide rights to the match from Main Bout for $175,000 and made Ali versus Folley the first-ever heavyweight championship fight shown live on U.S. home television during prime time. Main Bout made no profit from the fight and did not promote it. The organization acted merely to broker the worldwide rights to RKO and paid out the entire $175,000 rights fee to the two fighters—$150,000 to Ali and $25,000 to Folley. Ali also earned about 50 percent of the live gate. This was a good payday considering that Ali had fought only six weeks earlier and Folley was a sizable underdog.[45]

Looking for one last payday, Main Bout hastily arranged for an April 25 rematch between Ali and Floyd Patterson to take place just three days before Ali's scheduled induction into the Army. The Nevada State Athletic Commission (NSAC) agreed to sanction the Las Vegas bout, and Main Bout announced that it would be broadcast on closed-circuit television in the United States and beamed via satellite to Japan and Europe. Contracts called for Ali to receive $225,000. Malitz told reporters that with two weeks to go before fight time, Main Bout had already contracted eighty-five venues in the United States and a "large number of foreign outlets" to show the match, and he estimated that his company had already received $150,000 in fees. That number would rise, of course, once tickets began selling. It is a testimony to Ali's incredible drawing power that he was able to fight so frequently against such overmatched opposition and remain a moneymaker. His appeal was truly remarkable.[46]

As in Chicago a year earlier, however, an anti-Ali backlash ensued and the fight never took place. Politicians, backed by their cronies in the press, called for the match to be canceled. Jimmy Cannon labeled the bout a "sanctioned atrocity." Resistance was marked by a breakdown of official responsibility, as rogue administrators threatened to overlook their duties and disregard their subordinates. Referring to a brawl involving members of Ali's camp at the first Ali-Patterson fight, Las Vegas Sheriff Ralph Lamb warned local promoters: "[T]hey will not receive police protection from my department this time. Why should I risk some fine men getting hurt when the only ones who will profit from this fiasco will be the private promoters of the fight?" Nevada Governor Paul Laxalt ordered the NSAC to cancel the contest, and the body charged with regulating boxing in the state acquiesced. "It would give Nevada a black eye," claimed Laxalt, which was hard to believe considering the reputation that the state's gaming industry had for mob involvement. Main Bout shifted its attention to Pittsburgh. The Pennsylvania State Athletic Commission agreed to sanction the match, but Laxalt called Pennsylvania Governor Raymond Shafer and requested that he block it. Shafer did. Next, New York City was mentioned as a possible site. But New York State Athletic Commissioner Edwin Dooley, who less than a month later would order the revocation of Ali's license immediately after his May indictment for draft evasion, ended this speculation: "We have a reciprocity agreement with both the Nevada and Pennsylvania Commissions. They abide by our rulings and we abide by theirs." Dooley knew that such action would effectively bar Ali from fighting in the United States because of nationwide reciprocity agreements between state athletic commissions. Although New Mexico Governor David Cargo offered Albuquerque as a last-minute alternative, Main Bout had run out of time. The organization risked another Toronto-type flop with just two weeks remaining before Ali's scheduled induction. Defeated, Main Bout threw in the towel. Malitz told a reporter, "Once Pittsburgh was a dead issue, I felt it was all over."[47]

Main Bout had no choice but to accept its plight, but there were those in the black press who expressed outrage. Brad Pye of the *Los Angeles Sentinel* fumed, "Promoters, people who handle closed-circuit TV have punished Clay because of his religious beliefs. It's this writer's considered opinion that the primary reason Clay's fight was canceled in Las Vegas and blackballed in several other cities was strictly racial." Bill Nunn of the *Pittsburgh Courier* echoed similar concerns, "Last week the power of the white man was again displayed for those who would have you believe in the myth of this is 'my' country. When the states of Nevada and Pennsylvania, through their dictatorial governors turned thumbs down on the second Muhammad Ali-Floyd Patterson fight, they showed how they expect the game to be played. Either play by the way we set the rules or you don't play . . . period." The *Louisville Defender*, stalwart in its backing of Ali, echoed this sentiment in an editorial: "With the almighty dollar in sight (especially since Negroes had moved into the financial end—promoting and sponsoring—of the fight game through Muhammad Ali) these men forgot all about the 'American Way' in their haste to snatch the golden prize, the heavyweight crown, from a man whose performances had indicated that this was the only way it could be done for years to come." Muhammad Ali's conviction and five-year sentence for draft evasion in June ended Main Bout's run after only seventeen months and seven fights. State athletic commissions nationwide barred him following his May indictment, and he could not fight abroad because his status as a convicted felon rendered his passport invalid. Although Ali remained out of prison while his case was under appeal, his career as a fighter was finished for the foreseeable future. Realizing this, Arum, Malitz, and Brown left Main Bout to form a new company, Sports Action Inc., which wound up promoting the tournament designed to replace Ali as heavyweight champion. The NOI was not a part of the new organization. Like its most famous acolyte, it had been frozen out of professional boxing.[48]

Main Bout's tumultuous course was a glaring example of how Ali's cultural image was interconnected with the commercial intrigue surrounding his fights. The specter of Ali's making money for the NOI through Main Bout had given his opponents, both political and economic, the moral authority to try to destroy the organization, even through illegal means. The pockets of outrage that existed within the black press notwithstanding, it seemed as if most observers were happy to see the company destroyed. For it to have survived as long as it had, in the face of tremendous opposition, was noteworthy. Its destruction also indicated how strongly Ali's association with the Louisville Sponsoring Group influenced public perception of him. When Main Bout's existence indicated that his partnership with the LSG had dissolved, hostility toward the champion reached new levels.

It is difficult to gauge Main Bout's historical or cultural significance because it was short-lived and because its inner workings are largely unknown. Although Jim Brown certainly wanted the organization to become a vehicle for widespread black economic empowerment, there is no evidence that its other members felt the same way. Furthermore, it is almost impossible to discover if Main Bout's profits went anywhere besides the pockets of its officers. There is no proof linking it to any larger economic projects, and even had the corporation survived, it is unknown whether it would have been capable of making money and creating jobs for substantial numbers of African Americans. Nevertheless, it seems plausible to construe Main Bout's temporary success in the face of tremendous opposition as a symbolic victory for Ali and the NOI, if not for the black freedom struggle at large. Like the champion who founded the organization, it had faced challenges without compromising its principles. Although the company's ultimate defeat and Ali's ensuing conviction for draft evasion signaled a deep erosion of the champion's moral authority among large segments of American society, his plucky group of resolute defenders ensured that it never would be completely lost. Even though he had been barred from the ring, Ali never stopped asserting himself as a public figure. Over the next few years, he would begin to see himself as a kind of race leader, with his story being representative of the era's great issues. As his exile from boxing dragged on, more and more people began to follow his cue and frame him similarly, and Ali would begin to recapture the moral authority he had lost.

Carving Out Moral Authority

Ali's Race Man Phase

t is difficult to assess someone as a "race man," defined here as a person whose standing up for African Americans gains widespread recognition and legitimacy within black communities. Most observers would agree that Martin Luther King Jr. was one, but it is harder to analyze Muhammad Ali's status as such since he was primarily a boxer who never formally led any social movement. Nevertheless, I will try to make the case that in the period between his November 1965 victory over Floyd Patterson and his June 1967 conviction for draft evasion, Muhammad Ali began to see himself as a race man, and both rank-and-file Americans and people formally associated with the civil rights movement began to accept his self-definition. While it is impossible to gauge how widespread this acceptance was, I argue that it was significant enough, as it became quite clear to everyone that Ali was willing to forfeit his championship in defense of his principles, to develop newfound respect and moral authority among black people who once were skeptical of him.

Even though Ali made negative remarks about the civil rights movement and its leaders, especially as he first went public with his membership in the NOI, many key movement figures did not reciprocate. Ali was widely admired within the movement, mainly among its more progressive elements such as the Student Nonviolent Coordinating Committee (SNCC). While there was opposition to Ali, particularly before his draft resistance came to define him, the feeling that he was singled out by the government because of his outspoken militancy galvanized opinion among disparate elements in the black freedom struggle. Gradually, criticism of Ali by civil rights leaders lessened. Arthur Ashe, the tennis player turned sports historian, characterized the general feeling toward Ali by stating, "I can tell you that Ali was very definitely, sometimes unspokenly, admired by a lot of the leaders of the civil rights movement, who were sometimes even a little bit jealous of the following he had and the efficacy of what he did. There were a lot of people in the movement who wished that they held that sort of sway over African-Americans, but did not."[49]

The ambivalent relationship between Ali and the civil rights movement was evidenced by his statements about the movement and how some of its leading figures responded to him. Shortly before he won the championship, he said, "I like the Muslims. I'm not going to get killed trying to force myself on people who don't want me. I like my life. Integration is wrong. The white people don't want integration. I don't believe in forcing it, and the Muslims don't believe in it. So what's wrong with the Muslims?" The feeling among many integrationists was that Ali's loyalty was misplaced and that he was foolish to embrace the NOI's racial tenets. National Association for the Advancement of Colored People (NAACP) Executive Director Roy Wilkins said, "Cassius Clay may as well be an honorary member of the white citizen councils." Floyd Patterson, a supporter of the civil rights movement whose first bout with Ali degenerated into an ideological war of words, agreed: "I have every right to call the Black Muslims a menace to the Negro race. I do not believe that God put us here to hate one another. Cassius Clay is disgracing himself and the Negro race." SNCC's Julian Bond added: "I remember when Ali joined the Nation. The action of joining was not something many of us particularly liked."[50]

Because of his association with the NOI, few people within the civil rights movement respected Ali from the very beginning, although some were ahead of the curve. Wilkins and other key movement figures had abhorred Sonny Liston, but there was no sense of relief when the Louisville Lip dethroned him as heavyweight champion. Martin Luther King Jr. was the only civil rights leader who acknowledged Ali when he won the title, sending a congratulatory telegram. Even among skeptics, though, there were seeds of admiration that would eventually sprout into full-blown respect. While he found the NOI abhorrent, Julian Bond admitted, "But the notion that he would do it, that he'd jump out there, join this group that was so despised by mainstream America and be proud of it, sent a little thrill through you. . . . He was able to tell white folks for us to go to hell; that I'm going to do it my way." Mississippi organizer Lawrence Guyot shared this feeling: "We were down there in these small, hot, dusty towns, in an atmosphere thick with fear, trying to organize folk whose grandparents were slaves. A town where you had the Klan on one side, the local sheriff's department on the other, and more than a little intermingling between the two. And here was this beautifully arrogant young man who made us proud to be us and proud to fight for our rights."[51]

Central to doubts about Ali was the perception that his political agenda was inseparable from his belonging to the NOI. It was impossible for Ali's adversaries within the movement to credit someone who they felt represented an organization that was ideologically reprehensible and a danger to the very cause they had dedicated their lives to. However, as he began to be perceived as much as an anti-war symbol as a racial one, more and more people began to see Ali as a free thinker. The increased feeling that Ali was not necessarily a tool of the NOI was critical to his gaining respect from those who had previously disregarded him. As they separated Ali from the organization they so despised, his moral authority rose. Once Ali's draft case escalated, and he proved himself to be as much a man of action as one of rhetoric, those involved in the civil rights movement began to understand him as their peer, as someone who was willing to put his personal safety and livelihood on the line for a just cause. They then became his supporters, and their praise for him overwhelmed any initial misgivings they had about his membership in the NOI. Many of the civil rights movement's most esteemed figures have made it clear that they were admirers of Muhammad Ali.

John Lewis, SNCC's chairman during much of Ali's initial championship run and an integrationist protégé of Martin Luther King Jr. who went on to become a member of the U.S. House of Representatives, exemplifies how Ali helped galvanize disparate elements within the movement: "As chair of SNCC, I never considered working with Elijah Muhammad and the Black Muslims," said Lewis. "I never saw them as part of the movement. It would have been almost impossible, I think, to bring that group and the following of Muhammad under this umbrella." As Ali's draft resistance came into focus, however, Lewis began to separate him from the organization he so distrusted. "During the sixties, I grew to admire Muhammad Ali," he explained. Ali was "an exciting sports figure, but he also became a political activist to a certain degree by responding to what was happening around him." Lewis believes that this regard for Ali became widespread among black freedom fighters and anti-war activists. "I think many of the young people who came along and refused to be drafted, refused to take their stint, were deeply inspired by Muhammad Ali," he said. "Even me in the peace movement and many people in the civil rights movement looked to him as a symbol." Asked if Ali's NOI membership compromised his feelings about the boxer, Lewis responded, "No, not at all. I think Muhammad Ali was much bigger than his relationship with the Nation of Islam." In a short time, Ali had become a symbolic linchpin around which black freedom fighters of all ideological casts, even the staunchest of integrationists, could coalesce.[52]

SNCC's Julian Bond, who later became chair of the NAACP, shared Lewis's distaste for the Nation of Islam and his admiration for Ali. "We weren't big fans of the Nation," he said. "You know the Nation then was absolutely opposed to the nonviolent movement, and we were the Student Nonviolent Coordinating Committee. They were opposed to the notion of racial integration and we were an integrated organization. So while we saw [individual] Muslims on the streets in Atlanta where our headquarters was and had friendly relationships with them, we didn't have much affection for the organization." Being a longtime boxing fan, however, Bond had always been interested in the young fighter, and that interest reached new heights once Ali proved himself dedicated to the anti-war cause: "I followed him and admired him a great deal as a fighter and then when he became a political persona, I admired him all the more, because of all the people who spoke out against the war, he had the most at risk." Bond also asserts that he was hardly alone. "When Ali refused to take that symbolic step forward everyone knew about it moments later. You could hear people talking about it on street corners," he said. "It was on everyone's lips. People who had never thought about the war—black and white—began to think it through because of Ali. The ripples were enormous." Bond's feelings toward Ali's stand are even more impressive considering his antipathy toward the NOI and dedication to integration. They illustrate that when people began to consider the fighter separately from the organization, his moral authority blossomed.[53]

Bond had good reason to understand Ali as a race man, since the fighter's tribulations as a draft resister had paralleled Bond's experiences as an anti-war protester. When Bond won a seat in the Georgia House of Representatives, its members refused to seat him as they objected to his endorsement of SNCC's anti-war manifesto. Bond gained his seat in the assembly after two special elections and a U.S. Supreme Court order. Certainly, Bond could relate to Ali's unjust stripping of the heavyweight championship. A hero to the anti-war movement in his own right, Bond invoked Ali's story during speaking engagements and press conferences, even claiming that Ali deserved the Nobel Peace Prize. "A man like Muhammad, much more so than the others, has made a sacrifice most of us could not make if we wanted to, but Muhammad Ali is a man who has the respect and adulation of millions of peoples the world over and has an economic potential to which most people never come close. But he has sacrificed this voluntarily by following his conscience and his religious beliefs. He should have international recognition as a devoted man in the pursuit of peace," he told the National Conference of Negro Elected Officials.[54]

Martin Luther King Jr. also took seriously Ali's draft resistance. The two had been introduced by Chauncey Eskridge, who worked for both as an attorney. While in Miami at the champion's training camp in September 1964, Eskridge called King to discuss some business and then handed the phone to Ali. They had a brief conversation that was taped as part of the FBI's surveillance of King, and Ali told the civil rights paragon that he was his brother, invited him to his next title fight, and said that he was with him 100 percent. Elijah Muhammad repeatedly rejected King's attempts to reach out to the NOI and denounced him as a "deceiver [who] doesn't understand the Negroes' problem," but King nonetheless remained interested in Ali. He felt that Ali's refusal to be drafted would encourage thousands of other conscientious objectors to take prison over military service. He singled out the champion for praise in one sermon, impressed that, "He is giving up even fame. He is giving up millions of dollars in order to stand up for what his conscience tells him is right. No matter what you think of Muhammad Ali's religion, you have to admire his courage." King and Ali met for the only time in March 1967, a week before King's initial public refutation of the war and approximately a month prior to Ali's refusal to be inducted. King was in Louisville for a board meeting of his organization, the Southern Christian Leadership Conference (SCLC), which had chosen to gather there in support of a local open-housing campaign. They had a private meeting at King's hotel and held a joint press conference, with King praising the champion and telling reporters, "As Muhammad Ali has said, we are all—black and brown and poor—victims of the same system of oppression." Such praise from the era's leading civil rights spokesman further legitimized Ali as a race man. It was also remarkable because King had not always felt so positively about Ali. Although he had congratulated Ali privately on his victory over Liston, he was publicly critical of the new champion, telling the press, "When Cassius Clay joined the Black Muslims and started calling himself Cassius X, he became a champion of racial segregation and that is what we are fighting against." Three years had passed since then, however, and King seemed to have reconciled his ambivalence toward the young heavyweight, especially because his own decision to stand publicly against the war had been inspired by Ali's determined draft resistance. Charles Morgan Jr., a lawyer and SCLC board member, explained, "Martin had opposed the war for a long time but his hands were tied by our Board. Then Ali spoke out publicly, he took the consequences, and I believe it had an influence on Martin. Here was somebody who had a lot to lose and was willing to risk it all to say what he believed." Ali, perhaps bolstered by his visit with King, expanded his repertoire and shrugged off the NOI's prohibition against participating in civil rights protests when he toured Louisville's black neighborhoods afterward and addressed demonstrators. "In your struggle for freedom, justice, and equality, I am with you," he told one gathering. "I came to Louisville because I could not remain silent in Chicago while my own people—many of whom I grew up with, went to school with, and some of whom are my blood relatives—were being beaten, stomped and kicked in the streets simply because they want freedom, justice, and equality in housing."[55]

Later that day, as reporters followed him during his tour of black Louisville, Ali made his strongest anti-war statement to date. Ali critics are misguided when they question whether Ali wrote the statement, or whether he fully understood its implications. All that matters is that Ali chose to represent such views publicly. With his scheduled induction date still a month away, he said:

> Why should they ask me to put on a uniform and go ten thousand miles from home and drop bombs and bullets on brown people in Vietnam while so-called Negro people in Louisville are treated like dogs and denied simple human rights? No, I am not going ten thousand miles from home to help murder and burn another poor nation simply to continue the domination of white slave masters of the darker people the world over. This is the day when such evils must come to an end. I have been warned that to take such a stand would put my prestige in jeopardy and could cause me to lose millions of dollars which should accrue to me as the champion. But I have said it once and I will say it again. The real enemy of my people is right here. I will not disgrace my religion, my people or myself by becoming a tool to enslave those who are fighting for their own justice, freedom and equality. . . . If I thought the war was going to bring freedom and equality to twenty-two million of my people, they wouldn't have to draft me. I'd join tomorrow. But I either have to obey the laws of the land or the laws of Allah. I have nothing to lose by standing up for my beliefs. So I'll go to jail. We've been in jail for four hundred years.[56]

Members of the black press and community were beginning to take Ali seriously as a race man, even comparing his struggle to Dr. King's. The *St. Louis Argus* linked the two in an editorial claiming, "both national figures are together on the main basic point involving the civil rights issue—they believe that priority for the American Negro is the problem of 'survival in this country.' They employ different means to approach the ends. But they both are aimed at the same high domestic goal." Al Raby, a longtime key figure on the Chicago civil rights scene and one of the coordinators of King's efforts there the previous year, also likened Ali to King. "The whole hysteria around the concept of black power, the thrust of violence across America . . . the convictions of Muhammad Ali and Dr. King, are all indicative of an anti-Negro reaction in America," he said. Even Ali's critics were taking these developments seriously. Jackie Robinson, the baseball pioneer turned syndicated columnist, challenged King for praising the champion. "What values do you have in mind when you praise him [Ali] and say he has given up so much?" he asked. "I think all he has given up is his citizenship. I think his advisors have given him a bum steer." Unlike King, Robinson challenged Ali's position and refused to separate Ali from the Nation of Islam or accept that Ali really understood the implications of his anti-war stand. Months after Ali's conviction, Robinson still took the position that the champion didn't really know what was going on. "The tragedy is that an extremely talented young man has apparently allowed himself to be used," he commented. Because he saw Ali as a passive victim instead of an active participant in a freedom struggle, Robinson could not perceive Ali as a race man, much less a leader. His position, however, was becoming marginalized in the black community as increasing numbers of people took Ali's stance seriously.[57]

King wasn't the only SCLC leader to accept Ali as an important movement force. On that same trip to Louisville, Ali addressed the congregation at Antioch Baptist Church alongside SCLC co-founder Ralph Abernathy. SCLC's James Bevel, a longtime civil rights worker, told an audience at the University of Chicago, "I think Muhammad Ali is one of the great Americans. He has done [much] to bring light and hope to America. Few people have the courage and integrity to live by their own convictions." Positioning Ali as a galvanizing influence that would bring together disparate blocs of people of color in the United States, he predicted, "We will not stand by and watch Muhammad Ali lynched by the racists of this country. We are not going to stand by, as non-white people, while America lynches him."[58]

One of the most interesting things about Ali's standing within the black community during this period was the conscious effort by race leaders and the press to frame him as a unifying force rather than as someone whose ideas about black nationalism and integration were indicative of a larger rift within the civil rights movement. While in Louisville, Ali sparked controversy when he criticized the idea of open housing because he felt that it only meant blacks moving into white areas. When this threatened to deflate local protesters who had come to admire Ali, the *Louisville Defender* stepped in to "clear up some misconceptions over his remarks two weeks ago concerning the 'open housing' controversy." It printed an explanation of Ali's comments, in which the champion rescinded his initial misgivings about the campaign and told the hometown audience, "First, let me make it emphatically clear that I strongly support my people in their courageous struggle to secure some

measure of freedom, justice and equality by whatever means they find necessary." The newspaper also quoted the champion, "If by open occupancy, it is
meant the simple right of black people to live and occupy decent homes in
any area of Louisville or any other city . . . then I join with them in fighting
for that right." People took Ali's comments on open housing and the Vietnam
War seriously, and his opinions were becoming significant to growing numbers of people. His views no longer belonged only to himself, and community
forces were careful to present them in ways that would serve the larger civil
rights struggle rather than impede it.[59]

Open housing wasn't the only contemporary issue on which people sought
Ali's views, and the black community wasn't the sole group seeking his opinion. That summer in Chicago, Ali discussed the riots that gripped the nation's
cities. Careful not to offend those who sympathized with the rioters, he nonetheless told the audience, "I've got to tell you that it makes no sense at all for
black people to think that they can win a guerilla war in this country. This is
just what some white people want us to do. . . . They know we're not set up
for this kind of thing. . . . They've got everything in their favor when it comes
to fighting with guns . . . and we black people will be the ones to suffer the
most death and injuries . . . it'll be our homes that are destroyed." People
were interested in what Ali had to say, and he certainly influenced some of
the people who heard him speak. During his exile from boxing, he began to
reach larger audiences by appearing on political talk shows such as William
Buckley's televised *Firing Line*.[60]

Prominent integrationists like Lewis and King supported Ali, but he was
also strongly admired by black nationalists. One of Ali's biggest advocates
was Congress of Racial Equality (CORE) National Director Floyd McKissick. Like his peers within the movement, McKissick was impressed that Ali
would sacrifice so much for a cause, and he felt that Ali's "decision was made
with full knowledge of its implications." McKissick also believed that Ali's
case was indicative of the work that still needed to be done by freedom fighters. "Your dilemma dramatizes to me, as a Civil Rights leader," he wrote in an
open letter to the deposed champion, "that the Civil Rights movement has, in
fact, accomplished pathetically little." Ali accepted McKissick's invitation to
speak at CORE's annual convention in 1967, an important gathering that
brought together representatives from CORE, SNCC, and the Black Panther
Party. There Ali told the audience, "We can never have peace without freedom, justice and equality. And trying to get those things automatically brings
dissatisfaction . . . and fights." McKissick labeled him, "one of the greatest
living Americans because he is one of the few people who lives by his convictions," before presenting the champion an award on behalf of the organization, "for being the greatest heavyweight champion of all time and bringing

honor, glory and truth to millions by his willingness not to fight against other non-white people in the immoral and unjust war in Vietnam." At the convention, CORE drafted several official resolutions referring to Ali, and later that year its Chicago chapter declared that the organization would "advocate, promote and demand that each of the official and public bodies charged with the protection of Muhammad Ali's rights, privileges and immunities immediately recognize and grant to him the enjoyment and free exercise of those rights."[61]

Stokely Carmichael and H. Rap Brown, both successors of John Lewis as SNCC's chair after the organization moved toward black nationalism by the middle of the 1960s, also admired Ali's courage. Carmichael referred to him as "my hero" and stated, "No one risked or suffered like Muhammad Ali. I didn't risk anything. I just told people not to go." Carmichael's admiration dated back several years to 1965, when he had spearheaded a campaign to form a black political party in Alabama and SNCC volunteers had made bumper stickers reading "We're the Greatest" in reference to Ali's famous catchphrase. Under Brown's leadership, SNCC sent a formidable delegation, including Executive Secretary James Forman, to Houston for Ali's draft evasion trial because the organization wanted "to make sure justice is done." Brown also threatened that "black people everywhere will retaliate" if Ali were convicted, and he saw his trial as "a warning of what the American government intends to do to any of us who dare stand up." Declaring "Muhammad Ali one of the greatest symbols of our militant black youth and manhood," he promised that "SNCC stands ready to lend any assistance which our champ may deem necessary."[62]

Across ideological lines, it seemed as if a sizable majority of blacks within the United States, and their allies worldwide, were disturbed by the way Ali was being treated. Even those who found his black nationalism repugnant and refused to refer to him by his Muslim name, like Floyd Patterson, claimed that what was happening to Ali was wrong. "What bothers me is Clay is being made to pay too stiff a penalty for doing what is right. The prizefighter in America is not supposed to shoot off his mouth about politics, particularly if his views oppose the government's and might influence many among the working class that follows boxing," Patterson asserted. Such support for Ali extended beyond the national borders. In Guyana, there were pickets outside the U.S. embassy. In Pakistan, a demonstrator fasted outside the U.S. consulate. There were protests in Egypt. A newspaper in Ghana criticized the federal government. The first major anti-war demonstration in Britain featured leaflets reading, "LBJ Don't Send Muhammad Ali to War." Exiled black nationalist Robert F. Williams said in a statement from China, "What racist

America is doing to Ali, she is doing to all non-white humanity in the world."
Ali's power as a galvanizing force was remarkable.[63]

Ali's ability to bring together disparate elements within the black community was demonstrated by the palpable fear among civil rights leaders and politicians that Martin Luther King's stand against the Vietnam War would threaten to expose fault lines likely to endanger the freedom struggle altogether. Several prominent figures, including Roy Wilkins, Whitney Young of the Urban League, and Edward Brooke, the Massachusetts Republican who in 1966 became the first African American U.S. senator since Reconstruction, all argued that King's tying the stagnation of the movement to the escalation in Vietnam was irresponsible. The NAACP passed a resolution that declared, "To attempt to merge the civil rights movement with the peace movement and to assume that one is dependent upon the other is, in our judgment, a serious tactical mistake." Black newspapers shared this fear; the *Chicago Defender* asserted that King's move would endanger "the unity that once prevailed and gave effectiveness to the struggle for equality." Although one might argue that because similar trepidations were not attached to Ali's anti-war stance people did not take him seriously as a race leader, another argument might be that Ali was simply more effective than King in bringing people together. As far-fetched as that may seem to the unconvinced, Ali reached black nationalists that King did not, making him more credible to certain elements of the African American community than was King.[64]

Another way Ali's case unified disparate movement forces was through its shedding light on discriminatory laws connected with the draft. When Ali filed suit against his home state because the local board that had drafted him had virtually no black members, the *Pittsburgh Courier* noted in an editorial that the choice to do so "is scarcely different from that raised by civil rights activists in their demonstrations against unjust laws upholding racial segregation." Although Ali's claim was denied, it led to nationwide reform. Kentucky's government introduced legislation mandating the integration of state draft boards. South Carolina did the same. President Lyndon Johnson's Commission on the Draft recommended the abolition of imbalanced local draft boards; Stokely Carmichael and the NAACP, two forces on opposite sides of the nationalist/ integrationist divide, expressed their approval. Even when they clashed ideologically about the nature of Ali's draft resistance, movement figures found common ground on some of the issues embedded within his case.[65]

A pattern emerged in which the federal government reclassified a series of civil rights leaders as eligible for the draft and it became easier to see Ali, who twice previously had been declared ineligible, as their peer. SNCC's Bob Moses believes that his being drafted at age thirty-one was a direct response to his activism, particularly his appearances at anti-war rallies. He responded by fleeing the country for over a decade. Cleveland Sellers, another SNCC worker, was jailed when he refused military service, and he asserted that the draft was being used to silence dissent. Referring to SNCC, he claimed, "Seemingly there is a conspiracy on the part of the government to induct the whole organization." John Lewis was also reclassified as draft-eligible, and Julian Bond said that "[T]he president of the draft board was quoted in *Newsweek* as saying, that nigger Julian Bond, we sure let him slip through our fingers." By the time of Ali's trial, seventeen SNCC members were under indictment for refusing induction. Other sanctions against Ali paralleled similar actions taken by the federal government against leading civil rights figures. Ali's passport, like Stokely Carmichael's, was revoked. Ali was also placed on the U.S. House of Representatives List of Radical and Revolutionary Speakers. Claude Pepper, the Florida Democrat, said on the House floor, "If any one individual contributed to the contagious disrespect for law and love of country, then it would have to be our deposed fighting king." The FBI conducted surveillance and kept a file on Ali. The day after he had revealed his affiliation with the Nation of Islam, FBI Director J. Edgar Hoover had ordered his agents to inquire about Ali's draft status and obtained Ali's high school records in order to prove that the fighter was competent to serve in the military. That same day, the head of Ali's local draft board told reporters that the champion would be drafted within three weeks. It was not just rank-and-file citizens, the press, and important civil rights figures who were treating Ali like a race leader, but the federal government as well.[66]

There is evidence that the government's pursuit of Ali's case was related to his outspoken black nationalism and the feeling that he was a dissenter who might foment change and unrest. Ali's conscientious objector claim was rejected even though the judge presiding over his hearing recommended to the Department of Justice that Ali be legitimated as one because his opposition to the war was on religious grounds. Although such recommendations were rarely overruled, the federal government ignored this one, claiming that Ali's primary objections to the war were political. The perception that Ali was an activist, or a potential one, undoubtedly influenced the ruling. When after his conviction Ali sought permission to travel abroad to fight, federal courts again used his political involvement to rationalize their denial of his request. Although it was standard to strip felons of their passports, and the possibility existed that Ali would flee to a country that had no extradition agreement with the United States, it was also fair to say that he showed absolutely no indication of being a flight risk. He also had reason to believe that he would be able to find work overseas. Almost immediately after he was found guilty of draft evasion, the European Boxing Union announced, "In our view the case is still pending because Clay has appealed his conviction. Our feeling is that any decision should be postponed until his appeal is acted on." The Japanese Boxing Association also indicated that it would sponsor an Ali bout, as did Mexico's World Boxing Council. The federal government was not required to invalidate Ali's passport. But at a hearing to determine whether the ruling would be upheld, federal judge Joe Ingraham cited Ali's appearance at a Los Angeles anti-war rally to deny his reclassification request, claiming, "The defendant appears ready to take part in anti-government, anti-war activities. . . . I am concerned about his attending these rallies." Such treatment of Ali suggests that his reclassification was motivated not simply because his score on the Armed Forces Qualification Test became a passing one when the government rescaled its criteria for military eligibility.[67]

Floyd Patterson's allusion to Ali's appeal among the working class was no illusion. Unlike some civil rights leaders who appeared to be out of touch with the lives of rank-and-file blacks, Ali always had street credibility. He walked in what were perceived to be some of the country's most dangerous neighborhoods and always emerged unscathed. "You don't need protection from people who love you," he once said. In addition to his work in NOI temples nationwide, where he came into frequent contact with rough customers from the nation's black underclass, Ali intervened in a Chicago gang war, attempting to broker a peace by bringing together leaders of rival factions, including the notorious Blackstone Rangers. Shortly after his draft evasion conviction, Ali was selected as the grand marshal of the Watts Summer Festival, which drew over 80,000 participants. Responding to rumors that interracial violence was going to erupt in the Old Town section of Chicago, the exiled champion left his nearby residence, appeared on the street to create a diversion, and urged residents to "keep it cool tonight," which they did. Ali's celebrity, boxing ability, comfort among common folk, militancy, and affiliation with the Nation of Islam all contributed to his having widespread credibility among ghetto populations that was unrivaled by contemporary race leaders other than the late Malcolm X, Elijah Muhammad, and members of the Black Panther Party.[68]

Ali also held great sway among college students of all races. During his exile from boxing, dozens of universities invited him to speak on campus. At the University of Chicago, he denounced the war and distinguished between fighting in the ring and on the battlefields of Vietnam. "In the ring we have a referee and a doctor seeing to it that nobody gets hurt," he said. "In Vietnam, the intent is to kill, kill, kill, kill, kill, and kill some more." One thousand students gathered to hear him speak at Howard University, where he urged them to embrace black nationalism. Marion Jackson of the *Atlanta Daily World* commented, "Clay can be more effective than Stokely Carmichael in firing up a crowd. He is as motivated a pulpiteer as Dr. Martin Luther King, Jr." Ali's speech at Prairie View A&M, near Houston, drew 6,000 people. Following riots at nearby Texas Southern University, in which several people were killed and a number of buildings were burned down, Ali appeared at the school to cool down students and request that they not protest during his upcoming induction ceremony in downtown Houston. Ali's influence, especially among young people, transcended race and class lines. In a sense, he was becoming the voice of a generation.[69]

Ali's actions at Texas Southern and his speech at Prairie View A&M were reflections of his special relationship with the city of Houston, which became his adopted hometown while he sorted out his draft problems. He lived and fought there and cultivated ties with local residents. Following his bout with Cleveland Williams, the city even renamed Thomas Jefferson Street as Muhammad Ali Street, although the day after he refused induction the original name was restored. Ali took a special interest in an area orphanage, the Harris County Boys School, frequently visiting with the children there and serving as an honorary referee for one of its football games. Training for the Williams fight, he charged spectators to watch his workouts and made fans pay for his autograph, donating nearly $1,500 to the boys' home. Ali did similar work across the border, visiting a Monterrey orphanage run by Catholic priest Carlos Alvarez. The grateful Alvarez said about Ali's appearance, "It was so gracious of him . . . to fly down to Monterrey. The impact of his gesture, the inspiration he gave to these lads, cannot even be imagined." Nurturing his appeal to Houston's youth, Ali visited Booker T. Washington High School and stressed to students the importance of education. "I have a million dollars, but I can't spell. . . . Take your opportunity in high school," he said. He took the same message to the local Nation of Islam mosque, where he had replaced the regular minister, who was on a leave of absence. "The Negro will never be recognized, never be able to socialize without an education. To do it he needs money. . . . Because of our tax setup I can give 30 percent of my fight [revenues] toward educating the 22 million Negroes." Ali repeated himself at a historically black university. "You should never cease to learn. You should take every opportunity to advance an education," he said. Ali also entered more traditional leadership venues, speaking to the Houston Bar Association and attending a Republican Party fund-raiser alongside former president Dwight Eisenhower.[70]

Ali financially supported black education. In early 1967, the United Negro College Fund (UNCF) announced that the champion had become the largest single black contributor to the organization by way of a $10,000 donation. Said Ali, "Although I myself never had the opportunity to go to college, I give to the United Negro College Fund this $10,000 out of my love, admiration, and respect for their 34,000 dedicated students to help in some small way so that the seeds of immortality hidden within each one of them may be nourished and developed to their fullest capacity. To me, they are all 'The Greatest.'" When asked why he had been fighting so frequently during this period, Ali told reporters that he wanted more money to fund black education and had a goal of giving $100,000 to the UNCF. During this period, Ali also donated $150,000 to the Nation of Islam. "I'm a race man," he said. "It means more to me than personal gain or showing my teeth. If I end up with a quarter in my pocket I can look at myself and say I helped thousands of people."[71]

Ali also tried to use Main Bout to generate income for black colleges and the UNCF. Following his bouts in Europe, Ali made a standing offer to pay the expenses for black colleges that wanted to show closed-circuit telecasts of his fights. Six schools had accepted Ali's giveaway, at an estimated cost to Main Bout of $4,500 per closed-circuit installation, to screen his November 1966 title defense against Cleveland Williams. Ali pledged to donate a large portion of the receipts from that bout to black colleges and veterans' hospitals. He also coordinated a plan in which universities would participate in the closed-circuit telecast of his title defense against Ernie Terrell and donate the resulting revenues to the UNCF, but technological and logistical limitations prevented it from happening.[72]

Ali proposed fighting in exhibitions to help black charities but was blocked by politicians. Just days before the champion's draft evasion conviction, Michigan State Athletic Commissioner Chuck Davey announced that his state would host such a bout. Ali promised not to defend his championship, accept any money, or donate any of the revenues to the Nation of Islam. Said Davey, "He hasn't had his day in court yet, so I don't think I can pass judgment before he's had his day in court." The match, however, never materialized. Speaking at CORE's annual convention, Ali offered to help southern blacks by staging a benefit bout with the boxer who emerged victorious in the tournament designed to replace him as heavyweight champion. "Here before all the newsmen and television cameras," he said, "I challenge the winner of that tournament and promise to give every penny to feed people in Mississippi and throughout the South." He estimated that the event would raise over $1 million but was denied authorization by the California State Athletic Commission. Commissioner Jules Berman told reporters, "We all have religion, but my country comes first." Sam Lacy of the *Baltimore Afro-American* called the decision "just about as scurvy as anything the high-handed American political machine has done to its own needy."[73]

The promotional buildups to Ali's fights took on political significance as well. Ali bouts during this period sometimes had substantial ideological overtones, especially when he was challenged by opponents who disputed his claims to be a race man. It happened in November 1965 when he battled Floyd Patterson, and four months later, when his bout with Ernie Terrell was barred from Chicago, the challenger called him irresponsible: "[H]is comments about the draft were ridiculous. He made it sound like the Army was picking on him and that's not true." Refusing to call the champion by his new name, Terrell told reporters, "I really feel sorry for Clay. . . . It is wrong and harmful to promote religion or politics with your championship." By the end of the year, with his rescheduled bout against the champion looming, Terrell stepped up his attack, actually comparing Ali to Adolf Hitler and the devil, while the champion retaliated by calling Terrell an Uncle Tom. Not all of Ali's opponents, however, took the bait. In his next contest, against Zora Folley, both fighters refused to turn the promotion ugly. At a press conference, reporters asked Folley what he would call his opponent. When the challenger replied, "Muhammad Ali," the champion responded, "Thank you brother," and told the gathering, "He is a quiet dignified man. I respect him for respecting me." What impressed Ali most was that Folley resisted the temptation to seize upon a role that could make him into an American hero. "I know what they're telling Folley," he said. "That he has to beat that Black Muslim and he'll be invited to the White House to meet the President the next day. That's what makes the fight important politically."[74]

The Folley bout would be Ali's last for three-and-a-half years, but Ali's development beyond the ring would continue long after his conviction for draft evasion. He was somewhat apprehensive about his newfound political significance, once telling Robert Lipsyte, "I'm taking no credit as a leader. They're not going to make no Malcolm X out of me. If they make you a leader, they can catch you up," but it was also clear that he was headed in that direction. He did not depart from the public eye following his exile from boxing, and in many ways he became a larger figure during his three years outside the sport than he was while heavyweight champion of the world. During that period, Ali's symbolic importance would shift. As he became more involved with the anti-war movement and his relationship with the Nation of Islam faltered, his appeal to whites became as strong as his identification as a race man. In fact, these two things, his fading ties to the Nation of Islam and his increasing importance among whites who had been marginalized by the civil rights movement's turn toward black nationalism, would become the building blocks upon which his iconic status as an American superhero near the end of the twentieth century would rest. He generated unprecedented moral authority and earning power not as a racial symbol, but as one of integration and tolerance.[75]

III

Good People

Forty Years of Ali

The Making of an Icon

American public perception of Muhammad Ali has undergone a dramatic shift since his conviction for draft evasion. Although Ali was once a controversial figure, his image has stabilized over the last forty years. Hated by many during the late 1960s, Ali has come full circle in the new millennium, admired almost universally, excepting a handful of dissenters. Ali's makeover from a largely disliked figure into one now understood in more positive terms is nothing new. People who could be viewed as Ali's cultural peers, like former Nation of Islam (NOI) spokesman Malcolm X and Jack Johnson, the first African American world heavyweight champion, have been similarly reconstructed as misunderstood trailblazers who were ahead of the times. While interesting, America's forgiving of Ali is hardly unique.[1]

One factor that makes Ali's transformation worth studying is its intensity. Public sentiment toward Ali has skyrocketed past forgiveness into veneration. A vague collective understanding that previous generations were wrong about him has gushed forth into a full-blown movement to canonize him as a standard-bearer of American values and the embodiment of the best things this country has to offer. It is this sanctification that makes the rehabilitation of Ali's image unprecedented, going way beyond anything that has happened to Jack Johnson, Malcolm X, or any other once-controversial figure. The mainstream that once rejected Ali now embraces him. In American cultural history, there are simply no parallels to what has happened.

Thus, this final section of *Muhammad Ali: The Making of an Icon* is dedicated to making sense of this strange process, figuring out why this transformation has happened and what has sustained it, and speculating about its future. While understanding the evolution of Ali's image is important in itself, the more significant task is to use it as a window to view how American society works. Although the details of his life must be assessed in order to get to its larger significance, the big picture is not really about Ali, but rather about how economic concerns, race matters, and historiography come together to create symbols and folklore that influence the ways people perceive themselves and the world. The relationships between the commercial and cultural aspects of Muhammad Ali's life and career reflect the societies in which they have existed.

Although it encompasses a much broader period than previous parts have, this section maintains an analytical focus on the relationships between moral authority and financial interests. At the heart of the investigation are the questions of how and why Ali's moral authority, once largely shaped by the external forces with which he was associated, like the Louisville Sponsoring Group and the NOI, now rests primarily on Ali himself, despite the irony that he is less able to shape his own meaning than ever before because the tools that he once used to do so, boxing and speaking, are no longer available. Doubly ironic is that this change in public perception has occurred as the desires of those who stand to profit from his image have superseded Ali's in the public transmission of what he purports to represent. Ali has less control than ever before over his meaning, yet more than ever before people recognize him, and he is represented, as being its sole author and owner. It is the assessment of this paradox that ultimately drives my study of Ali's life and career during the past half century or so.

The Legacy of Ali's Exile
and the Nation of Islam

Muhammad Ali's moral authority, central to his appeal as an American hero, if not his gravity as a world-historical figure, draws a great deal of its strength from his three-and-a-half-year exile from boxing. His other outstanding attributes and accomplishments notwithstanding, it is the perception that Ali sacrificed his personal interests in the name of principle that has driven his cultural upgrade from legendary athlete to iconic model citizen and philosopher-guru. The exile has become the narrative linchpin of the Ali Story, transforming it from biography to allegory, defining its protagonist as heroic, and giving him an undeniable redemption point that marks him as a credible moral authority.

Because its meaning and consequences have changed with the times, Ali's exile from boxing, as a cultural text used to symbolize heroism, is hard to define precisely. Some forty years ago, the exile literally meant an impending jail sentence and the end of Ali's boxing career, but after a long, hard fight those threats vanished; Ali avoided prison and eventually regained his title. Today, the exile represents a much wider range of possibilities. In the commercial world, for example, it stands in as a reference point for various philosophies, character traits, and ideas, from courage to tolerance to intelligence. This versatility is critical to Ali's status as an attractive corporate pitchman, because his story can be used in myriad ways to engender feelings and moods that presumably help sell commodities.

Over time, the meaning of the exile expands and becomes ever more useful and accessible to a growing spectrum of interests. Ali's resistance to a war that according to the majority of Americans turned out to be unjust and fool-hardy resulted in the loss of peak ring years. The pain and the suffering Ali experienced are still at the core of his appeal as a heroic figure, but the terms of this appeal and the perception of what his exile means have changed as a result of new revelations. For example, any current use of Ali as a corporate spokesman must take into account his battle with Parkinson's syndrome. Ali's courageous coping with the condition is admirable in itself. But when coupled with the injustice of the exile, and juxtaposed with images of Ali in his prime—dancing, talking, radiating good looks and charisma—it becomes downright gallant.

These connections between the past and the present are easy to make, especially in the hands of professional advertisers. But even laypersons can do so. Ask anyone familiar with his story whether Muhammad Ali fought for too long and he or she will answer affirmatively. Although this overindul-gence had as much to do with his being a spotlight-addicted glory hog as anything else, it was also tied to his economic insecurity during the 1970s and 1980s. Ali fought on when he shouldn't have because he needed income, and these late-career bouts seem to have had a dramatically negative impact on his health. Whatever the reasons for Ali's financial problems were, they can be easily connected to his exile. Simply put, he needed money to com-pensate for three-and-a-half years of lost earning power, all the while generat-ing massive legal bills and other expenses. This cause-and-effect relationship may or may not be real, but in the hands of a capable marketer or good story-teller, it is easy to persuade people to believe it. The point is that the exile has become a profoundly adaptable cultural text that can be used to ascribe cour-age and positive values to Ali in a wide range of milieus, among them adver-tisements and other corporate endeavors. It is this versatility that helps keep the Ali legend relevant, and those who have tapped into it have been able to sell successfully the former champion, even to consumers who were born years after the relevant events had occurred.

At the heart of the equation of Ali's exile with heroism is his willingness to eschew money to follow his principles. More than the threat of a prison sentence, more than the discomfort of an uncertain future, it is the money that Ali gave up that has served as the ultimate barometer of his sacrifice and that has come to represent indelible proof of his commitment to uncommon moral standards. As time has passed, Ali's refusal to sell out has translated not only into symbolic capital but also into wealth. It is now acceptable for Ali to profit from his martyrdom because he withstood the temptation to do so in the past, thus insulating him from criticism suggesting that he currently ex-ploits his prior role as a race man and freedom fighter. Those who perceive this economic sacrifice as the marker of Ali's greatness are taking their cues from Ali himself, who was relentless in using it as a reference point to measure the magnitude of his effort. Although it wound up serving as the impenetrable foundation of Ali's claims to moral authority, and secured his place in the pantheon of American heroes, Ali's exile from boxing was an inglorious and miserable time for him. It was a period of great insecurity because he faced mounting legal bills and a five-year prison sentence, and because he rarely knew where his next paycheck would come from. Ali, who had always been preoccupied with money and treated it simultaneously with worship and disdain, became obsessed with it during his exile. "I started boxing because I thought this was the fastest way for a black person to make it in this country," he once said, and now that prospect was slipping away. Ali mentioned his deprivation repeatedly during the exile, as if he didn't want people to forget that standing up for one's principles came with a price. Despite this deprivation, however, stories of Ali giving away money, either to members of his entourage or to some other sad sack du jour, are legion. Although rarely in the foreground of narratives dedicated to his exile period, the economic pinch was the most dramatically discomfiting aspect of that sacrifice. It was at the core of Ali's consciousness on a daily basis.[2]

Ali's willingness to take the economic penalty that accompanied his draft resistance was also the opening that gave those who found his relationship with the NOI repugnant the chance to reverse ideological course and accept him in more favorable terms. Central to the underlying motivation behind public antipathy toward Ali prior to his exile was the belief that he was making a lot of money for the NOI. This feeling led to the near quashing of Main Bout and put people on guard that Ali had the potential to foment lasting change that could permanently alter the landscape of industries like professional boxing, not to mention the American racial order. Behind this threat was the belief that the NOI could not be co-opted. Although this was far from true, the uncompromising air that Ali had adopted throughout his draft trial and exile signified to the public that the NOI was intractable. The thought that it might become an economic power through the athletic works of Ali scared people.

Muhammad Ali's transformation from a contested figure to one that receives a near-universal stamp of approval could not have occurred without his separation from the NOI, a process he started in 1975, following Elijah Muhammad's death. Forgetting the heightened paranoia that accompanied public perception of the NOI during the frenzied civil rights era, even those who celebrate Ali today have to reckon with this past association. This view is evidenced by a sizable exhibit at the Muhammad Ali Center designed to address his bygone but irresponsible quotes about white devils and the evils of intermarriage. But hinting that Ali's black nationalist phase was anything but sincere is to undermine any pro-Ali mission, profit-driven or otherwise, because Ali's street credibility as an endorser will forever be linked with his NOI-driven draft resistance. While refutations of Ali's past indiscretions are part of the process of cleaning up his act, and he has said on numerous occasions that he no longer believes, for example, that whites are devils, there has been a far more subtle method used to exclude the NOI from the seminal narrative of the exile and disqualify it from sharing in Ali's redemption.

Both in retrospect and at the time, the exile has been positioned as the marker of Ali's outstanding character and the NOI's flawed one. If Ali's true sacrifice was his renunciation of money for principle, then the NOI's true failing was its refusal to stick by Ali once his earning potential dried up. Since the Ali legend rests primarily upon this period, the emphasis on such a contrast morally rescues Ali from his partnership with the NOI, even if it remained intact for years following his return to the ring. It has been a devastatingly effective tool within Ali narratives. Even though Elijah Muhammad was a legitimate draft resister who did prison time for refusing to fight in World War II, the portrayals of him and his organization during this episode, as seen in the *Ali* biopic and numerous biographies, are as unprincipled opportunists.

The key lesson is that the NOI refused to back Ali during his most important test, one that came about only as a result of his loyalty to the organization in the first place. For economic reasons, the NOI failed Ali, not unlike when its leaders had kept his membership a secret until he had defeated Liston, for fear of bad publicity if young Cassius were defeated. And once again, in a time of need, it had failed to summon the moral beneficence necessary to back a disciple in trouble. Ironically, although the stage had been set for Ali to become an admired moral authority by his being a member of the NOI, he achieved such status only when disassociated from that group. It was the NOI that terminated its relationship with Ali during the exile because he was no longer economically useful to them. While its leaders may have thought that distancing the organization from the unpopular and seemingly over-the-hill Ali was a good move, its backfiring still reverberates throughout the historical record.

For years prior to their dust-up, Ali had been identifying lost income as the key indicator of his commitment to the NOI. He felt that money was the true test of his loyalty. Shortly before his draft evasion trial, he commented:

This is what I sincerely believe. I've upheld my faith through the past years. I gave up one of the prettiest Negro women in the country; cost me $150,000 in alimony [Ali had divorced his wife in 1966 because she failed to follow the Nation of Islam's codes of conduct]. This was all controversy and publicity before the draft started. The white businessmen of Louisville, Kentucky will tell you that I've turned down eight million dollars in movie contracts, recordings, promotions and advertisements because of my faith. So I don't see why I should break the rules of my faith now.

Under oath in federal court, he told the presiding judge at his trial that the legitimacy of his draft resistance should be measured in economic terms: "If it wasn't against my conscience to do it, I would easily do it. I wouldn't raise all this court stuff and I wouldn't go through all this and lose the millions that I gave up and my image with the American public that I would say is completely dead and ruined because of us in here now." Ali had known well in advance of his conviction that his draft resistance was going to cost him. Gordon Davidson, on behalf of the Louisville Sponsoring Group, explained the situation. "On my desk right now, there must be a million dollars' worth of contracts. Endorsements, public appearances," he told the champ. "But they're going to be pulled if you do this. Plus, who knows what it'll do to your boxing career." Even after Davidson's assurances that arrangements with the National Guard, Army Reserve, Coast Guard, and Naval Reserve would allow him to fulfill his military obligation without facing combat, Ali would not be moved. Despite all of this, Ali refused to blame the NOI for his plight. Hounded by rumors that the organization was bleeding him dry, he insisted that he gave only 10 percent of his earnings to it, and that he was never asked for more. In fact, he claimed, the group had loaned him nearly $50,000 when he was short of funds.[3]

Ali also dismissed his civil rights–era contemporaries who hadn't made the economic sacrifices that he had. While Student Nonviolent Coordinating Committee (SNCC) Chairman H. Rap Brown led a pro-Ali demonstration outside an induction center in Houston, where his draft evasion trial was taking place, the champion seethed. "Rap Brown and these boys can say what they like because they're nobody," he said. "He don't care anything about race. He wants publicity." Leading movement figures concurred that Ali's sacrifice was remarkable. Former SNCC Chair Stokely Carmichael admitted, "No one risked or suffered like Muhammad Ali. I didn't risk anything. I just told people not to go." Another SNCC member, Bob Moses, asserted that what made people in the civil rights movement take Ali's anti-war stance seriously was "he was jeopardizing his actual status, titles were on the line."[4]

Even when addressing larger issues, Ali often would think about money first. His passport was voided, even though his case was still under appeal and he posed no flight risk. State athletic commissions refused to license him, even as they sanctioned bouts involving convicted felons who had committed violent offenses. Although he was convinced that these injustices violated his constitutional rights, Ali's major concern was that they prevented him from making a living. "They think they can bring me to my knees by taking away my title, and by not letting me fight in this country, and by taking my passport so I can't get to the three million worth of fight contracts that are waiting for me overseas," he said. "I say, damn the fights and damn all the money. A man's got to stand up for what he believes, and I'm standing up for my people, even if I have to go to jail."[5]

Ali's incredible loyalty to the NOI—as evidenced by his willingness to go to jail, his disposal of millions of dollars in endorsements, his refusal to blame the organization for his troubles, and his tithing to them—made their abandonment of him during his time of need even more objectionable. The relationship unraveled in April 1969. Needing money, Ali made a paid appearance on *Wide World of Sports* to talk to Howard Cosell about his future. When asked if he would consider returning to the ring, Ali said that he would if the money was right. Elijah Muhammad ordered Ali's immediate suspension from the NOI on the grounds that these comments indicated the former champion's willingness to sell out his principles. John Ali, the former Main Bout officer, released a statement that Ali's debts were the product of "ignorance and extravagance. . . . Even Muhammad Ali's sparring partners made better use of their monies than Muhammad Ali, who did not follow the wise counsel of Messenger Muhammad in saving himself from waste and extravagance." Absolving the organization from any blame, he added, "Neither Messenger Muhammad, the Nation of Islam, nor the Muslims have taken money from Muhammad Ali. In fact, we have helped Muhammad Ali." Herbert Muhammad informed the press that he had terminated his association with Ali, and that he was no longer his manager. A front-page headline in *Muhammad Speaks* said it all: "WE TELL THE WORLD WE'RE NOT WITH MUHAMMAD ALI." He was banned from all NOI meetings and activities and was barred from communicating with its members. For the next three years, Ali was persona non grata, and his name was mentioned neither in *Muhammad Speaks* nor in any NOI temple. In an editorial, and in his trademark capital letters, Elijah Muhammad warned, "LET THIS BE A LESSON TO YOU WHO ARE WEAK IN THE FAITH." Remarkably, Ali accepted his punishment, begging Elijah Muhammad's forgiveness, and further indicating that he was hardly weak in the faith, as his leader had claimed. "I made a fool of myself when I said that I'd return to boxing to pay my bills," he said. "I'm glad he awakened me. I'll take my punishment like a man. . . . I hope he'll accept me back." Ironically, Ali's dedication was far more steadfast than Herbert Muhammad's. Jim Brown reports that he received a phone call from Ali's manager in 1967 asking him to let the fighter know that it was possible for him to enter the military and keep his title. Herbert didn't want Brown to let Ali know that it was he who was trying to broker the deal, but he did want the ex-footballer to pass on the thought to the champion. Now it was Herbert Muhammad claiming that the champion lacked principle. While Ali's loyalty to the NOI compromised him at the time, costing him millions of dollars and untold anguish, not to mention making him look bad, it ultimately distinguished him as having transcended the organization without renouncing the principled draft resistance upon which his heroism would eventually come to rest.[6]

Both before and after his suspension from the NOI, Ali tried to find ways to return to the ring. He missed the money, yearned for the celebrity spotlight, and craved the athletic competition. Knowing, however, that Elijah Muhammad had accused him of selling out, and that state athletic commissions were wary of the political ramifications of licensing him, Ali had to be creative. He did so by volunteering to participate in benefit fights, which would pave the way for the resumption of his career while sending the message that he was keeping the faith. His publicist Harold Conrad reached an agreement with, of all people, the governor of Mississippi and the mayor of Jackson that would allow Ali to secure a boxing license and fight there in exchange for Ali's donating a share of his purse to the Salvation Army, but vigorous American Legion protests caused the politicians to renege. Similar patterns emerged in Nevada and Michigan. Between 1968 and 1970, Conrad unsuccessfully negotiated for an Ali bout in twenty-eight states, in addition to several Indian reservations and foreign venues.[7]

Having kept only about a tenth of the approximately $4 million in purses he had made while champion and facing enormous legal bills, Ali soon ran out of money. He was put into the difficult situation of having to earn income without compromising the very principles that had caused his economic hardship in the first place. His most steady stream of revenue came from speaking engagements at colleges and universities. He starred as the lead in the short-lived Broadway play *Buck White*, which was loosely based on the life of Jack Johnson, to whom Ali had grown fond of comparing himself. A movie about his boxing career, *a.k.a. Cassius Clay*, earned him $10,000, as did a motion-picture fantasy boxing match against retired champion Rocky Marciano, which ended with Ali being knocked out. There were also radio and television appearances, including a $450 payment for being a mystery guest on *What's My Line?* While these opportunities kept the public from forgetting him and paid some bills, the exile remained a time of great insecurity because he faced prison time and economic deprivation.[8]

Although he kept a stiff upper lip and was publicly defiant, anyone who knew Ali understood that he was having problems coping with the pressure.

His 1968 comments on being poor ring somewhat phony, but they emphasize Ali's very real spiritual devotion:

> I take my wife out and we eat ice cream. My wife [he remarried in August 1967] is such a good cook I never go to a restaurant. I give her twenty dollars for a whole week and it's enough for her. We can eat on three dollars a day. Look out there at that little robin pecking and eating. The Lord feeds the birds and the animals. If the Lord has this power, will the Lord let His servant starve, let a man who is doing His word go hungry? I'm not worried. The Lord will provide.

In a radio interview with former SNCC member Julius Lester later that year, Ali's frustration bubbled over as he blasted the greed and complacency of those who refused to take courageous stands as he had:

> This is our trouble today. All the so-called Negroes worry about is money. He's like the white man now. He'll blow up his mama for some money. Sell out his people for some money. That's why we're nowhere today because all the big Negroes with money are up on the hill with the white folks, riding with the white folks, going to church with the white folks, marrying the white folks. . . . And they forget all about the brother down there in Harlem.

Despite all of the rhetoric, Ali was in financial trouble. Legal bills were draining away any income he could generate and his lawyers sued him for unpaid fees. In 1969, after years of refusing its help but no longer able to afford private counsel, Ali finally accepted the National Association for the Advancement of Colored People (NAACP) Legal Defense Fund's offer to represent him. There were also a number of humiliating episodes. He was prevented from accessing his room at a New York hotel because he owed fifty-three dollars. He sometimes had to dip into his wife's meager savings account to meet expenses. It was a rough period for Muhammad Ali. While it would be ridiculous to characterize him as poverty stricken, it is clear that his life was in a degree of financial disorder.[9]

Although he never seemed to let bitterness get the better of him during his suspensions from boxing and the NOI, there is no doubt that it was one of the most trying times of his life. Publicly he was gracious. When the Supreme Court finally exonerated him in 1971, a reporter asked if he would seek legal recourse against the federal government. "No," he said. "They only did what they thought was right at the time. I did what I thought was right. That was all." But in 1984, when Ali was going through another rough patch, he filed a $50 million suit against the United States for damages incurred as a result of the exile. Four years later, citing the statute of limitations, a federal judge dismissed Ali's case. Shortly thereafter, however, the Ali renaissance began and he started to reclaim his long-lost financial independence.[10]

The Prodigal Son Returns

I n October 1970, three-and-a-half years after his previous bout, Muhammad Ali finally returned to the ring. Ali's homecoming, although it predated the Supreme Court's reversal of his conviction, was a product of the country's turning against the Vietnam War. Even to many of the people who were repulsed by his connection to the NOI, Ali's exclusion from the ring for taking a courageous stand had inspired sympathy and outrage. As the general public's views about the war aligned with Ali's, the idea that he was being unjustly punished for resisting an unjust war became common.

Ali's stance against the draft had been cutting-edge. Carelessly and forcefully articulated in February 1966, while he was preparing to fight Ernie Terrell, Ali's initial public opposition was at the forefront of black anti-war activism. SNCC, considered by many to be the most progressive of the contemporary civil rights organizations, had released its anti-war manifesto only a few weeks earlier. Martin Luther King Jr., the face of the movement, did not formally announce his opposition to the war until April 1967. By then Ali was deeply entrenched in the legal system, with his conviction coming ten weeks later.

King, who did not want to alienate President Lyndon Johnson's pro–civil rights administration, was hesitant to criticize the war, but he was still ahead of the political curve. Public opinion polls revealed that it was not until March 1968 that a majority of blacks, and November 1969 until a majority of Americans, opposed it. Only when anti-war sentiment reached this critical mass did Ali have the chance to return to the ring. Despite his tribulations, he was still identified as much by his brashness and allegiance to the NOI as his draft resistance, not to mention as a convicted felon who was clearly guilty of the charges brought against him. With the war becoming ever more unpopular, however, Ali was poised to be recast within American culture from primarily a racial symbol to a hero the anti-war movement could adopt as its own. The true signal that people were beginning to rethink what Ali meant was the resumption of his ring career. As throughout his professional life, Ali's moneymaking ability was the ultimate indicator of his moral authority.[11]

Ali's return to the ring came about directly as a product of the particular political peculiarities of Atlanta, Georgia, and indirectly as a result of growing public sympathy toward him. That Ali's cause seemed just to more people than ever before also weakened the inevitable backlash against his being allowed to fight. Georgia had no state athletic commission, which meant that any locality interested in hosting an Ali fight could do so without having to go through the governor's office. This was no small detail in Georgia, whose chief executive Lester Maddox was an ardent segregationist. Maddox, along with a number of members of Congress, did their best to get the Justice Department to block the fight, but the federal government had no jurisdiction over the matter, and any inclination its officers may have had to overstep their boundaries was checked by burgeoning support for Ali. In the end, Maddox declared an official day of mourning in the state but could do little else to impose his will. Leroy Johnson, a state senator who held considerable influence over Atlanta's sizable black voting bloc, in exchange for being given a financial piece of the promotion (which would turn out to be worth $175,000), pressured Mayor Sam Massell to approve an Ali bout in the city, promising to deliver votes to him in the upcoming election. Massell didn't like the position he was put into, but he realized that it was politically expedient for him to allow the fight to happen. And so it went. Ali made his comeback and defeated contender Jerry Quarry in three rounds.[12]

Ali's return to the ring was significant, but it neither exonerated him nor reduced his chances of going to prison. While it was a sign that public opinion toward him was evolving favorably, it was anybody's guess what kind of influence, if any, it would have on the ultimate arbiter of his future, the Supreme Court. Ali did not treat the Quarry fight as a vindication of his draft stand. He was, however, elated by the almost $1 million purse, which was the largest of his career and freed him from some of the financial pressure he was facing. When asked what was more important about his return to the ring, the money or the principle, he responded honestly, "The money. I'm not a kid no more. I've got a wife and three beautiful little children to support, I'm interested in buying them a nice house, I'm interested in security same as any of you. Of course, principle is important, too. They took my title away and gave it to [Joe] Frazier. If I can get by the second-best [ranked contender Oscar Bonavena] in six weeks, then I'm ready to give Frazier a chance."[13]

The Quarry bout reflected unprecedented interest in Ali's boxing career as well as recognition of him as a race man. The closed-circuit telecast was shown in 200 locations, with a buy rate of nearly 70 percent. For a bout that was perceived by many as a mismatch, with Ali installed as a significant 17–5 betting favorite, this was remarkable. Madison Square Garden was packed, with 17,800 fans paying over $200,000 to view it on the big screen. There were nineteen other New York City–area venues also showing it. The Inglewood Forum was another sellout, and the bout generated approximate total revenues of $4 million, coming close to the gates produced by his most lucrative pre-exile title fights. Ali received approximately 42.5 percent of the net profits, which translated into a purse approaching $900,000. It was the first American professional boxing match to be shown on Soviet television. After the bout, Clay was honored with the annual Martin Luther King Award by civil rights leader Ralph Abernathy, who called him "a living example of soul power, the March on Washington in two fists." Coretta Scott King added that Ali was "a champion of justice and peace and unity."[14]

The local government support Ali received was as important as money and public sympathy. The Quarry fight could not have happened without Ali's political allies using their influence to clear the way. Increasingly, individuals were beginning to break away from the once-unanimous boycott of Ali bouts, even though they risked retribution from voters and veterans' organizations. Some may have even felt that it was politically advantageous to get behind the former champion. Whatever their motivations, these maverick politicians were blazing a trail through the morass of forces that were trying to prevent Ali from ever fighting again. Their actions meant that Ali was closer than he had been in a long time to the levers of political and economic power, and they lent momentum to the growing belief that it was acceptable to publicly back him. The more he fought, the more it seemed that he had been wronged. This feeling also translated into Ali's becoming a bigger moneymaker than ever before. Interest in his boxing career was reaching the heights it had during his pre-championship years and would soon eclipse it.

Ali's next bout, six weeks later at Madison Square Garden, pointed to his growing legitimacy. Whereas in Georgia his return to the ring had indicated that he had friends within the legislative branch of government, the circumstances surrounding this fight pointed to the willingness of the judiciary to see things his way. The match came about as a result of a year-long effort by the NAACP Legal Defense Fund, which filed suit against the New York State Athletic Commission, claiming that its denial of Ali's boxing license violated his Fourteenth Amendment rights. The main piece of evidence was a list of licensed boxers in the state, which contained dozens of convicted felons, including murderers and military deserters. It made the case that Ali had been singled out for political reasons. Calling the refusal to license Ali "astonishing," a district court judge ordered that he be reinstated. The walls of resistance to Ali, hardly built upon a sturdy foundation in the first place, were beginning to crumble.[15]

With interest in his fights nearing an all-time high, Ali further engendered public support with a courageous and dramatic fifteenth-round technical knockout of the tough Argentine contender Oscar Bonavena, who had been the first man to knock down Joe Frazier. It was the only time in his career that Bonavena was stopped, and the spectacular nature of Ali's victory further endeared him to the public, because it embodied the same kind of resolve, endurance, and determination that had fueled him throughout the exile. The metaphoric relationship between this bout and Ali's larger showdown outside the ring was obvious. Against an indefatigable foe, he had called upon his deepest reserves to pull out a dramatic victory. Despite Bonavena's being a 6–1 underdog, Madison Square Garden was sold out, and the $615,000 live gate set an arena record. There were also 150 closed-circuit locations, including sixteen in the New York metropolitan area. With his draft case still unresolved, Ali signed to meet the undefeated all-time great Joe Frazier, who had taken over the championship in his absence.[16]

It was not the first bout to be labeled as such, and would not be the last, but the March 1971 match between Muhammad Ali and Joe Frazier was truly the Fight of the Century. It pitted two undefeated heavyweight champions of remarkable skill against each other, and its symbolic significance was heightened by Ali's draft case, which was reaching a crescendo. Those who both loved and hated the former Cassius Clay eagerly anticipated the outcome of the tussle. Both fighters earned titanic $2.5 million purses, then the largest in boxing history. The cost of the broadcasting rights, won by Hollywood talent agency chief Jerry Perenchio and sportsman Jack Kent Cooke for $4.5 million, took an unprecedented leap. The bout was seen in a record thirty-six countries, and 300 million people worldwide watched it. The closed-circuit take was an astonishing $16.3 million in the United States and Canada alone. The live audience at Madison Square Garden set an indoor boxing gate record of $1.35 million. It easily became the biggest-grossing bout in boxing history. Ali and his fans were disappointed when Frazier won the fifteen-round decision, but they also knew that Ali had been out of boxing for nearly four years and the speed with which his comeback bouts had been arranged had not given him time to get into condition. He had acquitted himself well in defeat, fighting valiantly despite absorbing tremendous punishment and signaling to everyone watching that he was still a great fighter.[17]

Ali's reconciliation with the NOI and Herbert Muhammad's return as his manager were surprisingly non-issues during the buildup to his showdown with Frazier. That there was little backlash to the reunion, and that veterans' groups were by far the most vocal opponents to the Ali-Frazier fight signaled that by this time Ali was as much an anti-war symbol as a racial one. His moral authority as such was powerful enough to mute public antipathy, so strong prior to his exile, to his enriching the NOI through boxing. As a result, it had no effect on the gate for the Frazier bout. However, the organization's return as Ali's earning power was rekindled suggests that the problem it had had with the fighter was not Ali's weakened faith, but the fact that he was not making money.

Taking seriously the relationships between earning power and cultural image requires that we regard Ali's massive purse share for the Frazier fight as a sign of his moral authority and as an indicator that public opinion was shifting in his favor. Although his Supreme Court case was still hanging in the balance, the Frazier gate portended the reversal of his conviction. Lifetime Supreme Court appointments are supposed to insulate opinions from sway by outside forces, but justices are human, and they may have been swept up in the zeitgeist blowing Ali's way. On June 28, 1971, some three-and-a-half months after the Frazier fight, the U.S. Supreme Court unanimously reversed Ali's conviction, making him a free man. The ruling did not declare Ali a conscientious objector, nor did it disparage the federal court's decision to convict him on draft evasion charges. Instead, the decision focused on a technicality that would allow Ali to go free, an obvious response to public outcry against his conviction, without setting a precedent that would make it easier for others to become conscientious objectors. In order to gain this status, such persons had to meet three criteria: they had to be opposed to war in any form, their beliefs had to be based in religion, and they had to be sincere. The Justice Department was responsible for telling rejected applicants which criteria he or she failed to meet. But the Justice Department never informed Ali of the basis of its ruling in his case. Thus, the court overturned the conviction. In doing so, it acknowledged Ali's moral authority. Indeed, Chief Justice Warren Burger admitted that his vote for overturning the conviction was motivated by his sense that it would be uplifting for black people.[18]

The decision allowed Ali to resume his boxing career full-time. His popularity in the United States and around the world, even against overmatched opposition, was mirrored by where he fought and the crowds he drew. His first two stateside matches were held in the Houston Astrodome, then the largest indoor arena in the world. Over the next few years, he fought in Zurich, Tokyo, Vancouver, Jakarta, and Dublin, drawing record numbers and making big money wherever he went. It was clear that he was becoming a world-historical figure, with influence that went far beyond his ring exploits. Still, the title proved elusive. For the next three years, Ali would not fight for the championship. But when Joe Frazier lost the crown to hard-hitting George Foreman, the stage was set for Ali to work his magic in one of the most memorable and misunderstood bouts in boxing history.

King of the World

The Consequences of Monarchy

Muhammad Ali's victory over George Foreman to regain the heavy-weight championship in the October 1974 Rumble in the Jungle is one of those historical moments that has developed its own mythology. Norman Mailer devoted a book to what he called *The Fight*. In 1997, the documentary *When We Were Kings* won an Oscar for its coverage of the event. These accounts, and others like it, place Ali at the center, as the transcendent conquering hero who reclaimed his throne as king of the world, once and for all banishing the forces of evil that had exiled him in the first place. Most observers simply cannot resist the temptation to let Ali's brilliant strategic victory over a seemingly impossible foe—in Africa, no less—pass without attaching to it some kind of biblical significance. Ali-Foreman is a natural for such passion plays.

The bout was a watershed that marked Ali's full-fledged arrival as a mainstream American hero. While there are always pockets of resistance to any public figure, no matter how revered, those who clung to the idea that Ali was a draft-dodger were pushed to the margins. Once a powerful enough force to drive Ali into exile, they now were on the wrong end of the conventional wisdom. Even to many who had once opposed him, the bout offered reason to celebrate. Athletically, it was a heroic performance. Politically and culturally, it dovetailed with the spirit of the times. For a country reeling from a series of crises—Watergate, race riots, the OPEC oil embargo—and having all but abandoned the Vietnam War, Ali was the perfect salve, someone whose redemption could resonate with the national consciousness and serve as a foil to the domestic and international events that were drowning American confidence. He protested the war well before most others had caught on. His honesty distinguished him from a presidential administration whose chief executive only months earlier desperately insisted that he was not a crook. He was black but appeared to transcend race without ever losing consciousness of its significance. He was Muslim but seemed neither foreign nor fanatical. The outpouring of affection toward Ali during this period underscored his effectiveness as a symbolic counterforce to disquieting domestic turmoil and worrisome shifts in the global order. Gerald Ford invited him to the White House. TWA made the bout its in-flight feature. Ali's reputation was rehabilitated.[19]

Some of the most celebrated versions of the Ali-Foreman narrative, such as *When We Were Kings*, star Ali in the role of transcendent cultural Renaissance man, a Pied Piper with the magical ability to align and unify African, American, and African American worldviews and values to everyone's betterment. While there is something to this perspective, it has obscured the fact that when it came to the Rumble in the Jungle, Ali was not really the force that made it happen, although it certainly could not have occurred without him. Zaire's true king of the world was President Mobutu Sese Seko, who ruled the country from 1965 to 1997. Mobutu was a dictator whose excesses were illustrated by his spending $10 million from the impoverished nation's treasury to host a boxing match. He suppressed those who opposed this far-fetched plan to spur investment in his kingdom. Mobutu's prince of darkness, the man who served as the go-between linking him with the two fighters, was the American boxing promoter Don King, whose reputation would be made by this event and who developed a talent for fleecing African American boxers. It was they, along with the fighters and their managers, who stood to profit from the bout.

Because it involved the politicized Ali and Foreman as his foil—a man who in response to the black power salute by Tommie Smith and John Carlos at the 1968 Summer Olympics took a flag-waving lap around the ring after clinching the gold medal—people failed to realize that those who injected symbolic meaning into Ali-Foreman were not the fighters, but rather Mobutu and Don King. While Americans, including Ali, latched on to the idea that the Rumble in the Jungle was something more than a boxing match, they were taking their cues from an unsavory duo. Although the bout increased American awareness of Africa, and the media attention produced positive images that countered Western ideas about African primitiveness, it is a stretch to assert that the Ali-Foreman bout, simply because it was held in Africa, represented black liberation. There is little evidence supporting this symbolism.

Mobutu and King tried to publicize the fight as a victory for black people. There is an irony behind these attempts because both men proved time and again to be injurious to that population. King had sold the fight to Mobutu as such, and Mobutu outdid him by installing roadside signs all around Kinshasa, the capital city where the fight took place, trumpeting the bout as something other than the marketing ploy it really was. In the capital letters that the era's demagogues seemed so fond of employing, as if using lowercase were a sign of weakness, Mobutu trumpeted philosophies such as:

> "A FIGHT BETWEEN TWO BLACKS IN A BLACK NATION ORGANIZED BY BLACKS AND SEEN BY THE WHOLE WORLD: THIS IS THE VICTORY OF MOBUTUISM."
>
> "THE COUNTRY OF ZAIRE WHICH HAS BEEN BLED BECAUSE OF PILLAGE AND SYSTEMATIC EXPLOITATION MUST BECOME A FORTRESS AGAINST IMPERIALISM AND A SPEARHEAD FOR THE LIBERATION OF THE AFRICAN CONTINENT."
>
> "THE FOREMAN-ALI FIGHT IS NOT A WAR BETWEEN TWO ENEMIES BUT A SPORT BETWEEN TWO BROTHERS."[20]

Although he exploited the race angle for promotional purposes, Ali fought in Africa for the money. "The true significance of why this fight is being fought in Africa," he admitted, "is because they came up with $10 million: $5 million for George Foreman, $5 million for me. London, England was trying to get it, promoters here in America were trying to get it, but none of them could surpass the $5 million mark." Herbert Muhammad added, "For five million dollars, Ali will fight anywhere on the planet Earth." It was Ali's moral authority and status as a race man, however, that lent legitimacy to the notion that the bout had political significance, and conned observers into giving Mobutu and King a free pass, even framing their efforts as hallmarks of the dawning of a new era in relations between Africa and the world. Politics were clearly an add-on, a convenient way of obscuring the profit motive and excusing Ali's association with figures as clearly corrupt as Mobutu and King, but many accounts portrayed black nationalism as the bout's raison d'être.[21]

The Rumble in the Jungle reveals the complex nature of Ali's moral authority. Just as his principles drove him to risk his freedom by resisting the draft, his principled reputation cloaked the wrongdoings of his associates under the guise of black nationalism and encouraged Ali to participate uncritically in the promotion. The reason that the Foreman fight is one of the most misinterpreted texts of the Ali Story is that although it appeared to have political significance, it in fact made blackness something to exploit for money. Ironically, Ali had been used like so many "great white hopes" that preceded him. Those reporting on the fight failed to examine the circumstances critically; any doubts were overridden by Ali's reputation for goodness, which in turn gave Mobutu and King carte blanche to take advantage of black people.

Of all of the foibles Muhammad Ali has lived down, the most difficult one to overcome has been his treatment of Joe Frazier, especially before their 1975 rubber match, the Thrilla in Manila. Cordial during Ali's exile, their relationship took a turn for the worse when Ali politicized Frazier as an Uncle Tom during the buildup to their first bout. The bad blood boiled over prior to their 1974 rematch, when they got into a televised scuffle on *Wide World of Sports* after Frazier took offense at Ali's calling him ignorant. But it was while hyping the third fight that Ali got out of hand, at least from Frazier's perspective. Without rehashing a story that has been told and re-told many times, it is safe to say that Ali more or less constantly referred to Frazier as a dumb, dark, ugly nigger who was too black physically and not black enough politically. It would be reasonable to argue that these charges were fair game and part of the psychological war that goes on between prospective rivals. One could also argue that Ali's attacks had nothing to do with boxing, were in bad taste, and revealed him to be a phony as a black nationalist and a self-hater. Frazier never forgave Ali for these comments, and a number of books written after the turn of the century that are critical of Ali have made Ali's attacks on Frazier the centerpiece of their argument.

Racial humor was always a staple of Ali's personal life; he especially loved jokes that zinged blacks and Jews. The harassment of Frazier folded neatly into Ali's affinity for such barbs. Howard Cosell described such an episode during a 1974 plane ride:

> Ali returned from the coach section. He was, as always, restless. "Those folks back there are crowded, they're uncomfortable. We've got to go back and entertain them. You call me nigger and boy, and we'll do our act." What I wanted to do was go to sleep, but instead I trailed him into the coach section and we went through a routine reserved for off-camera situations. "Look here, nigger," I would begin. "Did you say Trigger?" he would answer. "Now listen boy," I would say. "You mean Roy?" he would query. And the passengers loved it.[22]

While Ali usually referred to blacks positively as a racial group and often portrayed whites negatively as a racial group, he seemed to be more comfortable deprecating individual blacks than whites. Throughout his career, he more strongly criticized black than white opponents. There were reasons beyond race that he did this; for one thing his black opponents were a far greater threat to his ring career than his white ones. The better the fighter—think Frazier, Foreman, Liston, and Patterson—the harder Ali was on them. But for all his talk about white devils, Ali treated longtime white associates like Angelo Dundee with dignity and courtesy while heaping wrath upon black ones like Drew "Bundini" Brown. Dundee's consistent working relationship with Ali contrasted with Brown's blatantly and repeatedly taking advantage of the champion—he once hocked Ali's title belt—but there is no record of Ali treating any white person with the cruelty he dished out to Bundini, Frazier, Patterson, and others.

People like to construe Ali's international bouts as somehow informed by solidarity between him, the worldwide Islamic community, and people of color. Any investment of such symbolism in these fights, however, needs to be tested. Places like Malaysia, Indonesia, and the Philippines were appropriate for Ali bouts because they drew large crowds and were ruled by those with the money to pay him the purses he required. Whether these fights held any benefit for local people is ambiguous. One cannot fault Ali for earning a living, but it is significant that he possibly cashed in on his popularity at the expense of the world's poor people and received huge purses from dictators whose subjects may have been better off not having to shoulder the cost of an Ali bout. The interesting thing is not that Ali took part in such events, but that people have invented a progressive folklore to explain them. The ridiculous idea, which still seems predominant to this day, was that if Ali was involved it must be pure. This is the dark side of Ali's moral authority.

Ali left the NOI to become an orthodox Muslim following Elijah Muhammad's 1975 death. He maintained his close friendship with Herbert Muhammad, who remained his manager and spiritual adviser. Ali's defection from the NOI was vital to his becoming a lasting American hero, because it allowed him to renounce earlier statements about whites, politics, and interracial relations that are repugnant to the vast majority of Americans. He explained:

> I don't hate whites. That was history, but it's coming to an end. We're in a new phase, a resurrection. Elijah taught us to be independent, to clean ourselves up, to be proud and healthy. He stressed the bad things the white man did to us so we could get free and strong. Now, his son Wallace is showing us there are good and bad regardless of color, that the devil is in the mind and heart, not the skin. We Muslims hate injustice and evil, but we don't have time to hate people. White people wouldn't be here if God didn't mean them to be.[23]

Despite leaving the NOI and earning a series of lucrative purses, Ali still was losing ground financially during this period because of his spending habits. As a result, he kept fighting, which jeopardized his health and reputation.

A 1977 interview with Howard Cosell sounded just like the one they had done eight years earlier that led to Ali's suspension from the NOI. "The reason you'll fight again is because of the marital entanglement [Ali divorced his second wife in 1976 and then married Veronica Porche the following year] and your present need for money, isn't that true?" Cosell asked. Ali denied the accusation. A year later, he told Cosell, "If I sold everything I had, tomorrow, I'd be worth three-and-a-half million dollars." Ali had made over $40 million in purses, not to mention endorsements, appearance fees, and other earnings. Cosell said, "It has been written and written that you're dead broke, you have no money. Is this true?" Ali again denied it, but it was clear that he was having problems, and those who cared about him feared that he was on his way to physical and financial ruin.[24]

What should have been the most glorious period of Ali's life had become the preamble to one of the darkest. By patronizing Don King, keeping Herbert Muhammad as his manager, marrying Veronica Porche, and fighting far too long in order to pay these people and other hangers-on, Ali sowed the seeds for his own financial and physical ruin. As his money and health problems worsened, he became even more open to exploitation. It would eventually lead to the roughest decade of his life, the 1980s. What makes the period surrounding his victory over George Foreman so interesting is not that these things happened to him, but that it has been overwhelmingly misinterpreted as a glorious one.

Death of a Salesman

By the mid-1970s Muhammad Ali was severely compromised as a fighter. It was clear that Ali was not the man he used to be, but he fought on because he needed the money and the glory. Pitted repeatedly against soft and overmatched competition whose major qualification for receiving title shots was the ability to allow Ali to compensate for his inadequacies in the ring, the champion floundered when faced with quality tests. In 1978, Ali lost his title to upstart Leon Spinks, who had only seven professional fights and despite winning an Olympic gold medal two years earlier was a mediocre fighter. Although Ali defeated Spinks in a rematch later that year to regain the championship, and then retired, he would return to the ring eighteen months later to face new titleholder Larry Holmes, who dominated him for every second of every round before Ali's handlers refused to let him answer the bell for the eleventh round. There was one more fight after that, a loss to fringe contender Trevor Berbick, and then Ali slipped into an ignominious retirement.

The $8 million purse for the Holmes fight was the largest of Ali's career, and it should have been enough for him to live comfortably for a long time, but it wasn't. Don King, who promoted the fight, shorted Ali almost $1 million. Another third of the purse went to Herbert Muhammad. Ali whittled away almost all of the rest on training expenses and frivolities. The vultures that Ali had fed in Zaire were now feasting on his rotting corpse, and Ali showed little will to resist. Things got so bad that three years later, King paid Ali a mere $1,200 fee to hang around a title match between Holmes and Tim

Witherspoon. The former champion was on a sharp downswing toward mental, financial, and physical deterioration.[25]

Four days after the beating by Holmes, Ali checked into the hospital. There, it was discovered that his doctor, Charles Williams, who was also the personal physician of Herbert Muhammad and the late Elijah Muhammad, had misdiagnosed Ali with a hypothyroid condition and had given him medication that could have caused him serious health problems during the Holmes bout. Doctors also determined that before his rematch with Spinks, Ali's blood was found to be deficient in iron, potassium, and salt. While these complications were treatable, it was clear that Ali was not maintaining himself and was relying on unreliable people.[26]

Ali's precarious financial state made him vulnerable, and led him to trust seedy operators who proposed get-rich-quick schemes. In doing so, Ali diminished what are still his most valuable assets, his good name and his moral authority. In 1981, Ali became entangled in what was at the time the largest bank embezzlement case in U.S. history. He had endorsed a promotional organization called Muhammad Ali Professional Sports (MAPS), which paid him 25 percent of its net profits. The operation was unsuccessful, and investigators discovered that it had been funded by $21 million stolen by an employee from Wells Fargo Bank of California. Although he had received a number of payments from MAPS, it was clear to law enforcement officials that Ali was not in on the plot. But the episode was embarrassing and harmed Ali's reputation. The champ had become a chump.[27]

Ali's health problems also worsened as his body responded to the beatings he had taken over the prior twenty years. His hands trembled, his speech slurred, his pace slowed, and he felt perpetually tired. Amid false rumors that he was using drugs, in 1984, Ali checked into the hospital for a series of tests. After eight days of observation, doctors diagnosed Ali with Parkinson's syndrome. Although Ali denied that this condition, which threatened neither his life nor his mental faculties, was related to his too-long ring career, most outside observers thought otherwise. He was becoming a figure to be pitied, or worse, to be made fun of. A 1981 Saturday Night Live sketch featuring Eddie Murphy portrayed the former champion as delirious, punch-drunk, and pathetic—repeating himself, not making any sense, slurring his words, and reciting nursery rhymes. It was the type of disrespectful portrayal of Ali that you will never see today, but this was before the Ali renaissance of the 1990s.[28]

Ali also divorced for the third and last time during this period, and he got the worst part of the settlement. Although it appeared that his major real estate holdings and a sizable trust fund were protected as part of a prenuptial agreement that Veronica Porche had signed, Ali again allowed himself to be hustled. First, he ordered his lawyers to change his irrevocable trust fund to one with a five-year time limit, the expiration of which coincided with his wife's filing for divorce. Second, he ordered his lawyers to disregard the pre-nuptial agreement after Veronica convinced him that doing so would create hardship for their children. Third, he agreed to shoulder the burden of the tax payments that would stem from the distribution of family assets. As a result, when the divorce was finalized during the summer of 1986, Veronica walked away with significantly more than Ali did.[29]

Ali's name became associated with cheap schemes and goods, which cut into the very moral authority that gave these operations their most reasonable chances for success. One plan considered the sale of powdered milk to under-developed countries. Another was the creation of a Muhammad Ali Financial Corporation that would apply for a $100 billion loan to build mosques and low-income apartment buildings in cities around the United States. These projects never got off the ground. There were also all sorts of products that bore the Ali moniker: shoe polish, hamburger joints, popcorn, boxing equip-ment, candy. None of them caught on, his financial situation remained stag-nant, and the future looked bleak.[30]

The most scurrilous mix-ups Ali got into during this period were political. At first, his involvement was small-time and portended nothing illegal. Nev-ertheless, it was surprising to many of Ali's fans when the former champion endorsed a series of Republican candidates, starting in 1984 with the presi-dential re-election bid of Ronald Reagan. Four years later, he got behind George H. W. Bush's presidential run and Orrin Hatch's senatorial campaign. Although the NOI's ideas about independence through economic develop-ment were probably more Republican than Democratic, Ali was always a lib-eral darling, and progressives who looked at him as a moral symbol began to question his authority. Andrew Young, the former Southern Christian Lead-ership Conference member, claimed that it was wrong for Ali to support "candidates whose policies are harmful to the great majority of Americans, black and white." Former SNCC activist Julian Bond added, "I don't know why he's doing it, but it makes me feel bad. Ronald Reagan and George Bush have been tragedies for black Americans, and Orrin Hatch in my opinion is an awful person politically. I'd love to sit down with Ali and discuss it. I wish I could say to him, 'Listen, don't do that.'"[31]

It was when Ali linked up with an energetic attorney and huckster named Richard Hirschfeld that things turned ugly. Ali liked Hirschfeld because he regularly delivered on their joint business endeavors. It seemed as if every new project they embarked upon led to desperately needed cash in Ali's pocket. Their operations were highly diversified: Champion Sports Manage-ment, which trained and managed boxers, an Ali-brand car built in Brazil, a luxury hotel in Virginia Beach, a West German herpes vaccine, and an oil refinery in the Sudan. But once again, Ali's greed led him to involvement with someone who would ultimately damage his moral authority.[32]

The problem was that Hirschfeld was a criminal. Three times he was found guilty of fraud by the U.S. Securities and Exchange Commission; for this he was permanently disbarred. Hirschfeld's reputation had no effect on Ali, but the ex-champion soon found himself in a pickle. In 1988, Hirschfeld, who did a dead-on Ali impression, posed as the former champion in phone calls to six U.S. senators, a former governor, and the U.S. Attorney General, among others. In these telephone calls, Hirschfeld pursued an agenda that included the appointment of a University of Virginia law professor to a job in the Justice Department, the investigation of a special prosecutor in Virginia, and the enactment of legislation that would permit Ali to sue the federal government for damages resulting from his exile two decades earlier. Investigators eventually discovered that it was not Ali who had been making the phone calls. All of the items in question could be traced back to Hirschfeld: the law professor was his friend, the special prosecutor was investigating him, and as Ali's representative he would get a cut of any successful suit against the government. It also became clear that Hirschfeld was behind Ali's endorsement of various political candidates. But by then the damage had already been done to Ali's reputation. Hirschfeld eventually went to prison during the early 1990s for conspiracy and tax fraud. He then became an international fugitive when he fled to the Canary Islands after it was discovered that his 1995 parole had been driven by forged letters he had sent to the judges presiding over his case. Even in exile Hirschfeld caused Ali trouble. In 1999, with a Hollywood biopic about him on the drawing board, Ali successfully sued Hirschfeld to get out of a contract they had signed in 1988 that had given the rogue lawyer 40 percent of the rights to his life story. The suit finally ended Ali's obligation to the man who had run his name through the mud for a decade, but it was a reminder of the delicate relationship between commercial interests and cultural image. Even a legend like Ali had limits, and if he was ever going to capitalize on his moral authority again, he would have to be more careful about choosing his associates. Hirschfeld was eventually captured and wound up hanging himself in the laundry room of a Miami jail.[33]

One of the ironies of the relationship between Ali's commercial interests and cultural image during this period was that it led to the degradation of Ali's moral authority without his enjoying any profit. It would have been one thing if Ali had sold out and cashed in on his heroic past, but it was quite another for others to do so at Ali's expense and trash his reputation in the process. Ali's harnessing his iconic status into a fortune is a relatively new phenomenon, one that began as a result of his finally finding someone whom he could rely upon to defend his interests.

Lonnie Ali

The Savior

Perhaps the best thing that ever happened to Muhammad Ali took place on November 19, 1986, when he married his current wife, Yolanda "Lonnie" Ali. Without her intervention, there's a good chance that Ali would be financially insecure, convalescent, or dead. She saved her husband's life and engineered his becoming the icon he is today. When they married, there was much work to be done. Ali's health and reputation had to be salvaged. Such rehabilitation was only the beginning of repairing Ali's life. There was also the work of making him relevant to a new generation that had not lived through the civil rights movement and Vietnam War. With Lonnie's help, Ali has surpassed the influence he had achieved in the past as a commercial, moral, and cultural force.

The marriage was the culmination of a relationship that began in 1962. That year, Lonnie's parents moved to Louisville's West End into the home across the street from that of Odessa and Cassius Clay Sr. Five-year-old Lonnie idolized her famous twenty-year-old neighbor, who despite his brutal profession befriended the neighborhood kids. He took his young companion to the playground, bought her ice cream, and organized tricycle races in which she participated. Even after Ali won the championship, and well into the 1970s, he would socialize with her whenever he made one of his frequent visits home. Of course, she had a crush on him, but their relationship was that of a big brother and younger sister. He was instrumental in helping her select Vanderbilt University for her undergraduate work. After college she worked in sales for Kraft Foods, and eventually became an account representative. She also began an MBA program at the University of Louisville.[34]

Their relationship reached a new level in 1982, when Ali asked her to meet him for lunch during one of his visits to Louisville. Lonnie was stunned by what she saw; her idol was depressed and seemed to be in poor health. Only twenty-five years old, and with her career on the move, she nonetheless accepted an invitation to relocate to Los Angeles to become Ali's primary caregiver, transferring to UCLA to continue her graduate studies. Ali, with his wife Veronica's permission, agreed to pay all of her expenses. During this time, Lonnie also began to study Islam. Like Ali, she had been raised a Christian but through various shifts in her life had wound up a Muslim. After his marriage to Veronica Porche deteriorated, Ali asked Yolanda Williams to become his wife. Once his third divorce was completed, she accepted his proposal.[35]

They have been married over twenty years, and Lonnie Ali now serves as a caregiver for the former champion and the caretaker of his image and legacy. She has been remarkably adept in both roles, rebuilding the Ali name into a powerful industry and parlaying his reputation into wealth and prestige without compromising his dignity or moral authority. Knowing that Ali is prone to financial exploitation, she keeps the wolves away from him, as evidenced by a 1993 lawsuit against Herbert Muhammad for using Ali's name improperly.

In rejuvenating Ali's image, Lonnie has limited his availability to the media and public. Unlike in the past, when Ali was an open book, and anyone could gain access to him, it is now much more difficult to do so. At the same time, though, Lonnie knew that it was necessary to transform media coverage of Ali into narratives that emphasized his heroic past. She opened up the family home in Michigan, where they had moved shortly after getting married, to select reporters who she felt would portray Ali appropriately. Such control over who speaks to Ali on the record continues. My two requests for interviews with the former champion and his wife for this book, for example, were turned down, although one of the rejection letters included an autographed photo. One has to qualify to speak to Ali. Such protection has been integral in repairing the damage to Ali's image and moral authority that had occurred during the 1980s.

An early example of the media rehabilitation of Ali was a July 1988 *New York Times Magazine* piece by Peter Tauber, the late Hollywood screenwriter who was then making a television biopic about the former champion. The piece presented Ali as a man who was at peace, financially stable, physically healthier than people believed, and comfortable with his legacy. "Muhammad is fine," said Lonnie, "but people think he is dying." Ali's personal physician, the UCLA doctor Dennis Cope, told readers, "[F]rom the tests that we've done we have established that it is not punch-drunk syndrome—there's no evidence of deterioration of his ability to think. He's all there, and there's no reason to expect him to deteriorate." The article was important because it alleviated people's worst fears about Ali in a widely distributed magazine. The reformulating of his image had begun, but Lonnie's goal wasn't just to stabilize Ali's condition, but to make it stronger than ever before. In order to do that, though, she would need a permanent media envoy, someone whose job was to write about Muhammad Ali. Enter Thomas Hauser.[36]

Thomas Hauser

The Literary Rehabilitation of Ali's Legend

etween 1988 and 1998, nobody did more to publicly rebuild Muhammad
Ali's legendary image than writer Thomas Hauser. Charged by Lonnie
Ali to transmit her vision to a larger audience, Hauser served as Muhammad Ali's biographer and chief spokesperson for a decade. Hauser's writings during the 1990s were the ideological foundation of Ali's recoding as a sanctified American hero. They were—and still are—taken as proof of Ali's greatness and are key to his enduring cultural relevance. How Hauser was selected is something of a mystery, since Lonnie Ali has never publicly commented on the process, but by most accounts the partnership was mutually fulfilling. Hauser got a plum writing assignment, and the Ali camp got a book that jump-started the moribund movement to canonize the ex-champion as a global figure and all-time moral authority.

Although trained as an attorney, the Columbia University graduate had made a name for himself as a writer in the decade prior to his introduction to the Ali family. Hauser's 1978 literary debut, *The Execution of Charles Horman: An American Sacrifice*, was adapted into the 1982 movie *Missing*, starring Jack Lemmon and Sissy Spacek. Hauser's acclaimed 1986 book, *The Black Lights: Inside the World of Professional Boxing*, revealed a formidable understanding of how the fight business operates. In addition to his knowledge of law and impressive writing résumé, Hauser possessed an important criterion for becoming Muhammad Ali's authorized biographer: he idolized Ali. One of his biggest thrills as a young man was conducting an interview with the champion before his fight with Zora Folley.

The relationship between Ali and Hauser began in 1988, when Ali's best friend, the photographer Howard Bingham, contacted him. At a meeting, Lonnie Ali briefed Hauser about the assignment. She wanted a book "that would place Muhammad in context, not just as a fighter but also as a social, political, and religious figure" and highlight him as a gentle, caring, and spiritual person. With the mission outlined, and the writer completely authorized to conduct interviews, Hauser began the manuscript, frequently consulting with the Ali camp.[37]

Once he completed the initial draft, Hauser traveled to the Ali family farm in Michigan to meet with Bingham and the Alis and read them his manuscript. "By agreement," recalled the author, "there was to be no censorship. The purpose of our reading was to ensure that the book would be factually accurate." Hauser claims that if the Ali camp objected to something he had written, and he insisted on preserving it, then a rebuttal paragraph in Ali's words would be placed alongside such material. No such rebuttal paragraphs, however, exist in the book. Hauser also asserts that he retained final editorial control over the book and its release.[38]

Hauser's work, *Muhammad Ali: His Life and Times*, was the first serious Ali biography in fifteen years. Because it was authorized, Hauser had virtually unlimited access to Ali's inner circle and sizable group of admirers. The list of interviewees is extensive; Hauser names 178 people in an appendix, including fighters, actors, musicians, trainers, politicians, civil rights leaders, writers, journalists, comedians, and athletes, many of whom were towering figures in their fields. Among those listed are George Foreman, Sylvester Stallone, Bob Dylan, Angelo Dundee, Jimmy Carter, Julian Bond, James Michener, Robert Lipsyte, Dick Gregory, and Wilt Chamberlain. Simply put, Hauser was able to talk to virtually everyone alive who closely associated with Ali between 1960 and 1990. In fact, the only people unwilling to provide him with material for the book were Don King, Veronica Porche, and John Ali.[39]

Being an authorized biographer has advantages and limitations. Although he received unprecedented access and claims that the Ali camp had no undue influence on what he wrote, Hauser has been accused of being more of an advocate than a biographer. It is an allegation that he resents and categorically denies, but it is an important issue, because, as another Ali biographer wrote, "The foundations for the current Ali renaissance were laid by the publication of Thomas Hauser's biography." Unquestionably, Hauser's work has been the definitive source from which the overwhelming majority of interpretations of the former champion have since stemmed. Therefore, it is worth asking whether his book is hagiography. The motivations for writing a pro-Ali piece are obvious; doing so would give Hauser access to his idol, the literary chance of a lifetime, fame, and fortune.[40]

People raised this issue while the book was in production. Broadcaster Howard Cosell, well known for self-aggrandizement, was especially critical. Like Hauser, Cosell framed his advocacy of Ali as a product of the integrationist spirit of the civil rights movement, equating their relationship with his fighting for racial equality and justice. Also like Hauser, Cosell faced accusations of being an Ali shill, using his access for personal enrichment. Always known as a difficult and complex man, Cosell had a tendency toward cantankerousness that reached new heights as his health began to fail in the years prior to his 1995 death. Whether his hostility toward Hauser's work stemmed from professional jealousy, personal issues, or legitimate misgivings, Cosell was critical. In his 1991 best seller *What's Wrong with Sports*, he wrote, "My theory is that Hauser has gotten too close to his subject and is too enamored of Ali to write a completely honest and objective book." Cosell's criticism is instructional not because it was necessarily true, but because it illustrated the scrutiny that Hauser faced because his book was, as the *New York Times Book Review* called it, "the first definitive biography" of one of American history's most important popular cultural figures.[41]

Due to its breadth and its popularity, *Muhammad Ali: His Life and Times* remains the definitive Ali biography nearly twenty years after its publication. No book covers a broader expanse of Ali's life and career. It is unlikely that any Ali book has been more widely read, with the possible exception of David Remnick's *King of the World. Muhammad Ali and the Making of an American Hero*, which like Hauser's book made the *New York Times* best-seller list. By 2004, over 150,000 copies of Hauser's book had been printed in the United States alone. As a result of its widespread appeal and massive scope, *Muhammad Ali: His Life and Times* has achieved a status that other books have not. *King of the World* might also have claimed such reverence had it not covered only a short period of Ali's life, but it is Hauser's biography that stands alone as the authoritative Ali source.[42]

An indicator of the influence of Hauser's book is its formal dominance of the Ali genre. Its definitive characteristics—oral history, interview testimony, and hagiography—have become mainstays of both print and video versions of the Ali Story. Once primarily told as a narrative, the Ali Story is now usually presented as a series of recollections by Ali's contemporaries or as testimonies from younger people claiming to recognize Ali's significance. In source after source, these interviews, whether presented orally or in writing, have become the dominant vehicle to inform people about Muhammad Ali's life and times. There are numerous documentary-type films that intersperse footage of Ali in his prime with statements by people looking back on the era and praising the former champion. In effect, testimony stating Ali's greatness has become the primary evidence that he is great. Furthermore, in these sources, the respondents who have something positive to say about Ali vastly outnumber those who don't. All of these forms, which are now regularly practiced when telling the story of Muhammad Ali, more or less began with the Hauser book.[43]

Hauser's formula has proven so reliable over the past twenty years that it became the central storytelling mechanism of the Muhammad Ali Center, the nearly 100,000-square-foot downtown Louisville museum/shrine devoted to bolstering Ali's legacy. The ultimate Ali tribute, the pinnacle of Ali's renaissance, a one-man hall of fame, the Muhammad Ali Center is formatted much like Hauser's book in that its exhibits are dominated by first-person testimony confirming Ali's moral authority and greatness. Prior to its grand opening, the Ali Center's founders produced a book/video combination called *Muhammad Ali: Through the Eyes of the World*, which was distributed to major media outlets and members of the press. Yet another example of the classic arrangement of hagiographical oral interviews, it featured statements from the likes of James Earl Jones, Rod Steiger, Maya Angelou, and Dustin Hoffman, all waxing nostalgically about the greatness of the former champion. A *New York Times* article summarized its main themes: "Muhammad Ali has been called the greatest athlete of his century, but he was much more than a great boxer; he was one of the most compelling figures of his time, a leader in the civil rights movement, a fiercely principled man who nearly traded in his career rather than violate his religious beliefs, and a figure of remarkable charm and charisma in a sport hardly known for producing articulate men." I will analyze the Muhammad Ali Center in detail later, but the points here are that Hauser's book created standards still in place today, namely, that the way to tell Ali's story is through oral history, and that the evidentiary norm for measuring Ali's greatness is that his admirers say he is great. The Ali Center has become the decisive manifestation of this development and illustrates the ubiquity of Hauser's model.[44]

The potency of *Muhammad Ali: His Life and Times* shows the importance of literature to the construction and preservation of the Ali legend. At first glance it seems strange and counterintuitive that during an era dominated by online and cellular technological advances, books would drive the cultural rehabilitation of a made-for-television figure like Ali, whose speaking ability and in-ring grace were fundamental to his impact. It makes sense, however, that literature would help spur the remaking of Ali's meaning. Convincing a new generation of consumers to understand the staples of Ali's moral authority—his ties to the civil rights movement and the anti-war movement—takes the kind of argumentation that is well suited to book form. In fact, it could be said that the rehabilitation of Ali's image during the early 1990s was not self-contained, but part of a larger historiography that once and for all declared the civil rights and anti-war movements to have positively impacted American society.[45]

Literature became the opportune site to reconstruct a fallen champion who had lost the very assets that his television persona depended upon: looks, speaking ability, and fighting ability. Although these were the bases of Ali's popularity over the years, by the early 1990s he had taken on a new physical form, one that could not yet be transmitted visually to consumers. It would be impossible for Ali to sell products, or himself, without being redefined. Those who admired him as a boxer and talker, and were therefore most likely to be influenced into consumption at his behest, would also be most uncomfortable with his new embodiment. The Ali of the 1990s, unless carefully packaged, would more likely hurt than help product sales. Even today, as people grow comfortable with the wounded Ali, his video appearances are usually laden with images from his prime that ease the hard reality of his compromised physical condition. It is quite logical, then, that literature would be the site most effective in repackaging Ali as an icon in preparation for his return as a corporate force via visual media. It was the singular medium that didn't privilege Ali's physicality. In print, he remains as triumphant as ever, and video imagery today that harkens back to Ali's prime would not effectively confer moral authority upon him without its literary roots. Throughout the 1990s, Thomas Hauser was at the core of this process through the authorized biography and follow-up works like *Muhammad Ali in Perspective* (1996), which includes sections such as "The Importance of Muhammad Ali," and *Muhammad Ali and Company* (1998), which contains essays on such subjects as Ali's trip to Iraq to convince Saddam Hussein to forestall the first Persian Gulf War, Ali's visiting high schools to promote racial understanding, and Ali's trip to the United States Holocaust Memorial Museum.[46]

Sensing that Ali's legacy would depend in part on his literary past, Hauser savaged the champion's 1975 autobiography, *The Greatest: My Own Story*, claiming that it was mostly untrue and that Ali hadn't even read the ghostwritten work prior to its publication. Because the Ali Story presented in the autobiography was vastly different from the one Hauser offered, he had to undermine it in order to validate his own. *The Greatest* presents Ali as an uncompromising black nationalist who grew up in poverty, was distrustful of white people, and was used by the Louisville Sponsoring Group. All of these things contradicted Hauser's version of events. Furthermore, many myths about Ali that endure to this day, such as his throwing his gold medal into the Ohio River to protest segregation (he actually lost the medal), originated in *The Greatest*. Hauser claims that it was simply a matter of setting the record straight.[47]

Literary critic and essayist Gerald Early challenges this interpretation, asserting that Hauser had reason to dismiss the autobiography because his book purported to replace it. Early defends *The Greatest* not for its accuracy, but for its allegorical power, arguing that the book's meaning comes from the way it positions Ali, regardless of truth. Perhaps we should assess Hauser's book similarly. Although the material is presented as factual, its impact comes from its hagiographical representation of Ali. Its value does not lie in its truthfulness, but in the way it shapes and reflects public opinion toward Ali. In this regard, *Muhammad Ali: His Life and Times* is similar to *The Greatest: My Own Story*, despite Hauser's attempt to set them apart. The image of Herbert Muhammad signing off on every page of *The Greatest*, which Hauser uses as evidence of the book's worthlessness, resembles quite closely that of Hauser reading aloud every page of his manuscript to Lonnie and Muhammad Ali.[48]

By the turn of the century, the Ali camp had little use for Thomas Hauser and turned its back on him. Ironically, the effectiveness of Hauser's book sowed the seeds for his replacement as Ali's major media representative. While the movement to canonize Ali stemmed from and could not have happened without this literary preamble, it had to make its way into more lucrative worlds like video, television, cyberspace, retail, and brick-and-mortar structures if it were to expand into the phenomenon that exists today. Hauser maintains that "the relationship between Muhammad and myself has not changed." But he also admits that "the relationship between me and the people surrounding Muhammad has changed." Although he still sees his work to be "about finding a way that Muhammad could use his extraordinary persona to the maximum extent possible to promote tolerance and understanding between all people, and most significantly today, between America and the Islamic world," he blasts the Ali camp for commercializing the former champion. "Muhammad is uniquely able to contribute to this cause, which is far more important than selling athletic shoes. But you can't sell products for corporate America and, at the same time, sell hard truths to the world. The corporate image makers won't allow it." Rightfully or not, Hauser positions his own work not as part of, but in opposition to, a plan to recast Ali's cultural image in ways that would have commercial implications.[49]

It is tempting to dispute Hauser's explanation, however, because he became publicly critical of Ali's commercialization and skeptical of his heroic status only after the disintegration of their relationship. Hauser began early in the new century to report things about the former champion that he had overlooked or bypassed in his previous work. Perhaps disgusted by the monster he helped to create, Hauser has turned the majority of his Ali writing in recent years toward deconstructing Ali's saintly persona. In an online piece, for example, Hauser described in detail Ali's distasteful use of ethnic humor at a December 2001 fund-raiser for the Muhammad Ali Center. He also questioned Ali's growing significance as a human rights advocate: "Muhammad Ali leads best when he leads by example and by broad statements of tolerance and understanding among all people," wrote Hauser. "To ask more of him . . . is looking for trouble."[50]

The tension between Hauser and the Ali camp became public when Lonnie Ali censured him in 2003. Of course, the relationship had dissolved far earlier, as the fighter and writer hadn't spoken since 1998, and Hauser's pieces on Ali had gotten progressively more critical since then. But the latest episode made it clear to everyone that he had become persona non grata to the Ali people. It began when the publisher Taschen invited Hauser to submit an essay for one of the gaudiest displays of Ali commercialism ever witnessed, a seventy-five-pound, $4,000 coffee-table book made of ceramics, silk, and leather called *GOAT* [an acronym for "Greatest of All Time"]: *A Tribute to Muhammad Ali*. Robert Lipsyte, the former *New York Times* reporter and an acquaintance of Hauser's, explained that the author was "squeezed out of the inner circle" after Lonnie squashed his piece, which expressed discontent over the recent "soft-pedaling of Ali's early religious and social stands as well as the commercialization of his name." Hauser would eventually find homes for the commentary, first as an article in London's *Observer* and then in expanded form as a book called *The Lost Legacy of Muhammad Ali*. The thesis is that ever since "corporate America 'rediscovered' Ali . . . there has been a determined effort to rewrite history. To take advantage of Ali's economic potential, it has been deemed desirable to 'sanitize' him. And as a result, all the 'rough edges' are being filed away from Ali's life story." Hauser also accuses Ali of being a willing accomplice to this process, citing a 2002 television interview in which Ali was asked about politics and terrorism and responded, "I dodge those questions. I've opened up businesses around the country, selling products, and I don't want to say nothing and, not knowing what I'm doing, not being qualified, say the wrong thing and hurt my business." The disappointed Hauser commented, "It's hard to imagine Muhammad Ali in the 1960s withholding comment on the war in Vietnam for fear of jeopardizing his business interests."[51]

One of the more remarkable details about the evolution of Hauser's perspective toward Ali is his interest in preserving his own moral authority. By presenting Ali as compromised, Hauser reinvents himself as a lone soothsayer battling to safeguard the truth. All the others, including Ali, are sellouts looking to capitalize on the former champion's renewed importance, and Ali's cultural rejuvenation is akin to his ring comebacks: impressive on the surface but wholly lacking in substance. Yet Hauser's repositioning of his relationship to Ali is similarly misguided. Identifying Ali as a conduit between America and the Islamic world is ridiculous, considering, for example, that he accepted the Presidential Medal of Freedom from George W. Bush, whose decision to make war in Iraq antagonized Muslims worldwide. If Ali was ready for such political heavy lifting, he would have been warier of such recognition.

The ill-fated connection between Muhammad Ali and Thomas Hauser illustrates that those involved in the Ali industry are willing to reinvent themselves for profit, credibility, and moral authority. Even as the means of telling the Ali Story have changed over time, the ends have remained similar. Deception and money, as much as morality and tolerance, are at the heart of Ali's cultural re-emergence. The Ali who once falsely claimed to have thrown a gold medal into the Ohio River is not much different than the Ali who now claims to be a harbinger of world peace. Although the construction of the Ali Center and the ubiquity of visual imagery have meant a passing of the torch, the canonization of Ali as an American hero should be recognized as having a strong literary component. Some of the most powerful moments in Ali's post-boxing life, like his lighting of the Olympic torch to open the 1996 Summer Games, have been made for television. Yet without the literary context of books like the Hauser biography, the major product of such moments would have been people feeling badly for Ali. Perhaps one day, however, Ali's fall from grace will also result from his literary legacy. Hauser's more recent writing has sparked a growing backlash against the former champion, which includes such books as Mark Kram's *Ghosts of Manila: The Fateful Blood Feud between Muhammad Ali and Joe Frazier* (2001) and Jack Cashill's *Sucker Punch: The Hard Left Hook That Dazed Ali and Killed King's Dream* (2006), both of which seek to demolish any notion that Ali is worthy of the status he has achieved as an all-time moral authority.[52]

Olympic Torch

From Literature to Television

I t had been a long journey for the torch that was going to be used to ignite the cauldron signifying the start of the 1996 Summer Olympics in Atlanta. Some 10,000 people had handled and transported it 15,000 miles over the eighty-four days preceding the games. One of the most successful athletes in Olympic history, Al Oerter, who had won four consecutive gold medals in the discus throw between 1954 and 1968, carried it from just outside what is now known as Turner Field, and through the stadium's bowels before passing it on to a local favorite, boxer Evander Holyfield. Holyfield ran with the torch around the arena's track and then handed it to Janet Evans, the American gold-medal swimmer, who brought it up a steep ramp toward the cauldron, which loomed high above at the top of a winding trellis.

It appeared that Evans would have the honor of making the final run that would signal the conclusion of the opening ceremonies and the start of the games, but waiting at the top of the ramp was a special guest, ready to deliver the money shot, the moment that the National Broadcasting Company (NBC) hoped would galvanize its $456 million investment in the television rights to the event. In a surprise to all but those connected with the broadcast, amid a huge ovation, Muhammad Ali took the flame from Evans and triggered a mechanism that ignited the cauldron. Trembling and expressionless, but nonetheless a compelling figure, the champion had returned to the world stage as a pop icon. Announcer Bob Costas captured the moment: "Once the most dynamic figure in sports, a gregarious man, now trapped inside that mask created by Parkinson's syndrome. So, in one sense a poignant figure, but look at him, still a great, great presence. Still exuding nobility and stature, and the response he evokes is part affection, part excitement, but especially respect. What a moment." The Ali revolution would be televised after all.[53]

Getting Ali back on television and into the forefront of American cultural consciousness, as Costas's commentary illustrates, was something of a challenge. For an audience that was used to seeing Ali incarnated as a handsome, brash, young, loudmouthed, quick-witted, fleet-footed boxer, the reality of what he had become was sobering. Television is designed to be an entertaining escape from reality. Yet anyone watching Ali struggle to maneuver his torch was reminded that he was having severe physical difficulties, and it would be only natural for audiences to feel bad for him. The question facing the Ali camp, and corporate entities like NBC that wanted to use him for profit, was how to create narratives that would make his rediscovery palatable to viewing audiences. The Ali literary renaissance had provided the script necessary to recast him as a hero to an entire new generation, but if he were to truly catch fire, he would somehow have to be packaged for television in ways that transformed public understanding of his physical condition from a disability to yet another thing that made him great. Ali's lighting of the cauldron was the moment this process began.

Ali's handlers would also need to banish once and for all the lingering images of Ali as a member of the NOI and a black nationalist that distrusted white people. If he was to be recast as an all-American hero rather than an oppositional figure, whatever literary legacy was left by *The Greatest* would have to be put to rest. Particularly, the story about Ali throwing his gold medal into the Ohio River positioned him outside the mainstream. The story was born at a time when the Ali camp consisted primarily of Herbert Muhammad and the NOI and was exemplary of a black power moment when sticking it to whitey was in vogue. But by 1996 the tale had become a relic that no longer carried the symbolic weight it once had, in addition to being an outright phony. The time had come to set the record straight.

At halftime of the championship basketball game between the United States Dream Team and Yugoslavia, International Olympic Committee Chairman Juan Antonio Samaranch presented Ali with a gold medal to replace the one he had lost. As the crowd roared upon seeing the former champion courtside, Bob Costas clarified for fans what had really happened:

There is an apocryphal story that says that Ali, after returning from Rome as a teenager, having brought his country and himself glory, was turned away from restaurants because of segregation, faced racial slurs. That's not apocryphal, that undoubtedly happened. The story goes that in disgust, he took off his medal and threw it into the Ohio River. That is not true. The medal was simply lost. It makes a good symbolic story. It could have happened. It actually did not. But somehow the medal was misplaced. And now that situation will be rectified. Muhammad Ali, who electrified the crowd at the opening ceremony at the Olympic stadium, lighting the Olympic flame, taking the torch from Janet Evans . . . Although the Parkinson's syndrome slows his movements, leaves him virtually unable to speak, he is fully aware of everything that is going on, understands all conversations, understands this reaction, and look at the face, still handsome and smooth, at age fifty-four.

Now the world knew that Ali had not used that most patriotic of symbols, the gold medal, as a protest vehicle. He was back and ready to be marketed. The Olympic appearances successfully reintroduced Ali to television audiences and built upon the momentum that had started with Hauser's literary contributions.[54]

They also controlled proactively the damage that would have stemmed from the botched attempt to bring Ali back to television. A few months earlier, a piece had been taped for an August 4 showing on 60 *Minutes*, then the nation's highest-ranked television show, which coincided with the Olympic closing ceremonies. Although meant to be a heroic portrayal of the former champion, Ed Bradley's report on Ali was a marketing disaster. It was a classic example of how not to reintroduce Ali to the public, but it also proved to be a valuable lesson to the Ali camp. Its mistakes were never repeated by those who would try to remake Ali into a corporate entity.

The problem with the 60 *Minutes* segment was that it highlighted Ali's illness from Parkinson's syndrome without compensating for the pity it was sure to evoke from viewers used to seeing Ali in his prime. While the overall theme was that Ali was dealing with his physical problems gallantly, the piece did not come across as such, despite Bradley's opening monologue:

He called himself "The Greatest" and few argued. For a while he was, quite simply, the most recognizable person in the world. Born Cassius Clay in Louisville, Kentucky, he won his country a gold medal in boxing at the 1960 Olympics and then threw it into the Ohio River as a protest against his country's racism. At fifty-four, it is not surprising that he no longer, as he used to say, floats like a butterfly and stings like a bee. What is surprising about this most famous of all heavyweight champions who ever lived is how he has come to terms with the Parkinson's syndrome that doctors say comes from his years in the ring and by all rights should have laid him low and probably would have if he weren't Muhammad Ali.

This wasn't a bad start, but the constant emphasis on Ali's physical deterioration compromised the lesson that he was dealing with it heroically. Instead of shifting to Ali's past, as most current visual representations do, the focus remained on the hardships he was facing. While video of Ali at a memorabilia convention rolled, Bradley's voice-over explained: "Today it is increasingly difficult for him to talk. There is a constant shaking of his hands, rigid walk, sometimes a vacant stare. Still, people tend to dismiss his physical limitations and are respectful of the sometimes awkward silence that questions receive."

The middle part of Bradley's report anticipates what would eventually become the commonplace narrative that casts Ali as a mystical and godlike figure. But the 60 Minutes version does so clumsily, making him appear to be a dying man whose soul has left his body and is operating on a different plane than that of mere mortals. There are several references to Ali's seeing his good deeds—signing complimentary autographs, praying, making charity pilgrimages to impoverished areas of the world—as a means for him to get into heaven. It would be only natural for a viewer to be more concerned for his well-being than convinced of his transcendence. On the other hand, there are also some great illustrations of how Ali is still able to conjure up his own special brand of charisma under debilitating circumstances: doing magic tricks that impressed Fidel Castro, maintaining business interests that at the time earned him almost $1 million annually, and, in a beautiful and hilarious moment, convincing Bradley that he suffered from a sleep disorder that caused him to throw punches while unconscious.

Bradley's unsuccessful attempt to interview Ali at the end of the segment could have been disastrous to the former fighter's future currency as a corporate pitchman. Seated under the television lights, Ali backed out at the last minute after hearing Bradley's first question. "Can't do it," he said and walked off camera. Clearly shaken, Bradley explained to viewers that Ali didn't want his speech impediment to make people feel sorry for him, but that was exactly what the scene accomplished. Despite all the heroic rhetoric about Ali's ability to cope with his illness like the champion of old, the moment proved that he was having trouble coming to terms with his physical state.

In their attempt to undo the prevailing sadness, the final scenes wind up exacerbating the pathos. Asked about the situation, Lonnie Ali says, "I think he is very aware of how he sounds, and coming from where Muhammad came from, the Louisville Lip, and being as audible and as boastful as he used to be when he was boxing. I mean, he was always talking. And now to have a problem with his voice and speaking, I think it bothers him a great deal." To the follow-up question asking whether the former champ was embarrassed by his condition, Lonnie replied, "I would say yes, to some degree he is." Although the final images of the piece show Ali hitting a heavy bag in a manner that suggests he could knock out any regular person standing in the way of his punch, they are drowned out by Lonnie Ali's last words. Although meant to convince viewers of her husband's well-being, Lonnie's statement sounded more like something that someone would utter about a terminally ill relative eking out his final years in an assisted-living facility: "Muhammad is very well taken care of. He is a very independent individual, probably always will be until the day he dies. He makes his own decisions. He's not destitute. There are people who are more deserving of the public's sympathy than Muhammad. Muhammad is a happy man."[55]

The *60 Minutes* piece did not abort the Ali television revolution; actually, it wound up helping it. When an advance copy of the segment landed in the hands of Dick Ebersol, the president of NBC Sports, it inspired him to push for Ali to become the centerpiece of his network's coverage of the Summer Olympics. Ali's surprise emergence at the opening ceremonies was a made-for-television event, as evidenced by the intrigue surrounding negotiations to bring him on board. About a fortnight beforehand, he flew to Atlanta for a secret, pre-dawn rehearsal. Then, to fool those who might be suspicious of his presence in the city around the time of the Olympics, Ali returned about a week later to attend a United States Olympic Committee dinner. This visit gave him an excuse for being in town if anyone asked what he was doing there. Howard Bingham accompanied Ali, serving as the Ali's camp's representative. His job was to make sure that NBC would not aggravate the damage that was potentially looming as a result of the *60 Minutes* telecast. After Ali agreed to take part in the production, both he and Bingham signed confidentiality agreements to ensure that the event would have maximum impact.[56]

The deal culminated Ebersol's six months of lobbying real estate lawyer Billy Payne, who as chairman of the Atlanta Committee for the Olympic Games had final say on who would light the cauldron. Payne favored Evander Holyfield, the Atlanta native, evangelical Christian, and former world heavyweight champion, for the honor. "Billy didn't have a real fundamental appreciation of Ali beyond his being a boxer, and about his life now. Billy wanted to know what he represented now," said Ebersol. In an effort to change his mind, Ebersol sent Payne a campaign package that included the *60 Minutes* piece. But the segment raised doubts about whether Ali was an appropriate choice and whether he was physically up to the role. Payne, along with Don Mishner, the executive director of the opening ceremonies, met with Howard Bingham to discuss Ali's condition. "They wanted to know if Ali physically

could do it," said Bingham. "I told them Ali can do anything he wants to do."
Ebersol added, "Muhammad knew how it was going to be lit, that he wouldn't
have to run up any stairs," as was customary for many people in that position
to do. Ali, too, had doubts. "Initially, Muhammad had reservations about doing it because he doesn't like the image he projects on television and he realized that billions of people around the world would see him. But then he also
realized this was a way to help deliver his message of tolerance and understanding," said Thomas Hauser. Believing that it was his moral duty to accept
the honor, Ali anticipated the symbolic benefits of his participation: "Man-
kind coming together. Martin Luther King's home. Muslims seeing me with
the torch."[57]

It was a critical moment for the legacy of Muhammad Ali, marking his
evolution from public figure to icon. The responses to Ali's selection and the
event's execution were overwhelmingly positive, triggering a new and uplifting surge of affection toward him. George Vecsey of the *New York Times*
wrote, "Muhammad Ali floats above the Summer Games, no longer an elusive butterfly but a great glowing icon as large as a spaceship. He casts his
light on every athlete, every spectator, every volunteer, all the people who
walk these humid streets with just a little more zip in their step, now that
they have seen Ali." For those who had been wondering what had become of
Ali, or were troubled by rumors that he was dying, this moment was comfort-
ing. Certainly, Vecsey noticed, there was trepidation among the viewing audience: "Nobody wanted Ali to be remembered as the weakened legend who
dropped the Olympic torch in front of billions of people around the world. . . .
Hang on to the torch, Ali. That's what we said in my section." Ali's overcom-
ing his physical problems to complete the task at hand translated into a sign
of his transcendent moral authority, his ability to bring the races together, and
his symbolizing the infinite possibilities of life:

> Putting him on that platform was a stroke of genius that transformed
> a very nice ceremony into a celebration, a block party. I was sitting
> with a black male colleague and a white female colleague, and when
> we saw Ali shining on that platform, we exchanged high-fives at the
> audacious perfection of it. Ali was at the Games. Ali was on the hill.
> Raise the flame. Float like a butterfly, sting like a bee, all of us.

Even President Bill Clinton, on hand to declare an official start to the games,
was deeply moved when he saw the former champ. Embracing him, he said,
"They didn't tell me who would light the flame, but when I saw it was you, I
cried." Yes, Ali still invoked pity in some people, but overall, his ability to do
himself proud despite obstacles was seen as inspirational. That he had

achieved yet another unlikely victory, as he had against Liston and Foreman, brought a sense of hope to people. This sentiment would eventually be harnessed at the center of a 2004 advertising campaign by the sneaker company Adidas. The ad featured Ali and the tagline, "Impossible is nothing."[58]

Over a decade later, the impact of Ali's Olympic moment endures. The sports television network ESPN recently declared it the eighth most memorable moment in the past twenty-five years of sports. The event solidified Ali's standing as a moral force and American hero, a representative of his country on the world stage. During the next ten years, Ali received an avalanche of honors recognizing his national and international significance. In 1998, he was given the United Nations Messenger of Peace award. In Atlanta three years later, he became the initial torchbearer in the months-long processional that would culminate in the lighting of the cauldron to open the 2002 Olympic Games in Salt Lake City. In 2005, he traveled to Singapore to represent New York's campaign to host the 2012 Summer Games. Michael Bloomberg, the city's mayor, referenced Ali's Olympic past in a press statement:

> We are deeply honored that Muhammad Ali [is] part of the New York delegation in Singapore for the IOC [International Olympic Committee] Host City election. In 1996, Muhammad Ali's courageous lighting of the Olympic cauldron was one of the most powerful displays of the Olympic spirit ever. We are forever in awe of this great man who transcends all divides and touches us all. His athletic ability, indomitable spirit and grace have been an inspiration to tens of millions around the world.

The cauldron lighting proved that Muhammad Ali, if used correctly, was a powerful force that could drive the most important of made-for-television events. NBC had taken a huge financial gamble by using him, and its investment paid off royally. Over the next decade, Ali's career as an endorser, built around the themes of morality, inspiration, achievement, and perseverance, would reach unprecedented heights. In the meantime, his literary legacy was also evolving, as the notion of Ali as moral authority was developing into something far greater, the idea of Ali as godlike.[59]

Beyond Moral Authority

The Apotheosis of Muhammad Ali

By the onset of the new millennium, the idea that Ali was an otherworldly, divine mystic possessed of superpowers came into vogue among his biographers, admirers, cultural emissaries, and partners in commerce. The inkling has been floating around the culture for almost fifty years. Malcolm X had injected a significant amount of religious symbolism into Ali's title victory over Sonny Liston, as evidenced by the fighter telling the world during his post-fight interview, "I talk to God every day." While fighting for his life during his first match with Joe Frazier, he beseeched his implacable foe, "Don't you know I'm God?" Bundini Brown compared Ali to Jesus Christ and referred to him as a prophet during the buildup to his bout with George Foreman, as seen in *When We Were Kings*. It had usually been the Ali camp, or Ali himself, who floated this notion, but as the new century arrived, it became commonplace for people to perceive Ali as a supernatural force, as something more than just human.

As has been the case for the vast majority of meaning that has been made of Ali over the past two decades, the idea was rooted in literature. And as usual, it was driven by the work of Thomas Hauser, particularly his 1996 book *Healing: A Journal of Tolerance and Understanding*, for which Ali is somehow credited with co-authorship. It is a very peculiar volume. Other than an introductory essay framed in typical Hauserian fashion as "part of a multi-dimensional, international campaign to combat bigotry and prejudice," the book contains almost no material. It is really not much more than a glossy, illustrated planner consisting of page after page containing a single quotation and enough blank space to write grocery lists, recipes, or, I suppose, one's plans for ridding the world of bigotry and prejudice. The quotations emanate from philosophers, writers, religious texts, world leaders, and public figures. Whether it is unsettling to include Ali among this group depends on one's cultural orientation, but it was certainly a product of a particular historical moment to sell the former champion by positioning him alongside the likes of Seneca, Aristotle, Cicero, Voltaire, Thomas Jefferson, John Donne, Ralph Waldo Emerson, Henry David Thoreau, Walt Whitman, Leo Tolstoy, Frederick the Great, William Penn, Napoleon Bonaparte, Elizabeth Cady Stanton, Mark Twain, George Bernard Shaw, Albert Einstein, Frederick Douglass, W. E. B. Du Bois, Eleanor, Franklin, and Theodore Roosevelt, Martin Luther King, John F. Kennedy, Malcolm X, Pearl Buck, and James Baldwin. Quotes by Ali and, unbelievably, Hauser, close the volume. And if Ali's placement among such world-historical figures wasn't enough, Hauser's quote on the back cover pushes things over the top: "I look at this man and I say to myself, 'God is trying to tell us something.'" With a little literary license, Ali goes from human being to the lord's envoy.[60]

Over the next few years there emerged a book cycle thematically bound by author testimony that Ali has been sent from the heavens. Perhaps the most egregious of them was *The Tao of Muhammad Ali: A True Story* (1996) by Davis Miller. The author's note is a classic example of the genre:

> We struggle. Always. We are doing the best that we can. And we dream of transcendence. For me, there was a time when the dream was incarnate. And the dream's name was Muhammad Ali. This is the story of my time spent with that dream. Although the narrative is not always historically accurate, and although some chronology and numerous details have been changed for dramatic effect, it is, in essence, true.

There were also two books by Ali's daughter Hana, a product of his marriage to Veronica Porche. Her literary debut, *More Than a Hero: Muhammad Ali's Life Lessons Presented through His Daughter's Eyes* (2000), consists of typical Ali stories that foreground his sacred status—helping the homeless, dispensing wisdom, making people laugh, telling parables. "He's a prophet, a messenger of God, an angel," she writes more than once. "Throughout my life, there has never been one moment that the presence of my father's angelic soul has gone uncherished. He is a gift from God," reads another passage. Ali himself buys into the notion when he tells her, "[Y]ou're my daughter, so God takes extra care of you." A follow-up book called *The Soul of a Butterfly: Reflections on Life's Journey* (2004) provides more of the same.[61]

With the deification of Ali floating around the literary zeitgeist for a few years, the theme took hold in more blatantly commercialized forms such as television programs and advertising campaigns by the turn of the century. The most glaring example was the May 9, 1999, episode of the top-ten-rated, hour-long, primetime network television drama *Touched by an Angel*. The show, which ran for nine seasons and starred Della Reese, usually operated formulaically: a person facing a crossroads would be assisted by the main characters, who were angels sent from heaven to earth in human form to carry out God's will.

The Ali episode tells the story of an eleven-year-old boy named Tim, who lives in a run-down apartment with a loathsome older brother and an abusive uncle. Tim's life outside the home isn't much better, as bullies harass him constantly. In a last-ditch effort to preserve his dignity by learning to defend himself, the boy wanders into a boxing gym, where the angels are not coincidentally working as trainers. As the boy develops his skills, he becomes drawn to a poster on the gym wall featuring Muhammad Ali. One of the angels/trainers explains to him that Ali achieved true greatness not through boxing, but because he followed God's word and refused to kill people during the Vietnam War, even though he knew it would cost him his championship. The episode climaxes when Tim takes on one of the bullies in an amateur bout and emerges victorious. During the ensuing celebration, one of the angels produces Muhammad Ali, who appears in the ring to congratulate the boy. Knowing that the former champion is unable to speak, one of the angels relays Ali's message that Tim must now fight to save his family. Tim takes the directive to heart and goes home to confront his uncle, who realizes the error of his ways. Along with the older brother, the three reconcile and make peace, vowing to live more morally in the future.[62]

While the episode slightly twists the theme of Ali as godlike, since he is in human form throughout and the angels are the actual divine envoys, the representation of Ali as a supernatural agent of healing, introduced by Hauser three years earlier, is obvious. The angels purposefully draft him into service because they have never been children and therefore need a human being to handle this particular case. Furthermore, the angels read poetry to young Tim in order to teach him the importance of family, an obvious tip of the hat to the former champ. In essence, Ali is as powerful as the angels, if not more so, since they use his methods and person to accomplish things that they cannot. Regardless of the hierarchy, the point here is that Ali's running with the angels sets him apart from mere mortals. He is at the very least divinely inspired.

The other key text that deserves mention is the advertisement for the online company WebMD.com that aired during the Super Bowl in January

2000. The commercial, which featured Ali shadowboxing, is significant for two reasons. First, that the then-fledgling company's choice of Ali as its representative on what is perhaps the world's most expensive advertising platform illustrates the company's faith in him as a corporate pitchman. Even with millions of dollars on the line, Ali has emerged as a rock-solid endorser. Second, the decision to feature Ali performing athletically, even as he suffers from Parkinson's, reinforces his position as a transcendent figure of healing not bound by mortal constraints. That a Web site devoted to "Better information. Better health" would choose someone as famously ill as Ali as its representative emphasizes his godlike status.

Culture Meets Commerce

The Muhammad Ali Center, Naming
Rights, and the Price of Moral Authority

Without a doubt, the climax of the Ali renaissance that began in 1991 with the publication of Thomas Hauser's biography was the opening of the $80 million, 93,000-square-foot Muhammad Ali Center in downtown Louisville near the banks of the Ohio River. The major themes that had been developing around Ali during a fifteen-year period, most important of which was the idea of Ali as a moral authority, dramatically came to fruition with the opening of this shrine in November 2005.

Anyone walking through downtown Louisville could not miss that the city is Ali's hometown. There are signs everywhere touting the relationship, most notably headshots of the former champ flying high above lampposts and welcoming visitors along major avenues. There is also an important thorough-fare, the former Walnut Street now called Muhammad Ali Boulevard, named in his honor. The Muhammad Ali Center is the blue-chip showpiece of Louisville's investment in its favorite son, and it rests on a $10 million parcel of downtown riverfront property that was donated by the city.[63]

Unlike so many past ventures bearing his name, the Muhammad Ali Center is no fly-by-night operation. Its backers are among America's corporate blue chips, including Ford Motor Company, General Electric, and Yum! Brands. In addition to having an official partnership with the United Nations, the Ali Center has an advisory council filled with heavy hitters. Topped by the Dalai Lama, it also includes poet Maya Angelou, rock star Bono, rapper/entrepreneur Sean Combs, sportscaster Bob Costas, comedian Billy Crystal, former politician Mario Cuomo, television executive Dick Ebersol, president of the Carnegie Corporation of New York Vartan Gregorian, actress Angelina Jolie, record producer Quincy Jones, talk show host Larry King, entertainment mogul Jerry Perenchio, television reporter Diane Sawyer, talk show host Tavis Smiley, and comedian Robin Williams. This truly remarkable group, in addition to the various corporate heads and giants of philanthropy who sit on the Ali Center's board of directors, is testimony to how deeply entrenched the Ali legacy has become in our culture. Indeed, the Center, whose slogan urges visitors to "Find Greatness Within," reflects an all-out campaign to institutionalize the Ali legacy not only among corporate juggernauts and society's beautiful people, but also within the hearts and minds of individual citizens through their self-identification with the former champion.

The official literature of the Muhammad Ali Center builds upon the many ideas—the most important of which are those emphasizing Ali's moral authority—that had initially been revived by the Ali literature near the end of the twentieth century. The most telling texts produced by the Center are its purpose/mission statement, and the press releases defining its background, identity, function, and goals:

Purpose/Mission Statement

Serving as an international education and communications center that is inspired by the ideals of its visionary founder Muhammad Ali, the Muhammad Ali Center is a place that carries on Ali's legacy and inspires exploration of the greatness within ourselves. The Ali Center's innovative and immersive visitor experience, educational and public programming, and global initiatives carry on Muhammad's legacy and continue his life's work. Much more than a place that tells the story of one man's journey, the Ali Center reaches beyond its physical walls to fulfill its mission: To preserve and share the legacy and ideals of Muhammad Ali, to promote respect, hope, and understanding, and to inspire adults and children everywhere to be as great as they can be.

Background

Muhammad Ali's legacy is multifaceted. And his story is one of inspiration that touches individuals across the globe—regardless of one's age, ethnicity, religion, or culture. Ali has lived his life in accordance with his ideals and values. These values have guided him through the hard work necessary to be the best athlete he could be, and have given him the strength and courage throughout his life to stand up for what he believes. These values have inspired the work that he has dedicated himself to since he retired from the ring—encouraging peace, respect, and healing, and doing all he can to help children around the world.

Who We Are

The Muhammad Ali Center is both a destination site and an international education and cultural center that is inspired by the ideals of its founder Muhammad Ali. The Ali Center's innovative exhibits, educational and public programming, and global initiatives carry on Muhammad's legacy and inspire exploration of the greatness within ourselves. Much more than a place that tells the story of one man's journey, the Ali Center reaches beyond its physical walls to fulfill its mission. Like Muhammad Ali himself, the Ali Center focuses on what brings individuals together, not what sets them apart. We are a "global gathering place" where people come—both online and in person—to learn, share, celebrate our commonalities as human beings, and formulate ways of advancing humanity today and in the future. Ultimately, the Muhammad Ali Center's goal is to make a profoundly significant contribution to the global society.

What We Do

The Muhammad Ali Center's objectives focus on both educational outreach and a non-traditional visitor experience. Educational goals include various delivery methods and incorporate a wide range of topics from respect, diversity, and personal discovery to empowerment and conflict resolution. The on-site visitor experience incorporates as organizing elements, six prevailing core values of Ali's life: *respect, confidence, conviction, dedication, giving,* and *spirituality.* Through these theme-based pavilions, visitors can participate in a variety of interactive environments that parallel Ali's steps to personal greatness and challenge visitors to find the greatness within themselves. Some experiences affect participants on a deep emotional level and others are pure fun, energy, and excitement. All feature dramatic presentations that help illustrate the "how's" of Ali's life: how he found the courage, the dedication, and the discipline to become who he is today . . . how he found the conviction to stand up for what he believed . . . and how he turned his passion for excellence in the ring to a passion for peace on the world stage.

The official Ali Center literature is bound by themes that germinated within the Ali literary renaissance and have become fundamental to most people's understanding of him. Although stylistically and technologically it is a forward-reaching medium, the Muhammad Ali Center looks backward to prior written work in order to frame Ali according to certain ideological tenets. They are (1) Muhammad Ali is a dignified man of great moral authority, as evidenced by his lifelong core values of respect, confidence, conviction, dedication, giving, and spirituality; (2) Muhammad Ali is a unifying and healing force of tolerance and love, a symbolic and living example of how humanity should respond to diversity, and a medium through which people can transform the world into a better place by finding greatness via Ali and within themselves; and (3) Muhammad Ali is an inspiration whose significance comes from his good works and his positive effect on other people.[64]

Also like those of its literary predecessors, the evidentiary standards by which the Muhammad Ali Center evaluates Ali's greatness are based upon hagiographical interview testimony. As within the Hauser biography, Ali's greatness is presented as a function of people asserting his greatness. The exhibits purporting Ali's greatness are collections of images and opinions that present Ali in a positive light, and visitors are invited to see visual proof of his extraordinary nature. Such proof includes direct testimony and anecdotes by famous and ordinary people who have been touched positively by Ali, as well as official confirmations of his greatness, such as photographs of him receiving the Presidential Medal of Freedom and of him holding court with the Dalai Lama. The museum is also packed with images of Ali performing good deeds around the world. If the Hauser book could be incarnated into a structure, it would be the Muhammad Ali Center.

Because of the Muhammad Ali Center's vulnerability to criticism on account of its hagiographical nature and its unrelentingly positive coverage of the former champion, its creators have taken steps to assure patrons that it is an honest and objective site guided by the same moral authority as its namesake. At the main entranceway, where patrons first step into the Ali Center, there is prominent signage that declares:

> For more than 40 years, sportswriters, newsmen and biographers have told Ali's story from many angles. The Center conveys that story differently, through chapters that preserve Muhammad Ali's ideas and principles. Honest storytelling is supported by careful research and shaped by a concern for balance, integrity and accuracy.

Although the mission statement and other official literature do little to hide the founders' affection for Ali, the Muhammad Ali Center also tries to convince people that it truthfully represents his life. It never explicitly admits to serving a purely celebratory function.

There is no doubt, however, that the Muhammad Ali Center gives short shrift to those who don't share its vision, marginalizing and dehumanizing dissenting points of view. The museum's exhibits rarely discuss how Ali has veered—as he sometimes has—from his supposed core tenets of respect, confidence, conviction, dedication, giving, and spirituality. And when it does address such issues, it hardly ever attributes criticism of Ali to anyone in particular. There is no direct reference, for example, to the bitter nature of the rivalry between Ali and Joe Frazier. Instead, there is only vague mention of Ali's sometimes insulting his opponents. There are no names or faces attached to such criticisms of Ali, his history, and his place in society; we never get a sense of who might have been wronged by him and why they feel that way. While the Ali Center does not completely ignore those with dissenting points of view, it deals with them aggressively and proactively in ways that render them ineffective. In the photo-textual exhibit on Ali's core tenet of respect, for example, the museum has this to say:

> When Ali felt disrespected, he lashed out. His public views on "white devils," black superiority, and the status of women were anything but respectful. His loudmouth antics sold fight tickets but insulted opponents and many fans who didn't appreciate the sometimes cruel humor. Did Ali believe everything he said? People close to him say he didn't, and back their claims with examples. Muhammad Ali's journey of respect was one of personal growth, change, and maturation.

The Center also features predominantly a quote by Ali stating, "A man who views the world the same at fifty as he did at twenty has wasted thirty years of his life." The implications are obvious. Ali may have said and done bad things in the past, but he didn't mean them, and now he is above such things anyhow, so even if they happened, they are no longer relevant.[65]

At the core of the museum's message is the same rhetoric of equality and brotherhood that marked the early civil rights movement, when leaders were hopeful that morality would one day neutralize racial discrimination. The Ali Center holds a similarly utopian message. The assertion that rings throughout its halls is that if we all act as Muhammad Ali does, then diversity might one day cease being an impediment to equality, and we might be able to fully enjoy its benefits. While the Ali Center reaches back to Ali's draft resistance as a key qualification that indelibly marks him as a representative of the civil rights era, it is actually his battle with Parkinson's syndrome that ultimately carries the representational weight of his strength and morality. Ali's graceful fight in the face of serious medical issues is an underlying theme within the Ali Center and a series of recent advertising campaigns. This fight serves as a stand-in for virtually any struggle, whether with race, poverty, or disability. Even those battlegrounds upon which Ali took a less-than-progressive stand throughout his life, such as gender and homosexuality, are now presented as within his purview of healing.

In addition to bearing the fruits of the literary movement to sanctify him, the Muhammad Ali Center brings to light themes that have characterized Ali's public life and career for nearly fifty years. At its heart, it represents the merger of culture and commerce. While preserving Muhammad Ali's cultural legacy, the Muhammad Ali Center also furthers the commercial interests that accompany his iconic status. Not only does the center institutionalize and advance Ali's apotheosis, but it also caters to a fan base upon which its founders, advisers, and backers can capitalize. It provides a permanent and lasting headquarters from which to develop further commercial endeavors, since any failed venture, even one that potentially compromises Ali's moral authority, can be explained away within its walls. The Muhammad Ali Center is a propaganda vehicle whose existence will serve to clean up any mess that may come along to threaten its founders' version of the Ali Story. It is evidence of the Ali camp's masterful understanding of the relationships between moral authority and money.

The opening of the Muhammad Ali Center reinforced the Ali family's influence on the fighter's legacy. Cementing the future of Ali's cultural image gave them license to exploit their investment in it. In April 2006, Lonnie and Muhammad Ali reached an agreement with the entertainment firm CKX Inc. to sell for $50 million an 80 percent share in the fighter's name, image, and likeness, as well as the rights to all of his licensing agreements and some of his trademarks. The price of moral authority, which rather than athletic ability is now key to marketing the Ali name, is high. It is unclear whether the 20 percent portion retained by the Ali family gives them any veto over advertising campaigns stemming from this agreement, but it might not matter anyway, because as long as the Ali Center exists, it will serve as a counterweight to any negative publicity that might become associated with its namesake.

Even before this deal, Ali was a valuable commodity. In the five years prior to the agreement, the trademark and licensing businesses surrounding him had produced annual revenues between $4 million and $7 million. But the agreement earned Ali elite status. In 2004 CKX paid the Elvis Presley estate $100 million for a similar deal, and the following year it paid $174 million to acquire 19 Entertainment, whose holdings include the top-ranked *American Idol* television show. It wasn't even the largest endorsement deal ever offered a boxer; in 1999 the appliance company Salton paid George Foreman and his partners $137.5 million over five years for the right to use Foreman's name on cooking equipment, most notably the George Foreman Lean, Mean, Fat-Reducing Grilling Machine. Nevertheless, it was huge.

Although for a long time he has been one of the world's most recognizable figures, Ali's marketing value had never reached this magnitude. At the peak of his boxing skills, his membership in the NOI pre-empted most commercial possibilities, but even after he defeated George Foreman to regain the title there was no explosion of endorsements. His influence as a pitchman is stronger now than ever, thanks to the series of narratives that have successfully updated his profile from champion boxer to moral authority.

The size of the naming-rights deal surprised observers. Among commentators, two currents of opinion emerged. Carol Slezak of the *Chicago Sun-Times* reacted to the agreement as Ali's ultimate sellout, the corruption of a man once motivated by principle over money: "Not only did Muhammad Ali sell out, but he signed with the Elvis guys. How long before the first Ali mugs roll off an assembly line, headed for a Wal-Mart near you? How long before construction gets under way on Muhammadland, which surely will rival Graceland in tackiness? How long before Ali becomes yet another cheesy symbol of Americana?" The other school of thought, which has emerged as the more prevalent one, celebrated the deal as a form of justice and the rightful payoff to a man who once sacrificed untold millions to uphold his principles. As Kevin Blackistone of the *Dallas Morning News* wrote, "After he was robbed, as the Supreme Court's ruling proved, of his right to earn who knows how much during his forced exile from boxing, it is only fitting that this opportunity would drop into Ali's lap: an easy, not uneasy, payday. It was long overdue."[66]

What is strange about both readings of the situation is that they indicate the belief that Ali's business decision, one way or another, represents a break from the past. Nowhere is the understanding that this most recent venture is just another move by Ali to balance his carefully constructed cultural image with his financial interests. Ali has never been either a pure capitalist or a pure idealist. From the beginning, his career has been a negotiation between the two, rather than one or the other. Indeed, statements attributed to both Ali ("This relationship with CKX will help guarantee that, for generations to come, people of all nations will understand my beliefs and my purpose.") and his new managers ("Mr. Ali, together with his wife, Lonnie Ali, is expected to actively work with CKX to continue to promote his cultural and philosophical legacy throughout the world.") indicate their understanding of this phenomenon, even as observers misinterpret it.[67]

The Ali family and the people they have entrusted to market him realize that his strength as an endorser is based not on his relationship to given products but on the moral authority he brings to them. Ali's achieving such eminence is cumulatively built upon a lifetime of shifting meanings that have swirled about him, from fun-loving kid to black militant to anti-war figure to great boxer to disabled person. All of these identities have informed the current deification of Ali. Ali's endurance as a legendary cultural figure and relevant commercial player looks both backward to his boxing greatness and association with the civil rights era and forward to his current role as a figure of healing, love, tolerance, and never-ending possibilities.

The marketing of Ali prior to the signing of the naming-rights deal illustrates the contemporary standard of mixing past and present to produce an inspirational message. The three biggest advertising campaigns that Ali has participated in are Apple's "Think Different" campaign, Adidas's "Impossible is Nothing" campaign, and IBM's Linux "The Future is Open" campaign. Apple's turn-of-the-century "Think Different" commercials featured Ali shadowboxing and rapping in a clip from *When We Were Kings*. Adidas's "Impossible is Nothing" ads began in 2004. Another *When We Were Kings* clip rolls, although the Africans in the movie are replaced via computer-generated imaging by a multicultural group of joggers who accompany Ali on his roadwork. The voice-over plays:

> Some people listen to themselves, rather than listen to what others say. These people don't come around very often. But when they do, they remind us that once you set out on a path, even though critics may doubt you, it's OK to believe that there is no can't, won't, or impossible. They remind us that it's OK to believe impossible is nothing.

IBM's Linux "The Future is Open" commercial first aired during the 2004 Super Bowl. It shows a young boy watching TV highlights of Ali's rant after his first victory over Liston. The older Ali then joins him and counsels in person, "Shake things up," "Shake up the world," "Speak your mind," "Don't back down." All of these advertisements share the common theme that anything is possible with the moral authority that comes from Ali-associated core tenets such as confidence, dedication, and conviction. The selling of Ali's naming rights was a bold and shrewd stroke by the Ali family. It allowed them to maximize the value of Ali's moral authority, but it did so in a way that allowed them to retain considerable de facto control over his cultural image. It is doubtful that CKX will stray far from the Ali Center's model of representation. It is also difficult to imagine the public's turning against Ali or losing interest in him, even after his death, although there are people who feel that the whole Ali renaissance has been misguided.[68]

The Backlash

Exploring Contradictory Meanings of Ali

To a small band of dissenters, it is ludicrous that Muhammad Ali has become an American hero. They believe that Ali's achieving iconic status signifies a misguided society. Although few in number, and mostly without the cultural and commercial backing that has often accompanied works trumpeting forth Ali's glories, these critics have formed the literary and cultural backbone of a nascent backlash against Muhammad Ali. Surprisingly, they are not the types generally associated with the majority that once was hostile to Ali as a draft-dodging loudmouth. They are people who once admired Ali's anti-war stance and felt that he was exiled from boxing unjustly but are now troubled by his elevation to iconic status. The most extreme example is Thomas Hauser, who went from Ali's spokesman to outspoken critic, but there are others, like Robert Lipsyte, who fit this profile as well. The problem that members of this group usually have with Ali is either (1) that he was once legitimately heroic, and therefore the watered-down version of him now fed to the public is a lost opportunity to make the world a better place, or (2) that his image is hypocritical because he does not live up to, and never really has, the qualities that are attributed to him.[69]

The more common position that critics like Mark Kram and Jack Cashill have taken is that hypocrisy saturates our current perception of Ali as a purveyor of love, tolerance, and other heroic or godlike attributes. They believe that his image is at odds with reality, even as they admit that Ali has many good qualities. But they question why his darker side has been airbrushed from recent narratives that influence his impact on our culture. Ali's toughest critics, like Joe Frazier, whom Ali verbally savaged in hyping their three bouts, explicitly attack Ali as a demented character. Others merely point out instances in which Ali has not lived up to his reputation.

Certainly, there are hundreds of examples of Ali's behavior directly refuting the terms of his heroism as defined by sources like the Hauser biography and the Muhammad Ali Center. For all of the fanfare that heralds Ali as a figure of understanding, tolerance, and grace in the face of adversity, there are plenty of counter-narratives to challenge it. In this regard, it is vital to mention that those who would now position themselves as truth-seekers wanting to expose the real Ali were once his advocates. It would be silly to hold up Ali's NOI-driven statements from over thirty years ago about whites being devils as representative of his inability to represent tolerance today. People change, and Ali left the NOI. Therefore, it is no contradiction for him to serve as a world representative despite not living up to such an image in the past. Criticisms of Ali have no traction if they apply standards from decades ago to today's reality. Most of the Ali critics do not fall into this trap. It is not Ali's past conduct that troubles them or that they see as hypocritical, but the Ali of today that they judge as failing to make the grade. Granted, there is not a total separation between the Ali of the past and the present, despite the Muhammad Ali Center's best efforts to create one, but it is important for criticisms of Ali to be currently reasonable. Bashing someone's behavior of thirty years ago in order to make a point about his or her lack of goodness today is generally unconvincing. At the same time, however, there is something of a linkage between Ali's past and present, since so much of his current legacy is built upon what he did in his prime. Nevertheless, the Ali iconoclasts are on their most solid ground when they correspond Ali's behavior in the 1990s and twenty-first century to his portrayal as a hero during the same period. The least effective attempts to disparage the notion of Ali as great happen when people use past behavior to indict his current status.

It is something of a courageous position to challenge the hegemony that Muhammad Ali is a hero, and it is often difficult to get an audience sufficient enough to make broadcasting that position worthwhile. There is a relatively small market of people interested in reading about how Americans have been duped into thinking that Ali is great. Especially now, as Ali's alignment with powerful and wealthy corporate sponsors grows stronger, and the dissemination of his heroic image is tied to profits, those who wish to challenge such notions have to battle for airtime. And once they have gotten a public voice, these dissenters have been subject to backlashes of their own from those who would defend the good Ali name. Although it has been a marginal position to challenge Ali's current status, it is one that has been growing stronger over the years. While it is doubtful that Americans at large will do an about-face and rethink Ali to the point that he once again becomes widely disdained, it is worth studying the evolution of the nascent trend that would back such action. Why have people challenged Ali's rebirth?

Without putting them into context, let me present two examples of Ali's behavior contradicting his hype as a figure of tolerance. It is important to also point out, however, that these examples should not be perceived as wholesale indictments of Ali's reincarnation as a hero. Rather, they are chinks in the armor of perfection being ushered forth by his corporate sponsors and by Lonnie Ali. One of the mistakes that some of the Ali critics make is taking a small contradiction between Ali's behavior and his heroic billing and then trying to use it as a grand indictment of everything good Ali supposedly represents. On the other hand, I think it is safe to say that readers who are used to seeing and hearing Ali described in a certain way will be somewhat surprised by these images.

Example one: Ali ventures to North Korea during 1995, where he and a number of other Americans meet with a group of North Korean officials. When these luminaries begin speaking about the moral superiority and military strength of their country, Ali turns to his American peers and declares, "No wonder we hate these motherfuckers." Example two: At a 2001 fund-raiser for the Ali Center, Ali steps up to the dais and asks the crowd, "What's the difference between a Jew and a canoe?" The answer: "A canoe tips." Ali follows that one up with the question, "A black, a Puerto Rican, and a Mexican are in a car. Who's driving?" Answer: "The police." An Ali Center spokesperson claimed that Ali told the jokes to shock people and make a point, although she was unclear about what that point was. While situations like this are hardly enough to make the walls of the Ali Center come tumbling down, they illustrate that there is more to him than what is being presented within them. This is exactly the type of nuance and detail that the best critical assessments of the Ali legend explore. When Ali speaks, things come out differently than when his official representatives do. Similarly, his critics focus on such issues as Ali's mistreatment of Joe Frazier, his philandering, his profligacy, his choosing to side with Elijah Muhammad instead of Malcolm X, his anti-white statements during the 1960s and 1970s, his financial partnerships with criminals and scam artists during the 1980s, and that he fought too long, all of which are at the heart of the most recent cycle of books declaring the Ali legacy to be a farcical and artificial construct.[70]

So what will become of this backlash? Ali's fans outnumber his antagonists, but it is impossible to predict the future. Perhaps it is best to once more look backward, to an editorial from May 4, 1967, in the black newspaper the *St. Louis American*. The editorial, titled "Time Could Do for Muhammad Ali What It Did for Jack Demps[e]y," reasoned that it would be foolish to predict that the then-current backlash against Ali for his draft resistance would endure forever. Dempsey had been similarly demonized as a slacker during World War I but wound up a popular figure. The editorial board wrote presciently, "Another fifty years may do as much for Muhammad Ali as it has done for Jack Dempsey. Really, who knows what is 'right' and what is 'not right' through these muddled times?" These words hold true today. While it seems doubtful that America's love affair with Muhammad Ali will end anytime soon, it was equally doubtful forty years ago that he would ever attain the hallowed status he currently enjoys. In another forty years, who knows what will happen? You never can tell.[71]

Notes

PART I

1. Clay quoted in Thomas Hauser, *Muhammad Ali: His Life and Times* (New York: Simon & Schuster, 1991), 28.

2. David Remnick, *King of the World: Muhammad Ali and the Rise of an American Hero* (New York: Random House, 1998), 81–98.

3. Bettye Collier-Thomas and V.P. Franklin, *My Soul Is a Witness: A Chronology of the Civil Rights Era, 1954–1965* (New York: Henry Holt, 1999), 189; Remnick, *King of the World*, 81–98.

4. Earl Ruby, "Clay Wins Gold Medal in Olympic Boxing," *Louisville Courier-Journal*, September 6, 1960, 1:1; Hauser, *Muhammad Ali*, 18.

5. Dave Kindred, *Sound and Fury: Two Powerful Lives, One Fateful Friendship* (New York: Free Press, 2006), 34, 335n34; Muhammad Ali with Richard Durham, *The Greatest: My Own Story* (New York: Random House, 1975), 40–51; Remnick, *King of the World*, 91–111.

6. Dean Duncan, "Turkey Dinner Awaits Champion at the Clay Family Table Here," *Louisville Courier-Journal*, September 6, 1960, 2:1; "Cassius Clay Wins Olympic Gold Medal," *Louisville Defender*, September 8, 1960, 1; Clay quoted in Claude Lewis, *Cassius Clay* (New York: MacFadden-Bartell, 1965), 37.

7. Wilson quoted in Remnick, *King of the World*, 95; Hauser, *Muhammad Ali*, 22.

8. Clay quoted in Hauser, *Muhammad Ali*, 28; "Huge Civic Welcome Awes Olympic Champion," *Louisville Defender*, September 15, 1960, 1, 3, 16; Clarence Matthews, "Ambassador Clay," *Louisville Defender*, September 1, 1960, 13.

9. "Huge Civic Welcome," 1, 16; "Welcome Is Planned for Clay," *Louisville Times*, September 6, 1960, 2:6.

10. Burke and Chilton quoted in "Huge Civic Welcome," 3; "Welcome Is Planned," 2:6; "The Grand Avenue Neighbors," *Louisville Defender*, September 22, 1960, 7; "A

Singer Too," *Louisville Courier-Journal*, September 21, 1960, 2:6; Matthews, "Ambassador Clay," 13.

11. Hoblitzell quoted in Earl Ruby, "Hoblitzell Figures Way to Launch Cassius Clay in Professional Ring, Help Crippled Kids and Clay, Too," *Louisville Courier-Journal*, October 1, 1960, 2:7; "Back to Work," *Louisville Courier-Journal*, October 6, 1960, 2:29; "Clay to Face Ring Veteran in Debut," *Louisville Times*, October 11, 1960, 2:7; Clarence Royalty, "Best Sendoff in History Planned for Clay's Debut," *Louisville Courier-Journal*, October 16, 1960, 2:8; "Cassius Clay to End Amateur Career; To Turn Professional," *Louisville Defender*, October 20, 1960, 12.

12. Kroger executive's comments reported in Royalty, "Best Sendoff in History," 2:8; "Clay to End Training at Grace Center," *Louisville Courier-Journal*, October 20, 1960, 2:18; Larry Boeck, "Hunsaker's No Cream Puff," *Louisville Courier-Journal*, October 23, 1960, 2:12; Jimmy Brown, "Clay, Wilma Set Fast Pace Promoting Bout," *Louisville Courier-Journal*, October 28, 1960, 2:6; Ruby, "Hoblitzell Figures Way to Launch Cassius Clay," 2:7; Jimmy Brown, "Clay Tests Hunsaker in Pro Debut Tonight," *Louisville Courier-Journal*, October 29, 1960, 2:4.

13. Bob Weston, "Clay's Pro Debut Has Title Fight Complexion," *Louisville Times*, October 29, 1960, A-3; Jimmy Brown, "Clay Wins 1st Fight as a Pro," *Louisville Courier-Journal*, October 30, 1960, 1:1; Dean Eagle, "Clay Didn't Show Olympic Sharpness in His First Win," *Louisville Times*, October 31, 1960, 2:5; Unnamed spokesman for mayor's committee quoted in Bob Weston, "Boxing Show Nets $2,519 for Kosair," *Louisville Times*, March 4, 1961, 9.

14. Ruby, "Clay Wins Gold Medal," 1:1; Earl Ruby, "Champion Clay Due in New York for TV Thursday," *Louisville Courier-Journal*, September 7, 1960, 2:6. Clay quoted in both articles.

15. "Alberta Jones' Funeral Rites Held; Unsolved Murders Alarm West Enders," *Louisville Defender*, August 12, 1965, 1:1; "Alberta Jones' Death Ruled at Hands of Unknown Person," *Louisville Defender*, November 25, 1965, 1:1; "A Bright Light Is Extinguished," *Louisville Defender*, August 12, 1966, 1:4.

16. Jimmy Brown, "Clay Wins 1st Fight as a Pro," *Louisville Courier-Journal*, October 30, 1960, 1:1; "Clay to End Training at Grace Center," *Louisville Courier-Journal*, October 20, 1960, 2:18.

17. Although the autobiography has been convincingly debunked, I have chosen to believe some of the stories about the Reynolds estate simply because they constitute the most reasonable explanation, alongside Cassius Clay Sr.'s discomfort with Joe Martin, for why Clay ultimately rejected the offer. The Reynolds offer was almost identical to that of the Louisville Sponsoring Group. In fact, Reynolds's offer guaranteed about $30,000 more than the Sponsoring Group's did. The differences between the two contracts, even that which mandated Joe Martin as trainer, could easily have been worked out if Clay were convinced that Reynolds was the right person to manage him. After all, it's not as if Martin was going to be signed to a lifetime contract as Clay's trainer. Ali with Durham, *The Greatest*, 52–58. Martin quote is on page 54.

18. Remnick, *King of the World*, 104–105; Ali with Durham, *The Greatest*, 53; "The Dream," *Time*, March 22, 1963, 78; Dick Schaap, *Flashing before My Eyes: 50 Years of Headlines, Deadlines and Punchlines* (New York: Harperentertainment, 2001), 68–77; Mark Kram, *Ghosts of Manila: The Fateful Blood Feud between Muhammad Ali and Joe Frazier* (New York: HarperCollins, 2001), 69.

19. Dean Eagle, "Advice to Cassius Clay," *Louisville Times*, September 20, 1960, 2:5; Remnick, *King of the World*, 107.

20. Dean Eagle, "Patterson Clay's Goal," *Louisville Courier-Journal*, September 6, 1960; Eagle, "Advice to Cassius Clay," 2:5; Ruby, "Clay Wins Gold Medal," 1:1; Ruby, "Champion Clay Due in New York," 2:6; Larry Boeck, "Clay Has Three Contracts under Study But Is Still Undecided about 'Hook-Up,'" *Louisville Courier-Journal*, October 9, 1960, 2:11.

21. Boeck, "Clay Has Three Contracts," 2:11; Ali with Durham, *The Greatest*, 53, 58.

22. Huston Horn, "The Eleven Men behind Cassius Clay," *Sports Illustrated*, March 11, 1963, 62–70; Remnick, *King of the World*, 108–111.

23. Larry Boeck, "Juicy Contract Links Cassius, 'Brain Trust,'" *Louisville Courier-Journal*, October 27, 1960, 2:18; Earl Ruby, "'I Don't Want to Be a Joe Louis,' Says Louisville's Cassius Clay, 'Not with Income Tax Problems,'" *Louisville Courier-Journal*, November 2, 1960, 2:7; Hauser, *Muhammad Ali*, 30–31; Remnick, *King of the World*, 110; Telephone interview with Gordon Davidson (attorney for the Louisville Sponsoring Group), April 4, 2000, notes in possession of the author; Horn, "The Eleven Men behind Cassius Clay," 62–70; Clarence Matthews, "Clay Makes Professional Debut," *Louisville Defender*, November 3, 1960, 12.

24. Readers should note that calling Clay "boy" was not necessarily an insult. Boxers, black and white, were called "boy" during this era. It was a commonplace term in the sport. LSG press statement reprinted in Hunt Helm, "Louisville Remembers the Shy Kid from Central High," *Louisville Courier-Journal*, September 14, 1997, 1–7; Faversham quoted in Remnick, *King of the World*, 113

25. John Underwood, "Stardom-Bound Clay Chooses His Own Route," *Miami Herald*, December 21, 1960, D-1; Dean Eagle, "Cassius Clay Starts Career with Biggest Fanfare of All," *Louisville Times*, October 27, 1960, 2:21.

26. All quotes from Horn, "The Eleven Men behind Cassius Clay," 62–70.

27. Hauser, *Muhammad Ali*, 30; John Cottrell, *Man of Destiny: Muhammad Ali, Who Was Once Cassius Clay* (New York: Funk and Wagnalls, [1967] 1968), 46; Claude Lewis, *Cassius Clay*, 39; Ali with Durham, *The Greatest*, 61; Remnick, *King of the World*, 89; Ruby, "'I Don't Want to Be a Joe Louis,'" 2:7.

28. Yearlings statement quoted in Clarence Matthews, "Yearlings to Honor Clay," *Louisville Defender*, November 10, 1960, 12.

29. Unnamed LSG member quoted in Horn, "The Eleven Men behind Cassius Clay," 70.

30. "Clay Leaves to Talk Terms with Archie," *Louisville Times*, November 12, 1960, A-4; Hauser, *Muhammad Ali*, 33–36; Remnick, *King of the World*, 111–113; Paul Zimmerman, "Moore, Clay in Style Rift," *Los Angeles Times*, November 14, 1962, 3:2.

31. Faversham quoted in Zimmerman, "Moore, Clay in Style Rift," 3:2; unnamed backer quoted in Horn, "The Eleven Men behind Cassius Clay," 67.

32. Nick Tosches, *The Devil and Sonny Liston* (Boston: Little, Brown, 2000), 111–148; Remnick, *King of the World*, 43–68.

33. AP report, "Carbo Dictated to IBC, 'Influenced' Promoters, Gibson Tells Senators," *Miami Herald*, December 6, 1960, C-1; Chris Dundee quoted in John Underwood, "'Me and Frankie Carbo? I Never Been That Big,'" *Miami Herald*, December

6, 1960, C-1; Jimmy Burns, "Federal Control Would Help Squelch Racketeers in Boxing," *Miami Herald*, December 8, 1960, C-1.

    34. Hauser, *Muhammad Ali*, 36; John Underwood, "Title at Stake March 20,"
Miami Herald, December 18, 1960, D-1; "Dundee Left—Graciously," *Miami Herald*,
December 23, 1960, D-1; Jimmy Burns, "MacDonald Bids for Title Bout," *Miami
Herald*, December 18, 1960, D-1.

    35. Davidson quoted in Remnick, *King of the World*, 113–114; Hauser, *Muham-
mad Ali*, 35.

    36. John Underwood, "Stardom-Bound Clay Chooses His Own Route," *Miami
Herald*, December 21, 1960, D-1; "Clay's Second Victory Is by KO," *Louisville Times*,
December 28, 1960, 2:7; Tommy Devine, "Bowdry Causes Confusion," *Miami Herald*,
December 28, 1960, C-3; John Underwood, "Bowdry Turns Willie Into a Wishful
Wisp," *Miami Herald*, December 28, 1960, D-1; John Underwood, "No Room at Top,
Pastrano Still Reaching for Moon," *Miami Herald*, December 25, 1960, B-4.

    37. "Clay Signs to Fight 6-Foot, 6-Inch Boxer," *Louisville Times*, February 3, 1961,
2:8; "Cassius Feeds Upon Another Easy Victim," *Miami News*, February 8, 1961, C-4.

    38. "Olympic Champ to Box Ingo Monday on Miami Beach," *Miami Herald*, Feb-
ruary 5, 1961, C-1; John Underwood, "Title? Sure, But Johnson Still Wants Archie
Moore," *Miami Herald*, February 5, 1961, C-6; Olivieri quoted in "Clay Signs to Fight
6-Foot, 6-Inch Boxer," 2:8; Dean Eagle, "Third Time Is Charm," *Louisville Times*, February 6, 1961, B-2; "Ingemar on Display," *Miami Herald*, February 6, 1961, D-3; Clay
quoted in John Underwood, "Ingo Puffs, Misses and Loves It," *Miami Herald*, February
7, 1961, D-1.

    39. "I'm the Greatest, Says Cassius, But He Realizes Needs," *Miami News*, Febru-
ary 19, 1961, C-4; John Underwood, "'Old Spoiler' Maxim Sizes Up a Bigger, Matured
Patterson," *Miami Herald*, February 19, 1961, D-4; John Underwood, "Boastful Clay
Says He'll Clip Fleeman 'Easy,'" *Miami Herald*, February 21, 1961, D-2; "Clay Asks for
Rated Opponent," *Louisville Times*, February 22, 1961, 6; Tommy Devine, "Yon Cassius Has Lean, Hungry Look," *Miami News*, February 22, 1961, C-1, C-4; John Underwood, "Cassius Lets Fists Talk, TKO's Fleeman in 7th," *Miami Herald*, February 22,
1961, D-2.

    40. Larry Boeck, "Clark's Fists May Keep Cassius on the Move," *Louisville Courier-
Journal*, April 9, 1961, 2:7; Dean Eagle, "Is Clark a Clay Pigeon," *Louisville Times*, April
15, 1961, A-3; Earl Ruby, "'Cassius Clay Over His Head,' Says Jenson, Clark's Manager;
Thinks Ring Czar a Necessity," *Louisville Courier-Journal*, April 16, 1961, 2:1; King
quoted in Bob Weston, "'Clay Not Too Many Fights away from Title,' Says Beaten Foe's
Pilot," *Louisville Times*, April 20, 1961, 2:23; Larry Boeck, "Clay Dishes Out K.O. But
Also Can Take It," *Louisville Courier-Journal*, April 20, 1961, 2:20.

    41. Earl Ruby, "Now He's to Be a Movie Actor! This Cassius Clay Never Dull;
Besmanoff Bout Moved to Nov. 29," *Louisville Courier-Journal*, October 28, 1961, 2:4;
Clarence Royalty, "Sparring Mate May Help Clay," *Louisville Courier-Journal*, July
14, 1961, 2:6; Larry Boeck, "Gimmick? No, Alonzo Has Secret for Cassius," *Louisville
Courier-Journal*, July 19, 1961, 2:7; Larry Boeck, "Clay Gets Stiffest Test against Johnson Tonight," *Louisville Courier-Journal*, July 22, 1961, 2:3; Larry Boeck, "Confident
Cassius Decisions Johnson before a Hot 5,160," *Louisville Courier-Journal*, July 23,
1961, 2:1; Dick Schaap, "Happiest Heavyweight," *Saturday Evening Post*, March 25,
1961, 36+ ; "Wet Way to Train for a Fight," *Life*, September 8, 1961, 123–124; Huston

Horn, "Who Made Me Is Me!" *Sports Illustrated*, September 25, 1961, 40ff.; Faversham quoted in Larry Boeck, "Clay May Fight in November," *Louisville Courier-Journal*, October 12, 1961, 2:22.

42. Horn, "The Eleven Men behind Cassius Clay," 70ff.; Al Buck, "Cassius Clay Inc. Has Plans for Taking Title," *New York Post*, February 7, 1962, 81; Larry Boeck, "Clay Faces Toughest Foe of Career," *Louisville Courier-Journal*, October 4, 1961, 2:6; Cassius Clay, "Clay Sees Self as a Matador, Miteff as Bull," *Louisville Courier-Journal*, October 6, 1961, 2:15; Clarence Royalty, "Can Cassius Clout 'Em! Miteff Learns in 6th," *Louisville Courier-Journal*, October 8, 1961, 2:1; Larry Boeck, "Clay Scores T.K.O. in 7th; Ellis Loses," *Louisville Courier-Journal*, November 30, 1961, 2:24.

43. Hauser, *Muhammad Ali*, 28; Wagner quoted in Remnick, *King of the World*, 119–120; Arne K. Lang, "Ali Provided Quite a Vegas Spectacle," *Vegas Insider*, February 15, 2000, 1; Bob Weston, "Clay Impatient for Ranking Foes," *Louisville Times*, June 20, 1961, 2:5; AP report, "Clay Wins 10-Round Decision," *Louisville Courier-Journal*, June 27, 1961, 2:9; Dean Eagle, "Cockiness Only Thing against Cassius Clay, Boy Heavyweight," *Louisville Times*, April 25, 1961, 2:5.

44. Collier-Thomas and Franklin, *My Soul Is a Witness*, 163.

45. Remnick, *King of the World*, 43–68. For details about the impact that television had on small boxing clubs, see Truman K. Gibson with Steve Huntley, *Knocking Down Barriers: My Fight for Black America* (Evanston: Northwestern University Press, 2005), 251.

46. Al Buck, "Will Garden Sprout More Title Fights?" *New York Post*, May 15, 1962, 73; "Boxing Probe Opens Today," *New York Post*, May 21, 1962, 60; Milt Sosin, "Probe May Call Mrs. Paret," *New York Post*, May 24, 1962, 80; George Gallup, "Boxing Ban Favored by 4 out of 10," *Los Angeles Times*, April 25, 1962, 3:7; Jesse Abramson, "An Era in Boxing to End with Razing of St. Nick," *New York Herald Tribune*, May 20, 1962, 3:6.

47. Al Buck, "Liston Wants to Believe," *New York Post*, May 22, 1962, 85; "Archie 'Dethroned'; Title Vacated by N.Y." *New York Herald Tribune*, February 10, 1962, 11; William B. Conklin, "New York Strips Moore of Crown," *New York Times*, February 10, 1962, 17; "N.Y. to Take Title from Arch Today?" *New York Herald Tribune*, February 9, 1962, 25; Buck, "Cassius Clay Inc. Has Plans," 81.

48. Jim McCulley, "Rate Clay 5–1 over Banks," *New York Daily News*, February 10, 1962, 28; Al Buck, "Garden Swings Back to Age of Experience," *New York Post*, February 12, 1962, 40; Clay quoted in Al Buck, "Clay Out to Prove Fists Can Talk, Too," *New York Post*, February 11, 1962, 38; "Cassius Clay Gets Up from Canvas to Gain TKO over Banks in 4th Round," *Louisville Defender*, February 15, 1962, 18.

49. Pat Putnum, "Cassius Says He's Great . . . Wanna Argue?" *Miami Herald*, February 25, 1962, D-3; Pat Putnum, "Warner Has Confidence Back: 'Cassius Just Another Fight,'" *Miami Herald*, February 26, 1962, D-2; Dundee quoted in "Clay Has Special Following," *Miami Herald*, February 28, 1962, D-2; Pat Putnum, "Clay Says He'll KO Don Warner Tonight," *Miami Herald*, February 28, 1962, D-2; Pat Putnum, "'Angered' Clay Chills Warner," *Miami Herald*, March 1, 1962, C-1.

50. George Main, "Clay 6 to 1 over Logan," *Los Angeles Herald-Examiner*, April 23, 1962, C-1; George Main, "Clay Hides Out Before Big Bout," *Los Angeles Herald-Examiner*, April 22, 1962, G-5; John Hall, "Clay Stops Logan in Fourth," *Los Angeles Times*, April 24, 1962, 3:1; Melvin Durslag, "Cassius Not Bum, But Close to It," *Los Angeles Herald-Examiner*, April 25, 1962, B-10; Sid Ziff, "Big Mouth, Deaf Ears," *Los*

Angeles Times, April 25, 1962, 3:3; George Main, "Logan Stopped in Four," *Los Angeles Herald-Examiner,* April 24, 1962, C-1; John Hall, "Clay Boxes Logan Tonight at Arena," *Los Angeles Times,* April 23, 1962, 3:2.

51. "Clay 5–1 Over Daniels in St. Nick 10-Rounder," *New York Daily News,* May 19, 1962, 31; Dana Mozley, "Clay Clobbers Bleeding Daniels in 2:21 of 7th," *New York Daily News,* May 20, 1962, 134; Howard M. Tuckner, "Fight Is Halted Because of Cut," *New York Times,* May 20, 1962, 5:4; "Mercury Hits 99 Degrees for Hottest Day in 5 Years Here," *New York Times,* May 20, 1962, 1:1; "Clay Knocks Daniels Out in 7th Round," *New York Herald Tribune,* May 20, 1962, 3:1.

52. AP report, "Clay, Lavorante Square Off Tonight," *Louisville Courier-Journal,* July 20, 1962, 2:7.

53. Cottrell, *Man of Destiny,* 62; AP report, "Clay, Lavorante Square Off Tonight," 2:7; AP report, "Prophet Clay Wins in 5th," *Louisville Courier-Journal,* July 21, 1962, 2:6; Larry Boeck, "Clay's Win Was 'Turning Point,'" *Louisville Courier-Journal,* July 23, 1962, 2:9; John Hall, "George Tabs Clay to Beat Archie," *Los Angeles Times,* November 8, 1962, 3:2.

54. Kennedy quoted in Arthur R. Ashe Jr., *A Hard Road to Glory-Boxing: The African-American Athlete in Boxing* (New York: Amistad, [1988] 1993), 53.

55. Ibid.

56. UPI report, "Young Clay 2–1 Favorite over Moore," *Louisville Courier-Journal,* November 15, 1962, 2:24; John Hall, "Clay 3–1 to Beat Moore Tonight," *Los Angeles Times,* November 15, 1962, 3:1.

57. John Hall, "Mongoose Hits Deck Three Times," *Los Angeles Times,* November 16, 1962, 3:1; Sid Ziff, "King Cassius," *Los Angeles Times,* November 16, 1962, 3:3; "Now for the Champ?" *New York Post,* November 16, 1962, 1; AP report, "Clay Says He'll KO Liston," *Louisville Courier-Journal,* November 16, 1962, A-1; "Clay Calls It," *San Francisco Examiner,* November 16, 1962, A-1; Curley Grieve, "New Wizard of Schnoz Gets SF Ovation," *San Francisco Examiner,* November 16, 1962, 54; John Hall, "'Great Debate' Pays Off in Record Indoor Gate," *Los Angeles Times,* November 17, 1962, 2:1; UPI report, "Moore vs. Clay: Tall Profit for a Short Fight," *New York Times,* November 17, 1962, 19; Eddie Muller, "Classy Clay Calls His Shot: Stops Moore in 4th Round," *San Francisco Examiner,* November 16, 1962, 53; Eddie Muller, "Fistic Fame Shortcut," *San Francisco Examiner,* November 13, 1962, C-5; John Hall, "Clay 'Big' Enough for Now for Liston," *Los Angeles Times,* November 7, 1962, 3:4; Eddie Muller, "Ol' Arch, Clay Fight Tonight," *San Francisco Examiner,* November 15, 1962, 57; AP report, "Clay Has to Let Fists Talk Now," *New York Post,* November 15, 1962, 68.

58. Al Buck, ". . . Says Liston Must Fall in Eight," *New York Post,* November 16, 1962, 104; Bill Becker, "Winner Fulfills Early Prediction," *New York Times,* November 16, 1962, 36; Red Foley, "Garden Seeks Clay-Floyd Bout," *New York Daily News,* November 17, 1962, 26; AP/UPI report, "Clay-Floyd, Clay-Liston . . . Offers Pour In," *San Francisco Examiner,* November 17, 1962, 37; "Clay-Liston in '63?" *New York Herald-Tribune,* November 17, 1962, 15; AP/UPI report, "Garden Wants Clay to Meet Patterson," *Louisville Courier-Journal,* November 17, 1962, 2:4; Sid Ziff, "Off Day for All," *Los Angeles Times,* November 20, 1962, 3:3; John Hall, "Archie May Quit to Be Manager," *Los Angeles Times,* November 22, 1962, 3:3; "Clay Won't Fight Again This Year," *Louisville Courier-Journal,* November 26, 1962, 2:5; Larry Boeck, "No. 4 Clay Wants Machen," *Louisville Courier-Journal,* November 29, 1962, 2:21; "Clay Draws Big Offers," *Louis-*

ville Courier-Journal, November 30, 1962, 2:9; "Clay-Machen for SF?" *San Francisco Examiner*, November 30, 1962, 52; Zimmerman, "Moore, Clay in Style Rift," 3:2.

59. Arthur Daley, "'Put Up' Stage Nigh for Cassius, Archie," *Louisville Courier-Journal*, November 13, 1962, 2:5.

60. Ashe, *A Hard Road to Glory-Boxing*, 50–51.

61. UPI report, "Young Clay 2–1 Favorite over Moore," *Louisville Courier-Journal*, November 15, 1962, 2:24; AP report, "Clay Has to Let Fists Talk Now," 68.

62. Steindler and Clay ("Let them yell . . .") quoted in John Hall, "Cassius Clay Forces Gym Hecklers Out," *Los Angeles Times*, November 5, 1962, 3:7; Sid Ziff, "Archie in Character," *Los Angeles Times*, November 8, 1962, 3:2; Clay ("You tell him . . .") quoted in Sid Ziff, "Tortoise vs. Hare," *Los Angeles Times*, November 11, 1962, D-4; Sid Ziff, "Clay Says He'll Wait," *Los Angeles Times*, November 18, 1962, D-4; Clay ("People stop me . . .") quoted in Sid Ziff, "Aragon Tabs Clay," *Los Angeles Times*, November 14, 1962, 3:3; Clay ("I don't care . . .") quoted in AP report, "Clay Has to Let Fists Talk Now," *New York Post*, November 15, 1962, 68; *a.k.a. Cassius Clay*, directed by Jim Jacobs, with Muhammad Ali, 79 min. (United Artists, 1970). Clay quotes from multiple sources combined into single quote in text.

63. "Clay Backers Confident," *Louisville Courier-Journal*, November 2, 1962, 2:9; John Hall, "Clay's Trainer, Dundee, on Long Local Winning Streak," *Los Angeles Times*, November 13, 1962, 3:2; "Archie Jazzes Training Time," *Louisville Courier-Journal*, November 8, 1962, 2:20; "Cassius Clay Has Role in 'Requiem for a Heavyweight,'" *Louisville Defender*, November 8, 1962, 14; John Hall, "Jazz Band to Swing for Ol' Archie Today," *Los Angeles Times*, November 9, 1962, 3:2; AP report, "Liston May Be There and Clay Is Delighted," *Louisville Courier-Journal*, 2:12; John Hall, "Liston Possible Ringsider for Fight between Clay and Moore," *Los Angeles Times*, November 15, 1962, 2:3; "Clay, Moore Getting Big Dose of Ballyhoo," *Louisville Courier-Journal*, November 11, 1962, 2:10; Ali with Durham, *The Greatest*, 82.

64. Clay quoted in Sid Ziff, "Clay's Forte: Big Mouth," *Los Angeles Times*, April 17, 1962, 3:3.

65. Clay quoted in Paul Zimmerman, "Cassius Clay's Moral Code," *Los Angeles Times*, April 23, 1962, 3:2; Jim Murray, "Cassius on Clay," *Los Angeles Times*, April 20, 1962, 3:1.

66. "Snow Wave Grips U.S., District," *Pittsburgh Press*, January 23, 1963, 1, 2; "18 Below Sets Record Here," *Pittsburgh Press*, January 24, 1963, 1; "Below-Zero Wave Holds Area in Grip," *Pittsburgh Post-Gazette*, January 24, 1963, 1.

67. Al Abrams, "Sidelights on Sports," *Pittsburgh Post-Gazette*, January 21, 1963, 20; Al Abrams, "A Sports Phenomena," *Pittsburgh Post-Gazette*, January 23, 1963, 18.

68. Jimmy Miller, "Clay Does It; Kayo in 3rd," *Pittsburgh Post-Gazette*, January 25, 1963, 1; Thomas Hennessy, "Arena Packed in Return of Bigtime Boxing Here," *Pittsburgh Post-Gazette*, January 25, 1963, 1; Al Abrams, "Sub-Zero Weather Fails to Hold Back Fight Fans," *Pittsburgh Post-Gazette*, January 25, 1963, 18.

69. Al Abrams, "First Post-Mortem," *Pittsburgh Post-Gazette*, January 26, 1963, 10; Miller, "Clay Does It, 1, 18–19; Jimmy Miller, "Clay Insists He's Ready for Liston," *Pittsburgh Post-Gazette*, January 26, 1963, 10; Remnick, *King of the World*, 135; "'I'll Chop That Big Monkey to Pieces . . .' Says Cassius Clay," *Life*, February 15, 1963, 62.

70. Horn, "The Eleven Men behind Cassius Clay," 62–70; Jimmy Miller, "Clay Guaranteed Pay in Contract," *Pittsburgh Post-Gazette*, January 16, 1963, 21.

71. UPI report, "Scalpers Cashing in on Clay vs. Jones," *Chicago Daily News*, March 11, 1963, 37; Anthony Marenghi, "'Bush-Leaguer' Clay First in History to Sell Out Garden in Advance," *Newark Star-Ledger*, March 12, 1963, 27; UPI report, "SRO Sign Out for Clay-Jones Scrap," *Los Angeles Times*, March 12, 1963, 3:5; "Clay Captivates New York Like Joe Louis of 1935," *Pittsburgh Courier*, March 16, 1963, 15; Paul Zimmerman, "Cassius Still Question Mark," *Los Angeles Times*, March 15, 1963, 3:2; "Dream Time," *Time*, March 22, 1963, cover + 78–81; Teddy Brenner, *Only the Ring Was Square* (Englewood Cliffs: Prentice-Hall, 1981), 82; AP report, "Clay Solid 3–1 Choice over Jones," *Los Angeles Times*, March 13, 1963, 3:3; Cottrell, *Man of Destiny*, 95; Huston Horn, "A Comeuppance for the Cocksure Cassius," *Sports Illustrated*, March 25, 1963, 16.

72. Zimmerman, "Cassius Still Question Mark," 3:2.

73. AP report, "Clay Solid 3–1 Choice over Jones," 3:3; Liston quoted in AP report, "Liston Fear: 'I Might Murder Him,'" *Newark Star-Ledger*, March 14, 1963, 21.

74. Clay quoted in Les Matthews, "Sports Whirl," *New York Amsterdam News*, March 16, 1963, 30.

75. Pete Hamill interview quoted in George F. Brown, "'I'm No Jim Meredith' Says Clay," *Pittsburgh Courier*, March 30, 1963, 1.

76. Henry Lee Moon letter quoted in Brown, "'I'm No Jim Meredith,'" 1.

77. Chuvalo biographical information and Chuvalo quotes from *The Originals: George Chuvalo—A Portrait in the First Person* [television series], directed by Jim Hanley (Toronto: City TV, 1990).

78. Clay quoted in AP report, "Clay Is Criticized for Refusal to Box," *New York Times*, October 12, 1963, 16.

79. Gerald Walter, "Clay Seals the Lip and Trains for Nine," *London Daily Mirror*, June 4, 1963, 23; "Cassius Gets a Warning," *London Daily Express*, June 7, 1963, 17; Cooper quoted in Sydney Hulls, "Cooper Loses Spar-Mate Joe," *London Daily Express*, June 5, 1963, 18; Peter Wilson, "It Must Be Cassius," *London Daily Mirror*, June 18, 1963, 23; Sydney Hulls, "Police Guard Clay," *London Daily Express*, June 19, 1963, 11; Peter Wilson, "Clay Wins in Five with a 'Bare' Fist," *London Daily Mirror*, June 19, 1963, 23; Henry Langdon, "The 100,000 Pound Fight," *London Daily Express*, June 18, 1963, 13; Desmond Hackett, "Gallant Cooper Has Clay Down—Then a Cut Eye Ends It," *London Daily Express*, June 19, 1963, 16; Robert Daley, "Clay Keeps Word and Stops Cooper in 5th Round before 55,000 in London," *New York Times*, June 19, 1963, 27; Robert Daley, "Boxer's Immaturity Is Seen as Chink in His Armor," *New York Times*, June 20, 1963, 36; BBC radio comment from "As B.B.C. Reported the Fight," *New York Times*, June 19, 1063, 27; BBC television comment taken directly from film of the bout.

80. Wilson, "Clay Wins in Five," 23; "The Winner on His Back," *London Daily Mirror*, June 19, 1963, 22; Daley, "Clay Keeps Word," 27; UPI report, "Liston's Man Promises Clay September Fight," *New York Times*, June 19, 1963, 27.

81. Davidson quoted in Desmond Hackett, "Surprise . . . Clay the Talker Can Move Fast Too!" *London Daily Express*, June 17, 1963, 14; Faversham on Clay spending quoted in Sydney Hulls, untitled article, *London Daily Express*, June 19, 1963, 14; Faversham at ringside quoted in Daley, "Clay Keeps Word," 27.

82. Clay quoted in "'Fed-Up' Clay Set to Forsake South," *Pittsburgh Courier*, July 6, 1963, 15.

83. UPI report, "Liston Is Expected to Sign Next Week for Bout with Clay," *New York Times*, November 1, 1963, 36; AP report, "Liston-Clay Fight Finds New Site: Mi-

ami Beach," *New York Times*, December 7, 1963, 20; "The Man, the Rabbit & the Boy," *Time*, August 2, 1963, 52; "Clay to Get Chance with Sonny Liston," *Pittsburgh Courier*, December 7, 1963, 15.

84. Liston quoted in Arthur Daley, "Reciprocal Reaction," *New York Times*, September 25, 1963, 52; UPI report, "Fatigue, Racial Queries Brought Liston Home," *New York Times*, October 3, 1963, 42; Arthur Daley, "How Long Will It Take?" *New York Times*, November 11, 1963, 17; Clay quoted in AP report, "Blow Is for Show," *Los Angeles Herald-Examiner*, February 20, 1964, F-1.

85. Information about the historical underpinnings of the Nation of Islam's economic nationalism can be found in John Bracey, August Meier, and Elliot Rudwick, *Black Nationalism in America* (Indianapolis, Bobbs-Merrill, 1970); Wilson J. Moses, *The Golden Age of Black Nationalism* (New York: Oxford University Press, 1978); August Meier, *Negro Thought in America 1880–1915: Racial Ideologies in the Age of Booker T. Washington* (Ann Arbor: University of Michigan Press, [1963] 1966); August Meier and Elliot Rudwick, *Along the Color Line: Explorations in the Black Experience* (Urbana: University of Illinois, 1976); Sterling Stuckey, *Slave Culture: Nationalist Theory and the Foundations of Black America* (New York: Oxford University Press, 1987); Raymond W. Smock, ed., *Booker T. Washington in Perspective: Essays of Louis Harlan* (Jackson: University of Mississippi Press, 1988); Tony Martin, *Race First: The Ideological and Organizational Struggles of Marcus Garvey and the Universal Negro Improvement Association* (Westport: Greenwood Press, 1976); Rodney Carlisle, *The Roots of Black Nationalism* (Port Washington: Kennikat Press, 1975).

86. AP report, "Cassius Confused, Dad Says," *The Louisville Times*, February 7, 1964, 11; Sid Ziff, "Clay's Dad Speaks Up," *Los Angeles Times*, February 23, 1964, C-3; Angelo Dundee quoted in Dean Eagle, "Fanfare Is Tonic to Young Boxers," *Louisville Times*, February 24, 1964, 2:4; Sid Ziff, "Is Clay for Real?" *Los Angeles Times*, February 20, 1964, 3:3; Leonard Koppett, "Clay Ends Drills, But Not His Talk," *New York Times*, February 22, 1964, 25; Cecil Blye, "Writer Calls Cassius' Black Muslim Antics Phony," *Louisville Defender*, February 6, 1964, 8; Dean Eagle, "Will Cassius Clay Be Afraid of Liston?" *Louisville Times*, February 25, 1964, 2:4.

87. Clay quoted in UPI report, "Police Prevent a Noisy Clay from Crashing Liston's Camp," *New York Times*, February 8, 1964, 18; Robert Lipsyte, "Clay's Act Plays Liston's Camp and Sonny Is a Kindly Critic," *New York Times*, February 20, 1964, 33.

88. Faversham quoted in Gerald Eskenazi, "Loss of Bicycle Got Clay Rolling," *New York Times*, February 26, 1964, 26.

89. Peniel Joseph, *Waiting 'Til the Midnight Hour: A Narrative History of Black Power in America* (New York: Henry Holt, 2006), 96.

90. Davidson quoted in Remnick, *King of the World*, 110–111.

91. Gordon Davidson to Archibald Foster, November 4, 1960, George Barry Bingham Papers, Collection MSSA B613a, folder 1657, The Filson Historical Society, Louisville (hereafter Bingham Papers); James Ross Todd to Louisville Sponsoring Group, January 17, 1962, Bingham Papers, folder 1657; Bill Faversham to Worth Bingham, January 26, 1961, Bingham Papers, folder 1657; Bill Faversham to Louisville Sponsoring Group, May 15, 1962, Bingham Papers, folder 1657; Bill Faversham to Louisville Sponsoring Group, August 20, 1962, Bingham Papers, folder 1657.

92. William Cutchins to Wilbur Mills, July 22, 1963, Bingham Papers, folder 1657, Gordon Davidson to William Cutchins, July 23, 1963, Bingham Papers, folder 1657.

93. Bill Faversham to Louisville Sponsoring Group, April 23, 1964, Bingham Papers, folder 1658.

94. Archibald Foster to Arthur Grafton, August 9, 1965, Bingham Papers, folder 1661.

95. Gordon Davidson to William Cutchins, July 23, 1963, Bingham Papers, folder 1657.

96. Gordon Davidson to William Cutchins, July 23, 1963, Bingham Papers, folder 1657; Gordon Davidson to Archibald Foster, December 9, 1964, Bingham Papers, folder 1658; Lester Malitz to Muhammad Ali, January 18, 1965, Bingham Papers, folder 1659; Lester Malitz to Gordon Davidson, February 9, 1965, Bingham Papers, folder 1659.

97. James Ross Todd to Louisville Sponsoring Group, December 19, 1960, Bingham Papers, folder 1656; James Ross Todd to Robert Worth Bingham, January 12, 1961, Bingham Papers, folder 1656; James Ross Todd to Louisville Sponsoring Group, February 2, 1962, Bingham Papers, folder 1656; James Ross Todd to Louisville Sponsoring Group, January 30, 1963, Bingham Papers, folder 1656; James Ross Todd to Louisville Sponsoring Group, April 30, 1964, Bingham Papers, folder 1656; Worth Bingham to David Hacker, undated, Bingham Papers, folder 1662.

98. Louisville Sponsoring Group to Muhammad Ali, January 6, 1965, Bingham Papers, folder 1659.

99. Gordon Davidson to Drew Brown, December 18, 1964, Bingham Papers, folder 1658; Gordon Davidson to Drew Brown, November 25, 1964, Bingham Papers, folder 1658; Gordon Davidson to Drew Brown, February 16, 1965, Bingham Papers, folder 1659.

100. Gordon Davidson to Louisville Sponsoring Group, May 4, 1964, Bingham Papers, folder 1658; Gordon Davidson to Louisville Sponsoring Group, July 29, 1964, Bingham Papers, folder 1658; Gordon Davidson to Don Ulmer, March 4, 1965, Bingham Papers, folder 1659; Gordon Davidson to Don Ulmer, March 15, 1965, Bingham Papers, folder 1659; Gordon Davidson to Don Ulmer, April 12, 1965, Bingham Papers, folder 1660; Gordon Davidson to Don Ulmer, June 3, 1965, Bingham Papers, folder 1660; Arthur Grafton to Louisville Sponsoring Group, June 23, 1965, Bingham Papers, folder 1660; Arthur Grafton to Louisville Sponsoring Group, September 9, 1965, Bingham Papers, folder 1661.

101. Bill Faversham to Louisville Sponsoring Group, June 7, 1961, Bingham Papers, folder 1657; Bill Faversham to Louisville Sponsoring Group, September 19, 1963, Bingham Papers, folder 1657.

102. William Cutchins to Louisville Sponsoring Group, September 24, 1963, Bingham Papers, folder 1658.

103. Gordon Davidson to Archibald Foster, December 9, 1964, Bingham Papers, folder 1658; Gordon Davidson to Angelo Dundee, December 22, 1964, Bingham Papers, folder 1658.

104. Gordon Davidson to Joe Thomas, February 8, 1965, Bingham Papers, folder 1659; Gordon Davidson to Louisville Sponsoring Group, March 10, 1965, Bingham Papers, folder 1659.

105. Ali and Faversham quoted in untitled newspaper clipping from *New York Post*, May 26, 1965, Bingham Papers, folder 1660; Archibald Foster to Arthur Grafton, February 8, 1966, Bingham Papers, folder 1662.

106. Gordon Davidson to Chauncey Eskridge, February 16, 1965, Bingham Papers, folder 1659; Gordon Davidson to Chauncey Eskridge, March 9, 1965, Bingham Papers, folder 1659; Gordon Davidson to Mrs. Cassius M. Clay, March 9, 1965, Bingham Papers, folder 1659; Gordon Davidson to Cassius Clay, May 13, 1965, Bingham Papers, folder 1660.

107. Gordon Davidson to Louisville Sponsoring Group Executive Committee, January 11, 1966, Bingham Papers, folder 1662; Arthur Grafton to Louisville Sponsoring Group, February 16, 1966, Bingham Papers, folder 1662.

108. Arthur Grafton to Louisville Sponsoring Group, February 16, 1966, Bingham Papers, folder 1662; Faversham quoted in "Clay's Father Thinks Son Made the Right Decision," *Baltimore Afro-American*, May 6, 1967, 9.

109. Gordon Davidson to Worth Bingham, December 9, 1964, Bingham Papers, folder 1658.

110. Bob Evans to Worth Bingham, December 7, 1965, Bingham Papers, folder 1662; Clay quoted in "Ring Group May Strip Clay of Title," *Louisville Times*, March 23, 1964, 1, 18; Evans quoted in Dana Mozley, "WBA Head Calls Clay Unfit, Acts to Take Crown Away," *New York Daily News*, March 23, 1964, 3, 48.

111. Bill Faversham to Archibald Foster, July 8, 1965, Bingham Papers, folder 1661; Garland Cherry to Gordon Davidson, December 20, 1963, Bingham Papers, folder 1657; Gordon Davidson to Richard Wanner, September 25, 1964, Bingham Papers, folder 1658.

112. Hauser, *Muhammad Ali*, 65–67; Remnick, *King of the World*, 170–171, 185; Ashe, *Hard Road to Glory-Boxing*, 56.

113. "Who Can Beat Him?" *Newsweek*, August 5, 1963, 68.

114. Louis quoted in Jack Mann, "Clay Goofed Up the Gate with Hysterics—Louis," *New York Herald Tribune*, February 26, 1964, 26.

115. Robert Lipsyte, "Ticket Sale Slow at Site of Fight," *New York Times*, February 25, 1964, 34.

116. "Record Crowds Expected to See Liston-Clay Title Fight Tuesday," *New York Times*, February 23, 1964, 5:3; Halpern quoted in AP report, "Promoter's Bath Cost 400 Grand," *San Francisco Examiner*, February 26, 1964, 56; UPI report, "Record $3,200,000 Likely to Be Topped for Bout TV," *New York Times*, February 26, 1964, 27; UPI report, "Broke Record," *Chicago Tribune*, February 26, 1964, 3:2; Leonard Koppett, "All the World's a Stage, via TV, for Title Fight," *New York Times*, February 23, 1964, 5:1; AP report, "Majors Boost TV 'Take,' But Eye New Deal," *Los Angeles Times*, February 25, 1964, 3:2; "Odds Hold at 7 to 1 on Liston," *San Francisco Examiner*, February 25, 1964, 52.

117. Robert Lipsyte, "Each Slice of Fight Pie Is Rich, But Promoter's Going Hungry," *New York Times*, February 24, 1964, 30; Jesse Abramson, "Clay Is the Greatest—Stops Sonny in 7," *New York Herald Tribune*, February 26, 1964, 24.

118. A note on these figures: It is difficult to reconstruct the figures and profit shares from closed-circuit-television bouts. Contemporary newspapers and periodicals reveal wildly different estimates, and since closed-circuit companies were not obligated to reveal final sales to the press, and never did, the only thing to go on are these speculative press reports. Whenever these reports have conflicted, I have tried to aggregate them into the most reasonable estimates possible, which I then insert into the

text. I write "or so it seemed" alongside my comment that Liston was the biggest winner because it is probable that the mob took much of his purse. Tex Maule, "Yes, It Was Good and Honest," *Sports Illustrated*, March 9, 1964, 24.

119. Gerald Eskenazi, "Theater-TV Tickets for Fight Expected to Make Good Showing," *New York Times*, February 25, 1964, 34.

120. Norm Miller, "Theatre TV Fans Got a Fistful," *New York Daily News*, February 26, 1964, 71; Crehan quoted in Jim McCulley, "85,000 Here to See Fight on TNT-V," *New York Daily News*, February 25, 1964, 44; Joseph Sheehan, "TV Crowds Cheer Clay," *New York Times*, February 26, 1964, 28.

121. "Large Screen TV of Title Fight Set at 20 Local Sites," *Los Angeles Times*, February 18, 1964, 3:3; John Hall, "Plenty of Theater TV Seats Left for Liston-Clay Fight Tuesday," *Los Angeles Times*, February 23, 1964, C-18; Sid Ziff, "Better Be Early," *Los Angeles Times*, February 24, 1964, 3:2; John Hall, "Fight to Lure 100,000 Here; Don't Be Late," *Los Angeles Times*, February 25, 1964, 3:1; "Orange County Traffic Snarls around TV Site," *Los Angeles Times*, February 26, 1964, 3:2; "Fight Success on Local TV Outlets," *Los Angeles Times*, February 27, 1964, 3:3; George Main, "Watch Your Step, Sonny," *Los Angeles Herald Examiner*, February 23, 1964, F-5; John Hall, "On to Bellevue," *Los Angeles Times*, February 26, 1964, 3:3; Bud Furillo, "Steamer Visits Palmist: Sees Liston Win in First," *Los Angeles Herald-Examiner*, February 21, 1964, F-2; Hurst quoted in "Theater Fight Fans in Melee," *Los Angeles Herald-Examiner*, February 26, 1964, A-1.

122. "26,000 See Fight Here on Television," *Chicago Tribune*, February 26, 1964, 3:2.

123. Red Smith, "Long, Long Arms," *New York Herald Tribune*, February 25, 1964, 22; Jesse Abramson, "Odds at 11–10 That Cassius Won't Last 5," *New York Herald Tribune*, February 25, 1964, 22; AP report, "165 Million Europeans Watch Fight," *New York Times*, February 26, 1964, 3:2; "Fight Facts," *Chicago Tribune*, February 25, 1964, 3:3.

124. Browitt quoted in Kelly Cocanougher, "Fight Fans Prompt and Partial," *The Louisville Times*, February 26, 1964, 27; Editorial page, "Hail Cassius, The New King," *Louisville Times*, February 26, 1964, 1:16; Dean Eagle, "Cassius Is Champion and Eagle Eats Crow," *Louisville Times*, February 26, 1964, 2:6.

125. Faversham, Clay, and Clay Sr. quoted in Eagle, "Cassius Is Champion and Eagle Eats Crow," 2:6; Martin quoted in "'Clay Would Do It Again, Only Quicker,' Martin" *Louisville Times*, February 26, 1964, 2:6; Phil Pepe, *Come Out Smokin': Joe Frazier—The Champion Nobody Knew* (New York: Coward, McCann & Geoghegan, 1972), 156.

126. Kindred, *Sound and Fury*, 75–77. Clay quoted on page 76.

127. "Integrated New Orleans Crowd Sees Fight TV without Incident," *New York Times*, February 26, 1964, 28; AP report, "CORE Victory: 2 New Orleans Theaters Cancel," *New York Herald Tribune*, February 25, 1964, 22; AP report, "Cancel 2 TV Casts over Racial Row," *Chicago Tribune*, February 25, 1964, 3:1; "2 Theaters Drop Telecast of Bout," *New York Times*, February 25, 1964, 34; Nilon and Halpern quoted in Leonard Koppett, "Fight TV Facing Integration Snag," *New York Times*, February 24, 1964, 30.

128. "Integrated New Orleans Crowd," 28; Liston and Farmer quoted in AP report, "CORE Victory," 22; AP report, "Cancel 2 TV," 3:1; Theater statement re-

printed in "2 Theaters Drop Telecast," 34; Koppett, "Fight TV Facing Integration Snag," 30.

PART II

1. Ali quoted in H.J. McFall, "Cassius Clay Tells Plans to Form a Negro Company," *Louisville Defender*, January 13, 1966, 1.

2. Discussion of the finances of Ali-Patterson can be found in Eddie Muller, "Fight Talk Today Is $," *San Francisco Examiner*, November 19, 1965, 58; Al Buck, "Cassius Clay: The 'Champion,'" *New York Post*, November 24, 1966, 48; "The Fight of TV," *Chicago Sun-Times*, November 24, 1965, 17; AP report, "Fight Facts and Figures," *Louisville Courier-Journal*, November 22, 1965, B-7; Paul Zimmerman, "Clay, Patterson to Offer Defense," *Los Angeles Times*, November 22, 1965, 3:1. Financial information on Ali's rematch with Liston can be found in AP report, "Facts on Title Fight," *New York Times*, May 26, 1965, 49, 54. For financial statistics on Ali's first bout with Liston, see AP report, "Fight Facts, Figures," *San Francisco Examiner*, February 25, 1964, 52; Robert Lipsyte, "Each Slice of Fight Pie Is Rich, But Promoter's Going Hungry," *New York Times*, February 24, 1964, 30; Leonard Koppett, "All the World's a Stage, via TV, for Title Fight," *New York Times*, February 23, 1964, 5:1.

3. Although Main Bout had only five members, the organization was split into six voting shares in order to give the Nation of Islam 50 percent control. Some reports reverse the shares of Brown and Arum, claiming that Brown was a 20 percent shareholder while Arum controlled 10 percent of Main Bout. Jimmy Cannon, "Theater TV, the Muslims . . . and Jim Brown," *Los Angeles Herald-Examiner*, January 10, 1966, C-2; Thomas Hauser, *Muhammad Ali: His Life and Times* (New York: Simon & Schuster, 1991), 150–152; Robert Lipsyte, "Clay's Main Bout, Inc., Seen Final Step in a Project to Bolster Negro Business," *New York Times*, January 9, 1966, 5:4; George Vass, "TV Firm Dictated Date of Title Bout," *Chicago Daily News*, January 28, 1966, 22; Taylor Branch, *Pillar of Fire: America in the King Years, 1963–1965* (New York: Simon & Schuster, 1998), 479.

4. Ali quoted in AP report, "Clay to Put Title on Line in Fight against Terrell," *New York Times*, January 9, 1966, 5:1, 4; Telephone interview with Gordon Davidson, April 4, 2000, notes in possession of author; Grafton quoted in Jack Olsen, "All Alone with the Future," *Sports Illustrated*, May 9, 1966, 42.

5. Brown (first quote) cited in Vass, "TV Firm Dictated Date," 22; Lipsyte, "Clay's Main Bout," 5:4; UPI report, "Cleveland Grid Star Brown Retires," *Montreal Star*, July 14, 1966, 21; AP report, "Brown to Help Negro Economy," *Baltimore Sun*, July 15, 1966, C-1; Earl Ruby, "Has Brown Left Door Ajar? No Ex-Athletes in His Plan," *Louisville Courier-Journal*, July 22, 1966, B-8; Milton Gross, "Curiouser and Curiouser," *New York Post*, February 3, 1967, 77; Jim Brown (subject). *Beyond the Glory* [television series]. (New York: FOX Sports, airdate August 14, 2005); Brown (second quote) cited in *The Last Round: Chuvalo vs. Ali*, directed by Joseph Blasioli, 100 min. (Toronto: National Film Board of Canada, 2002); Herman Graham III, *The Brothers' Vietnam War: Black Power, Manhood, and the Military Experience* (Gainesville: University Press of Florida, 2003), 86. Also see "Plan 3,000 Jobs for Youth by NIEU," *Los Angeles Sentinel*, June 22, 1967, A-7.

6. Gene Ward, "Heavy Title, TV and All, Taken Over by Muslims," *Chicago's American*, February 13, 1966, 10; Jimmy Cannon, "Malice Disguised as Banter in

Clay's Evil Strain of Wit," *Miami Herald*, February 19, 1966, C-2; Cannon, "Theater TV, the Muslims," C-2; Jack Olsen, "Learning Elijah's Advanced Lesson in Hate," *Sports Illustrated*, May 2, 1966, 38, 52; Doug Gilbert, "Clay-Terrell Package Wrapped in Muslims?" *Chicago's American*, February 5, 1966, 11; Red Smith, "N.Y. Merits Clay-Terrell, It's Claimed," *Chicago Sun-Times*, February 7, 1966, 72; Editorial page, "Throw the Bums Out," *Chicago Daily News*, February 5, 1966, 14; Editorial page, "Sucker Bait," *Chicago Tribune*, February 14, 1966, 1:20.

7. One critical article from the black press is "Clay Opens New 'Kettle of Fish,'" *New York Amsterdam News*, January 25, 1966, 25. Cal Jacox, "From the Sidelines," *Cleveland Call and Post*, January 22, 1966, 22; Ric Roberts, "Change of Pace," *Pittsburgh Courier*, February 19, 1966, 14; "'Mob' Ruled Boxers Retire Flat Broke," *Pittsburgh Courier*, February 12, 1966, 15.

8. Hauser, *Muhammad Ali*, 142; UPI report, "Clay, Namath Targets in Draft Legislation," *Louisville Courier-Journal*, February 10, 1966, B-5; Chip Magnus, "Congressmen Seek Khaki for Clay, Namath," *Chicago Sun-Times*, February 10, 1966, 116; UPI report, "Draft Heat On, But Lip Still Zipped," *Los Angeles Times*, February 12, 1966, 2:7.

9. Ali quoted in Tom Fitzpatrick, "Cassius Appeals; 'Muslims Not at War,'" *Chicago Daily News*, February 18, 1966, 29; Ali quoted in "Clay Sees Self as Boon to U.S. in Civilian Dress," *Chicago Tribune*, February 21, 1966, 1:3. All quotes from Fitzpatrick except for last one.

10. Dick Young, "Young Ideas," *New York Daily News*, December 31, 1966, 38; Jack Clary, "Frothy Facts," *New York World-Telegram and Sun*, February 21, 1966, 37; Red Smith, "Folk Hero," *New York Herald-Tribune*, February 21, 1966, 28; Gene Ward, "Ward to the Wise," *New York Daily News*, February 20, 1966, 153; Arthur Daley, "Instant Bile," *New York Times*, February 24, 1966, 42.

11. Melvin Durslag, "A Fight to Help the Worthy," *Los Angeles Herald-Examiner*, February 21, 1966, C-1; Milton Moss, "Emergency Operation on Clay," *Los Angeles Herald-Examiner*, February 22, 1966, C-2; Red Smith, "The Patrioteers," *New York Herald-Tribune*, February 23, 1966, 28; Jimmy Cannon, "Too Much at Stake; Muslims Silence Clay," *Chicago Daily News*, February 22, 1966, 17; Editorial page, "Clay's Tough Assignment," *Chicago's American*, February 25, 1966, 10; Editorial page, "He's All Yours, Louisville," *Chicago Tribune*, February 25, 1966, 18.

12. Editorial page, "Cassius vs. the Draft," *Chicago's American*, February 19, 1966, 4; Editorial page, "The Reluctant Hero," *Chicago Tribune*, February 19, 1966, 1:10; "News Chiefs Rap Kerner, Boxing Board," *Chicago Tribune*, February 21, 1966, 1:3; "VFW Urges Kerner to Block Clay Fight," *Chicago Tribune*, February 21, 1966, 1:2; "2 Legislators Rip Clay Bout License," *Chicago Tribune*, February 21, 1966, 1:1; "Senator Asks Kerner to Cancel Clay Bout," *Chicago Tribune*, February 22, 1966, 1:1; Siragusa quoted in "Siragusa Raps Clay on Draft," *Chicago Tribune*, February 23, 1966, 1:1; Wilson quoted in "Wilson Fears Disorders at Clay Fight: Joins Opposition with Howlett," *Chicago Tribune*, February 24, 1966, 1:1; James R. Ralph Jr., *Northern Protest: Martin Luther King, Jr., Chicago, and the Civil Rights Movement* (Cambridge: Harvard University Press, 1993), 87; Daley quoted in Editorial page, "Mayor Daley's Good Advice," *Chicago Tribune*, February 23, 1966, 1:16; Kerner quoted in "Clay Due Tomorrow as Fight Furor Grows," *Chicago's American*, February 23, 1966, 37.

13. Bentley quoted in AP report, "Cassius Is Still Single; Regrets Draft Popoff," *New York Daily News*, February 21, 1966, 117; Triner quoted in AP report, "Clay Gives Apologies to Illinois," *Miami Herald*, February 22, 1966, B-1; Ali quoted (first quote) in UPI report, "Illinois Delays Fight Decision Pending Personal Clay Apology," *Miami Herald*, February 22, 1966, B-1; Ali quoted (second quote) in Lester Bromberg, "Clay's New 'Quiet Man' Role May Save Fight," *New York World-Telegram and Sun*, February 22, 1966, 8.

14. Larry Merchant, "Clay Pigeon," *Philadelphia Daily News*, February 22, 1966, 58; UPI report, "Clay Apologizes for Draft Remarks," *Atlanta Daily World*, February 22, 1966, 1; Moss, "Emergency Operation," C-2; Cannon, "Too Much at Stake," 17; Editorial page, "Whoever Wins, Illinois Loses," *Chicago Daily News*, February 23, 1966, 8; Ray Sons, "Shy Clay to 'Avoid' Muslim Meeting Here," *Chicago Daily News*, February 23, 1966, 49; Jack Mabley, "Plans Apology before Athletic Commission Here," *Chicago's American*, February 24, 1966, 1; AP report, "Clay Not Expected to Attend Black Muslim Convention," *New York Times*, February 24, 1966, 44; Daley, "Instant Bile," 44; Sid Ziff, "One Fight He Wants," *Los Angeles Times*, February 25, 1966, 3:3; Ali quoted in Pat Putnam, "Muslim Clay to Stay Away?" *Miami Herald*, February 24, 1966, D-5; "News from the Camp of the Champ," *Muhammad Speaks*, March 4, 1966, 9; "Champion Silent on Arrival for State Hearing," *Chicago's American*, February 25, 1966, 1.

15. Ed Stone, "Suspicion Clouds Clay-Terrell Sanction Here," *Chicago's American*, February 25, 1966, 25; "Champ Refuses to Apologize to Commission," *Chicago Daily News*, February 25, 1966, 3:25; Ali and Triner quoted in "Clay Fight Ruled Illegal," *Chicago's American*, February 26, 1966, 1:1, 25; David Condon, "In the Wake of the News," *Chicago Tribune*, February 26, 1966, 2:1; Ali quoted (final quote of paragraph) in Ed Sainsbury, "Illinois: Fight Is Illegal . . . Clay No Apology," *New York World-Telegram and Sun*, February 25, 1966, 25.

16. Bentley and Schoenwald were the only members of the National Sports Promotion Corporation, which promoted the live, on-site event. According to Clark, the licensing problems were the following: Ali didn't file a certificate of a resident physician with his license reapplication; Ali answered a "moral character" question insufficiently; Ali failed to include his proper ring record in the license reapplication; and he signed the application "Muhammad Ali" instead of "Cassius Clay." Clark also cited Terrell for failing to file a physician's certificate. Clark quoted in "Attorney General Clark's Statement," *Chicago's American*, February 25, 1966, 25; Jesse Abramson, "The Championship Fight Almost Nobody Wants," *New York Herald-Tribune*, March 2, 1966, 27; Daley quoted in Doug Gilbert, "Clay Title Fight on Ropes Here, Pittsburgh Next?" *Chicago's American*, February 26, 1966, 1:1; Editorial page, "A Wise Decision at Last," *Chicago Tribune*, March 3, 1966, 20.

17. Arum quoted in Jack Berry, "Clay: He Wouldn't Crawl," *Detroit Free Press*, March 10, 1966, D-2; Robert Lipsyte, "Clay-Terrell Fight for Title Is Shifted to Louisville for March 29," *New York Times*, March 1, 1966, 30; Robert Lipsyte, "Louisville Rejects Plans for a Clay-Terrell Go," *New York Times*, March 2, 1966, 36; Sullivan quoted in UPI report, "Kentucky Senate Urges Clay to Enlist," *Philadelphia Daily News*, February 24, 1966, 58; Gilbert, "Clay Title Fight," 1:1; UPI report, "Clay-Terrell Bout Gets No Pennsylvania Welcome," *New York Times*, February 27, 1966, 5:2; AP report, "Boxing's Big Bout Bangor Bound?" *Los Angeles Herald-Examiner*, February

28, 1966, D-1; AP report, "No Decision on Clay Bout," *Baltimore Sun*, March 1, 1966, C-1; Reed quoted in AP report, "Heavy Fight Bounces Back," *Baltimore Sun*, March 2, 1966, C-1.

18. Muhammad quoted in "Muslim Leader Raps Viet Policy While Clay Listens," *Chicago Tribune*, February 27, 1966, 1:3; David Condon, "In the Wake of the News," *Chicago Tribune*, March 28, 1966, 3:1. Also see Paul Sisco, "Muslim Chief Backs Clay's Draft Stand," *Louisville Courier-Journal*, February 27, 1966, A-1.

19. UPI report, "Clay Is Granted Permission to Leave Country for Bout," *New York Times*, March 18, 1966, 47. Also see Milton Gross, "Cassius Clay at the Brink," *Chicago Daily News*, March 28, 1966, 29.

20. For explanations of the fight's rejection by various Canadian cities, some of which were political, some of which were logistic, see Jesse Abramson, "The License Hasn't Been Granted Yet," *New York Herald-Tribune*, March 3, 1966, 20; Combined wire services, "Funny Thing Happened to Clay Title Bout on Its Way to the Forum," *New York Herald-Tribune*, March 4, 1966, 21; Jesse Abramson, "Clay Fails to Pass at Verdun, Tries New Front," *New York Herald-Tribune*, March 5, 1966, 13; AP report, "5 Sites Considered for Clay Title Bout," *New York Herald-Tribune*, March 6, 1966, 4:6; UPI report, "Montreal May Take Clay Bout," *Los Angeles Herald-Examiner*, March 3, 1966, D-2; Norm Miller, "Ill. Wind Blows: Clay-Terrell Go to Montreal," *New York Daily News*, March 3, 1966, 66; AP report, "Sorrels, Edmonton Display Interest," *New York Times*, March 5, 1966, 19; Berry, "Clay: He Wouldn't Crawl," D-2; Lester Bromberg, "Toronto: We'll Accept Clay-Terrell Fight," *New York World-Telegram and Sun*, March 8, 1966, 18; *The Last Round: Chuvalo vs. Ali*.

21. *Donohue's Legends: Requiem for a Heavyweight* [television series], directed by Tom Aziz (Calgary: CTV, 1991); Chuvalo quoted in *The Originals: George Chuvalo—A Portrait in the First Person* [television series], directed by Jim Hanley (Toronto: City TV, 1990); Marciano quoted in Hauser, *Muhammad Ali*, 149.

22. Chuvalo ("I know I beat Terrell . . .") quoted in *Donohue's Legends: Requiem for a Heavyweight*; Chuvalo quotes Luftspring in *The Last Round: Chuvalo vs. Ali*; *The Originals: George Chuvalo—A Portrait in the First Person*.

23. Kilroy quoted in AP report, "Cal. Charges Terrell Controlled by Thugs," *San Juan Star*, November 19, 1965, 55–56; Bob Sales, "Terrell's Manager Ripped by California Commission," *New York Herald-Tribune*, November 19, 1965, 26; Jim McCulley, "N.Y. Denies Terrell's Bid for Title Bout with Clay," *New York Daily News*, January 29, 1966, 26; Tape-recorded in-person interview with Ernie Terrell, Chicago, IL, July 5, 2002. An excellent overview of the intrigue surrounding Terrell appears in Robert Lipsyte, "State Commission Denies License to Terrell," *New York Times*, January 29, 1966, 17.

24. Lester Bromberg, "Clay-Terrell Fight for Title Appears Dead," *New York World-Telegram and Sun*, March 10, 1966, 12; Jesse Abramson, "Clay Fights Chuvalo for Peanuts in Toronto," *New York Herald-Tribune*, March 29, 1966, 22; Arthur Daley, "Is This Trip Necessary?" *New York Times*, March 29, 1966, 47; Eddie Muller, "Clay-Chuvalo Talk Negative," *San Francisco Examiner*, March 25, 1966, 67; Lester Bromberg, "Price Is 6–5 Chuvalo Will Go 15 Rounds," *New York World-Telegram and Sun*, March 28, 1966, 27; Prescott Sullivan, "Who'd Want to Miss It?" *San Francisco Examiner*, March 23, 1966, 61; Robert Lipsyte, "Bettor's Eye View of Chuvalo: A Big Bum with a Lot of Heart," *New York Times*, March 26, 1966, 19; Bob Stewart, "Just Maybe," *New*

York World-Telegram and Sun, March 25, 1966, 27; John P. Carmichael, "The Barber Shop," *Chicago Daily News*, March 26, 1966, 3:29; Red Smith, "The Action," *New York Herald-Tribune*, March 29, 1966, 23; Robert Lipsyte, "Patterson Gains Unanimous Decision over Chuvalo in 12 Rounder," *New York Times*, February 2, 1965, 36; "64 Theater Sites to Show Patterson-Chuvalo Bout," *New York Times*, January 27, 1965, 39; *The Last Round: Chuvalo vs. Ali*.

25. AP report, "Clay Beats Chuvalo in 15 Rounds," *Baltimore Sun*, March 30, 1966, C-1; Melvin Durslag, "A Good Lively Match," *San Francisco Examiner*, March 30, 1966, 78; Robert Lipsyte, "Clay Outpoints Chuvalo in Bruising, No-Knockdown 15-Rounder at Toronto," *New York Times*, March 30, 1966, 49; "Clay Quiet, Chuvalo Proud," *New York World-Telegram and Sun*, March 30, 1966, 26; *Donohue's Legends: Requiem for a Heavyweight*; Brown and Dunphy quoted from film of Ali vs. Chuvalo closed-circuit telecast, March 29, 1966.

26. AP report, "Fight Facts and Figures," *Chicago Daily News*, February 9, 1966, 45; AP report, "Fight Theater TV a Resounding Dud," *San Francisco Examiner*, March 30, 1966, 78; *N.Y. Times-Chicago Tribune* dispatch, "Advertisers Boycotting Clay Fight," *Chicago Tribune*, March 15, 1966, 3:3; AP report, "Ad Sponsors Cool to Bout," *Baltimore Sun*, March 16, 1966, C-3.

27. Brown quoted from *The Last Round: Chuvalo vs. Ali*; Arum quoted in Gil Rogin, "A Battle of the Lionhearted," *Sports Illustrated*, April 11, 1966, 37; Mike Marqusee, *Redemption Song: Muhammad Ali and the Spirit of the Sixties* (London: Verso, 1999), 178.

28. AP report, "Miami Legion Post to Picket Theaters," *New York Herald-Tribune*, March 6, 1966, 4:6; Jack Olsen, "A Case of Conscience," *Sports Illustrated*, April 11, 1966, 90; Gregory Allen Howard, ed., *Ali: The Movie and the Man* (New York: Newmarket Press, 2001), 80; Tex Maule, "Showdown with a Punching Bag," *Sports Illustrated*, March 28, 1966, 35; Berry, "Clay: He Wouldn't Crawl," D-2; Eddie Muller, "Chargin, Ms. Eaton Swing Clay TV Ban," *San Francisco Examiner*, March 10, 1966, 56; Norman Ross, "How to Vote against Boxing: Don't Spend Money on It," *Chicago Daily News*, February 25, 1966, 12; Robert Lipsyte, "Coast Backs Boycott," *New York Times*, March 10, 1966, 37; Clark quoted in Marqusee, *Redemption Song*, 177; Dave Kindred, *Sound and Fury: Two Powerful Lives, One Fateful Friendship* (New York: Free Press, 2006), 94.

29. Abramson, "Clay Fights Chuvalo," 47; AP report, "Clay Beats Chuvalo," C-1; AP report, "Theater-TV Lays an Egg at the Box Office," *New York World-Telegram and Sun*, March 30, 1966, 26; AP report, "Clucking Sound at Clay Box Office," *San Francisco Examiner*, March 12, 1966, 33; Chargin/Eaton statement quoted in John Washington, "Olympic Bans Clay TV," *Los Angeles Herald-Examiner*, March 8, 1966, F-1; Eddie Muller, "Clay Fight Blackout," *San Francisco Examiner*, March 8, 1966, 51; Muller, "Chargin, Ms. Eaton," 56; *The Last Round: Chuvalo vs. Ali*; Syufy quoted in Eddie Muller, "Syufy Spurns Clay Tee-Vee," *San Francisco Examiner*, March 19, 1966, 31; Sullivan, "Who'd Want to Miss It?" 61; AP report, "Experts Flock to Chuvalo Camp," *San Francisco Examiner*, March 22, 1966, 48; "Fight Tickets on Sale," *Los Angeles Herald-Examiner*, November 21, 1965, E-7; Emerling and Seguin quoted in Lester Bromberg, "Only 1 Local Theater Chain Has Clay TV," *New York World-Telegram and Sun*, March 9, 1966, 34; Paul Weisman, "Fight Facts . . . or Just Fiction?" *New York Herald-Tribune*, March 17, 1966, 24; Dick Young, "Young Ideas," *New York Daily News*,

November 17, 1965, 113; Paul Weisman, ". . . Bout Also Flops on the Popcorn Circuit," *New York Herald-Tribune*, March 29, 1966, 23.

30. Figures from Red Smith, "The Zillion-Dollar Fight Gate, Jacksonville Style," *New York Herald-Tribune*, March 15, 1964, 4:2.

31. AP report, "Fight Theater TV," 78; Abramson, "Clay Fights Chuvalo," 47; AP report, "Clay Beats Chuvalo," C-1; AP report, "Theater-TV Lays an Egg," 26; AP report, "Clucking Sound," 33; Muller, "Clay-Chuvalo Talk," 67; Malitz quoted ("Made enough to pay the bills" and "grossly underpaid") in Dave Brady, "Home TV Carries Clay-Cooper Fight," *Washington Post*, April 27, 1966, C-3; Rogin, "A Battle of the Lion-hearted," 34; Malitz ("We lost money . . .") quoted in Hauser, *Muhammad Ali*, 152; Mark Kram, *Ghosts of Manila: The Fateful Blood Feud between Muhammad Ali and Joe Frazier* (New York: HarperCollins, 2001), 49.

32. Bob Stewart, "Flop in the Making," *New York World-Telegram and Sun*, March 9, 1966, 35; Eddie Muller, "Fight Empire Not That Bad," *San Francisco Examiner*, March 6, 1966, 3:8; Jim Murray, "'Enery Might Shut Him Up," *Des Moines Register*, April 26, 1966, S-2; A. S. Young, "Aw F'Heavens Sake," *New York Amsterdam News*, April 2, 1966, 31. Newspaper articles comparing Main Bout unfavorably to the Louis-ville Sponsoring Group include Larry Boeck, "Association with Muslims Has Cost Clay $2 Million over Last Two Years, Backer Says," *Louisville Courier-Journal*, November 20, 1965, B-9; "Clay, Muslim Pals Figure to Strike It Rich Here," *Chicago Tribune*, February 21, 1966, 3:1; "Clay Group to Stay with Him for Now; Reveal Appeal Plan," *Chicago Tribune*, February 22, 1966, 3:1; Gene Ward, "Ward to the Wise," *New York Daily News*, March 1, 1966, 51; Dick Young, "Young Ideas," *New York Daily News*, June 4, 1966, 35. The most extravagant lambasting of Main Bout and the Nation of Islam in comparison to the Louisville Sponsoring Group is from Jack Olsen, *Black Is Best: The Riddle of Cassius Clay* (New York: Dell Publishing Co., 1967), 209–243.

33. Clarence Matthews, "Muhammad Ali Wins," *Louisville Defender*, April 7, 1966, 30; Marion Jackson, "Views Sports of the World," *Atlanta Daily World*, March 13, 1966, 8; "Champ Ali on Threshold of New Achievements," *Muhammad Speaks*, April 5, 1966, 6; Moses J. Newson, "Cassius Clay, Main Bout, Inc. and a Boxing World Miracle," *Baltimore Afro-American*, April 9, 1966, 10; Brown quoted in "Jim Brown Charges Fight Foes Oppose Negro TV Promoters," *Chicago Daily News*, March 10, 1966, 27; "Jimmy Brown Defends Clay on Capitol Hill," *New York Herald-Tribune*, March 11, 1966, 20.

34. Robert Lipsyte, "Boxing's Bogeyman's Back," *New York Times*, January 30, 1966, S-3; Berry, "Clay: He Wouldn't Crawl," D-2; Jimmy Cannon, "This Mismatch Is for Title, Despite Toronto's Billing," *Chicago Daily News*, March 29, 1966, 40.

35. In his tape-recorded interview with the author, Terrell denied being threatened by gangsters and claimed that Glickman had no mob ties. Terrell also denied talking to the FBI about his withdrawal from the Ali fight. The FBI, with help from the U.S. Department of Justice (it is unclear whether or not they were responding to Adam Clayton Powell's request) investigated the promotion and held grand jury hearings into alleged death threats against Terrell, claiming that Chicago gangsters had threatened to murder him if he faced Ali in Toronto. It also probed whether mobsters had threatened to kill Glickman after he flew to the Big Apple for a licensing hearing on the same plane as Terrell, thus ruining Terrell's chances to get a license in New York. Law enforcement officials and the New York State Athletic Commission knew that Glickman was a mob associate and his carelessly flying with Terrell suggested that the

fighter was connected. The mob wanted the bout to take place in New York for financial reasons.

In all, eleven witnesses from the often-interrelated worlds of organized crime and professional boxing were subpoenaed to appear before the grand jury. They were: Glickman; Irving Schoenwald; Bob Arum; Teddy Brenner and Harry Markson, who together ran Madison Square Garden's boxing division; Joseph Glaser, a New York theatrical agent and boxing manager; Julius Isaacson, Terrell's former manager and a New York underworld associate; Tony Accardo, the Chicago crime syndicate's "godfather"; Felix Alderisio, Accardo's second-in-command; Gus Alex, the boss of the Chicago crime syndicate's gambling operations and a notorious fight fixer; and Gus Zapas, a top Chicago aide to labor leader Jimmy Hoffa. The government wanted to know if Accardo, Alderisio, Alex, Zapas, and perhaps some of their New York affiliates had violated federal gambling and racketeering laws in their attempt to hijack the March 29 promotion. U.S. Attorney Edward Hanrahan sought indictments against anyone who used "terror tactics" to tamper with "the arrangements to promote in New York City the ill-fated [Ali-Terrell] fight."

The United Press International reported that the underworld would have received half of Terrell's $300,000 purse had the fight been held in New York. The government's key witness was Glickman. If he testified, the prosecution would have a reasonable chance to indict gangsters who might have interfered with the promotion. Witness Isaacson proved to be no help, and Zapas and Alex exercised their Fifth Amendment rights. The statements by Brenner, Markson, and Schoenwald were taken on March 30. Glickman told his story on March 31, discussing his entry into the fight game, his associations with boxers, and his relationships with fellow witnesses. After Glickman's testimony, Hanrahan announced that he would postpone further hearings to consider the evidence. He reserved the right to call the witnesses again and ordered federal protection for Glickman. On April 15, Glickman entered the hospital for exhaustion and released himself from the FBI's protective custody, which the government feared signaled a deal between him and the gangsters he had offended. According to unnamed officials working the case, Glickman agreed not to implicate Accardo and Alderisio in exchange for his life. With its star witness suddenly uncooperative, hamstrung investigators had no case and were forced to retreat. The only indictment they could muster was of Gus Alex, who later went free. Members of the black press were disappointed by the government's failure to make more of an impact on mob control of professional boxing, while white reporters were silent about the investigation's conclusion.

For descriptions of Terrell's and Glickman's problems in New York, see Ed Stone, "Glickman Denies Terrell Controlled by Underworld," *Chicago's American*, November 19, 1965, 33; AP report, "Ernie Says Charge 'Lie,'" *Atlanta Journal*, November 19, 1965, 22; UPI report, "Deny Terrell License to Fight in New York," *New York World-Telegram and Sun*, January 28, 1966, 24; McCulley, "N.Y. Denies Terrell's Bid," 26; Lipsyte, "State Commission Denies License to Terrell," 17; Lipsyte, "Boxing's Bogeyman's Back," S-3; Dave Nightingale, "Ernie Denies Glickman Ties," *Chicago Daily News*, February 1, 1966, 31; Phil Pepe, "The Terrell Case," *New York World-Telegram and Sun*, February 17, 1966, 15; Jesse Abramson, "Terrell Lost Date by Coincidence," *New York Herald-Tribune*, February 17, 1966, 23.

For discussions of the FBI grand jury hearings, see Cannon, "This Mismatch Is for Title," 40; AP/UPI report, "Probe on Terrell Death Threat," *San Francisco Examiner*,

March 26, 1966, 31; AP report, "U.S. Probes Threat to Terrell's Life," *New York Herald-Tribune*, March 27, 1966, 4:1; UPI report, "Inquiry Ordered on Boxing Threat," *New York Times*, March 27, 1966, 5:1; "Who's Who in Federal Probe of Mob's Link to Boxing," *Chicago Daily News*, March 30, 1966, 5; Edmund J. Rooney, "Boxing Probe Opens Here after Last Minute Site Shift," *Chicago Daily News*, March 30, 1966, 1; "Glickman Tells Jury of Mob's Boxing Links," *Chicago Daily News*, March 31, 1966, 6; Norman Glubok, "'I'll Talk, I'm Not Afraid,' Says Terrell," *Chicago Daily News*, March 28, 1966, 1; Robert Lipsyte, "Showdown in Boxing," *New York Times*, March 28, 1966, 45; UPI report, "Ring Pilot Gives Extortion Terms," *New York Times*, March 28, 1966, 45; UPI report, "In This Corner—The Mafia," *San Francisco Examiner*, March 28, 1966, 65; Edmund J. Rooney, "Glickman in City—Guarded by FBI," *Chicago Daily News*, March 29, 1966, 1; Combined news services, "Glickman's Hobby Goes Sour, Business Fails," *St. Louis Post-Dispatch*, March 31, 1966, C-8; "Glickman Hospital Stay 'Indefinite,'" *Chicago Daily News*, May 4, 1966, 5; "Fear Mob Promised Glickman Protection to Stop Testimony," *Chicago's American*, April 16, 1966, 3; "Boxing Jury Indictment," *Chicago Daily News*, April 15, 1966, 1.

For a note on the indictment of Gus Alex, see "Boxing Jury Indictment," 1. For the *Pittsburgh Courier* commentary, see "Terrell 'Intimidation' Exposes Ring Problem," *Pittsburgh Courier*, May 14, 1966, 14.

36. Lipsyte, "Showdown in Boxing," 45; UPI report, "Ring Pilot Gives," 45; UPI report, "In This Corner," 65.

37. Ali quoted in Phil Pepe, "Uneasy Lies the Head," *New York World-Telegram and Sun*, March 8, 1966, 16; Milton Gross, "Clay Distressed Now," *Chicago Daily News*, March 8, 1966, 35; Ali quoted in Milton Gross, "Clay Heaviest of Career," *Chicago Daily News*, March 29, 1966, 39; Ali quoted in Earl Ruby, "Ruby's Report," *Louisville Courier-Journal*, March 2, 1966, B-4; Ali quoted in Larry Merchant, "A Day with Clay," *Philadelphia Daily News*, March 8, 1966, 64; Ali (words before "more than money") quoted in Robert Lipsyte, "Youngsters' Chatter Helps Clay Endure Camp Drudgery," *New York Times*, February 20, 1966, 4:3; Ali ("I'm not disturbed . . .") quoted in Robert Lipsyte, "Clay Says He Is a Jet Airplane and All the Rest Are Prop Jets," *New York Times*, March 25, 1966, 49.

38. For reports on ABC's negotiations with Main Bout, see Brady, "Home TV Carries," C-3; AP report, "Clay, Cooper Home TV Is Discussed," *San Francisco Chronicle*, April 28, 1966, 56; UPI report, "Clay Bout on Satellite Relay to US," *San Francisco Chronicle*, April 29, 1966, 60; Milton Gross, "Rolling in the Isles," *New York Post*, May 24, 1966, 93. For financial particulars about the Ali-Cooper fight, see Arthur Veysey, "See Sellout Crowd for Cooper and Clay Battle," *Chicago Tribune*, May 12, 1966, 3:1; AP report, "Cassius Wants Jones as Next Opponent," *Hartford Courant*, May 23, 1966, 22; Gene Ward, "Clay in 6—Henry's a Bloody Mess," *New York Daily News*, May 22, 1966; "Cooper's Share May Remain a Secret," *Irish Times*, May 24, 1966, 3; "Big Fight Finance," *London Daily Express*, May 23, 1966, 4; AP report, "Clay 11–2 Choice to Retain World Heavyweight Crown over Cooper," *Wichita Eagle and Beacon*, May 15, 1966, D-5; John Rodda, "Why Clay Is Coming Here," *Manchester Guardian*, April 18, 1966, A-1; "Bookies Say It's Clay," *London Daily Mirror*, May 21, 1966, 2; "The Clay Fight May Go on TV," *London Daily Mirror*, May 9, 1966, 24; "British Broadcast Is Set Up for Clay-Cooper Title Bout," *New York Times*, May 9, 1966, 53; Ken Irwin, "Big Fight 'Live' on the Radio," *London Daily Mirror*, May 14, 1966, 11; Mike Grade, "Sport-

light," *London Daily Mirror*, April 26, 1966, 20; Desmond Hackett, "'Enry's 'Arvest," *London Daily Express*, April 18, 1966, 18; AP report, "Clay, Beatles Rate Same Tax Category," *Wichita Eagle*, May 27, 1966, D-5; Eddie Muller, "Shadow Boxing: Clay's Purse Well-Bitten," *San Francisco Examiner*, June 7, 1966, 60; UPI report, "Title Bout May Pay $140,000 to Cooper," *Washington Post*, April 26, 1966, C-2. Details about Ali's relationship with ABC are in Jim Spence and Dave Diles, *Up Close and Personal: The Inside Story of Network Television Sports* (New York: Atheneum Publishers, 1988), 92, 102–103, 231.

39. "He's a Mere Mortal," *San Francisco Examiner*, August 5, 1966, 49; Arthur Daley, "A Visit with Brian London," *New York Times*, August 5, 1966, 22; Arthur Daley, "Britain Showing Little Interest," *New York Times*, August 6, 1966, 23; Sydney Hulls, "Frozen London," *London Daily Express*, August 8, 1966, 11; UPI report, "Clay-London Mismatch Was Financial Bomb, Too," *Washington Post*, August 10, 1966, D-3; AP report, "ABC to Televise Clay Title Bout," *Washington Post*, July 7, 1966, B-4; AP report, "Clay on TV," *Louisville Courier-Journal*, July 7, 1966, B-5; AP report, "Clay Title Bout on Live TV," *San Francisco Examiner*, July 20, 1966, 41; Milton Gross, "Cassius 203 1/2, Karl 194 3/4," *New York Post*, September 10, 1966, 80; Sydney Hulls, "Angelo Predicts a K.O. Win," *London Daily Express*, August 4, 1966, 11; Red Fisher, "British Board Should Have Blocked Bout," *Montreal Star*, August 11, 1966, 26; Gene Ward, "Terrell Outpoints Jones, Fans Boo 'Champ' for Fouls," *New York Daily News*, June 29, 1966, 107.

40. "Clay to Get 50 Percent for Bout with Mildenberger," *New York Times*, July 10, 1966, S-8; Fred Tupper, "Fight Expected to Draw 40,000," *New York Times*, September 10, 1966, 23; Gross, "Cassius 203 1/2," 80; Hugh McIlvaney, "Clay Wins in 12th Round," *London Observer*, September 11, 1966, 20; AP report, "Mildenberger Accepts Sept. 10 as Date for Title Fight with Clay," *Washington Post*, June 25, 1966, E-1; AP report, "Clay Stops German in 12th Round," *Washington Post*, September 11, 1966, C-5.

41. Figures from Maule, "Showdown with a Punching Bag," 102.

42. Ali and unnamed LSG member quoted in Olsen, "All Alone with the Future," 39, 42, 45; Muhammad quoted in Hauser, *Muhammad Ali*, 155–156; Marqusee, *Redemption Song*, 87; Kindred, *Sound and Fury*, 75.

43. Al Buck, "Cassius Puts Out the Cat; Terrell Next—In Garden?" *New York Post*, November 15, 1966, 96; "Title Crowd Shatters Indoor Fight Record," *New York Post*, November 15, 1966, 92; "Clay-Williams Bout Is Slated for 24 Metropolitan Theaters," *New York Times*, November 13, 1966, 5:2; AP/UPI report, "Clay Rates Williams Fifth among Foes," *San Francisco Chronicle*, November 16, 1966, 50; Al Buck, "Cat Can't Win, Odds Insist," *New York Post*, November 14, 1966, 88; AP report, "Clay-Williams to Be on Radio Monday," *Newark Star-Ledger*, November 11, 1966, 36; UPI report, "Mutual Radio Carries Clay Bout," *Washington Post*, November 11, 1966, G-2; Gene Ward, "Clay 5–1 to Skin a Cat in Title Fight," *New York Daily News*, November 14, 1966, 72; Gene Ward, "Another Clay Pigeon: Cat KO'ed at 1:08 of the 3d," *New York Daily News*, November 15, 1966, 86; "Branford Set to Televise Clay-Williams," *Newark Star-Ledger*, November 13, 1966, 8:2; Jack Fiske, "A Shuffle, Some Fun, and a Fight," *San Francisco Chronicle*, November 15, 1966, 45; "Clay TV," *San Francisco Chronicle*, November 12, 1966, 39; Brown quoted in Frank Mastro, "TV Viewers Cheer Clay's TKO Victory," *Chicago Tribune*, November 15, 1966, 3.2, "A Compound Problem Confronts Cassius!" *Los Angeles Herald-Examiner*, November 1, 1966, D-2.

44. "Facts on Houston Fight," *New York Times*, February 8, 1967, 23; "Fight Facts, Figures," *Houston Post*, February 8, 1967, 3:3; "Clay Now Eyes Old Man Folley," *Los Angeles Herald-Examiner*, February 7, 1967, B-3; Gerald Eskenazi, "Telecast Highlight: Close-Ups of Terrell's Face," *New York Times*, February 7, 1967, 46; Jesse Abramson, "Acoustical Dud in Garden," *New York World Journal Tribune*, February 7, 1967, 29; Jim McCulley, "Garden TV: A One-Rounder," *New York Daily News*, February 7, 1967, 52; George Bernet, "Ali's Crowd Cheers Hero in Theater," *Newark Star-Ledger*, February 7, 1967, 22; Steve Cady, "30,000 Expected at Houston Fight," *New York Times*, February 6, 1967, 36; "Garden among 25 Nearby Sites Presenting Title Fight on TV," *New York Times*, February 5, 1967, 5:3; Advertisement, *Los Angeles Herald-Examiner*, January 22, 1967, D-4; William Jackson, "Now Ali Is Undisputed Champ," *Cleveland Call and Post*, February 11, 1967, 1; "Clay or Louis: Who Was the Greatest Fighter?" *Los Angeles Sentinel*, January 26, 1967, B-3; Marion Jackson, "Views Sports of the World," *Atlanta Daily World*, January 21, 1967, 5.

45. Jim McCulley, "Clay Right to Jaw KO's Folley in 7," *New York Daily News*, March 23, 1967, 70; Kay Gardella, "Clay-Folley Bout to Revive Home TV," *New York Daily News*, February 22, 1967, 78; Jim McCulley, "Cassius Pockets $264,838," *New York Daily News*, March 24, 1967, 54.

46. "Champion Is Set for 10th Defense," *New York Times*, April 4, 1967, 51; "Clay and Floyd Do It Again on April 25 in Las Vegas," *New York World Journal Tribune*, April 4, 1967, 45; Robert Lipsyte, "After Patterson, the Field Lies Fallow," *New York Times*, April 3, 1967, 53; Joe O'Day, "Clay, Pat Sign for Encore; Ali's Swan Song," *New York Daily News*, April 5, 1967, 99; AP report, "Clay and Patterson Sign for Rematch," *Chicago Tribune*, April 5, 1967, 3:1; Malitz quoted in Deane McGowen, "Patterson Fight with Clay Is Off," *New York Times*, April 13, 1967, 56.

47. Jimmy Cannon, "Clay-Floyd Fight: A Sanctioned Atrocity," *New York World Journal Tribune*, April 5, 1967, 45; Lamb quoted in UPI report, "Won't Police Fight, Vegas Sheriff Says," *Philadelphia Daily News*, April 6, 1967, 53; Laxalt quoted in UPI report, "Nevada Cancels Clay Title Bout," *New York Times*, April 12, 1967, 53; Dooley and Malitz quoted in McGowen, "Patterson Fight," 56; UPI report, "Clay Title Fight Is Counted Out," *New York Times*, April 15, 1967, 23.

48. Brad Pye Jr., "Will Clay Ever Fight Again?" *Los Angeles Sentinel*, April 27, 1967, B1; Bill Nunn, "Change of Pace," *Pittsburgh Courier*, April 22, 1967, 14; Editorial page, "Move with Indecent Haste," *Louisville Defender*, May 11, 1967, A-6. For information about the tournament to replace Ali, see Gene Ward, "Ward to the Wise," *New York Daily News*, April 20, 1967, 95; Robert Lipsyte, "Boxing's New Era: The Gold Rush Is On," *New York Times*, April 30, 1967, 5:1; Robert Lipsyte, "Patterson Bout Slated July 15," *New York Times*, May 9, 1967, 58; Gene Ward, "Seven Stalking Clay's Title Willingly; Frazier Stalls," *New York Daily News*, May 10, 1967, 97; "'Not Guilty,' Says Clay in Draft Case," *Newark Star-Ledger*, May 9, 1967, 1, 14; UPI report, "Ring Tourney Moves Closer to Reality," *Louisville Courier-Journal and Times*, May 7, 1967, C-6; Nicholas Von Hoffman, "Clay Refuses Induction, Stripped of World Title," *Washington Post*, April 29, 1967, A-1, C-4; Dave Brady, "8 So-So Heavyweights Bounce into Title Picture," *Washington Post*, April 30, 1967, D-5.

49. Ashe quoted in Hauser, *Muhammad Ali*, 204–205.

50. Marqusee, *Redemption Song*, 76; Ali, Wilkins, Patterson, and Bond quoted in Dave Zirin, *Muhammad Ali Handbook* (London: MQ Publications Ltd., 2007), 116–117, 121.

51. Marqusee, *Redemption Song*, 79; Bond and Guyot quoted in Zirin, *Muhammad Ali Handbook*, 117, 123.

52. Tape-recorded in-person interview with John Lewis, Washington, DC, March 21, 2002.

53. Tape-recorded telephone interview with Julian Bond, March 18, 2002; final Bond quote of paragraph from Zirin, *Muhammad Ali Handbook*, 198.

54. Bond quoted in "Julian Bond Speaks on Need for Black Struggle against American Injustice," *Muhammad Speaks*, October 20, 1967, 27; UPI report, "Bond Proposes Proclaiming Victory, Leaving Vietnam," *Norfolk Journal and Guide*, May 13, 1967, 15.

55. Marqusee, *Redemption Song*, 132–133, 212–214; Branch, *Pillar of Fire*, 478–479; UPI report, "Rev. King, Muhammad Join in War on Slums," *Norfolk Journal and Guide*, February 26, 1966, 1; "Elijah Blasts King, U.S. Peace Aim," *Chicago's American*, February 27, 1966, 1:1; Muhammad quoted in "King 'Deceiver,' Elijah Charges in New Attack," *Chicago's American*, February 28, 1966, 2; Robert Lipsyte, "Clay Puts His Affairs in Order as Day of Decision Approaches," *New York Times*, April 27, 1967, 54; "Cassius Clay Draws King's Praise," *Los Angeles Sentinel*, May 4, 1967, A-2; King ("He is giving up even fame. . . .") quoted in "King Denounces U.S. Position on Viet: Praises Heroic Stand of Muhammad Ali," *Muhammad Speaks*, May 12, 1967, 2; King ("As Muhammad Ali has said . . .") quoted in Zirin, *Muhammad Ali Handbook*, 192; King ("When Cassius Clay joined . . .") quoted in Howard Bingham and Max Wallace, *Muhammad Ali's Greatest Fight: Cassius Clay vs. The United States of America* (New York: M. Evans and Company, 2000), 92, 136, 166 (quote is on page 92, information about relationship between King and Ali is on pages 136 and 166); Ali quoted in Pan African Press, "Champion Takes Greatest Struggle," *Muhammad Speaks*, April 28, 1967, 9. For background on King's role in the Louisville open-housing campaign, see Ralph, *Northern Protest*, 215–216.

56. Ali quoted in Marqusee, *Redemption Song*, 214–215.

57. Editorial page, "Two in One," *St. Louis Argus*, April 28, 1967, 12; Raby quoted in "Black Leaders Blast Unjust U.S. Conviction of Heavyweight Champion Muhammad Ali," *Muhammad Speaks*, June 30, 1967, 9; Robinson ("What values do you have . . .") quoted in Marqusee, *Redemption Song*, 222; Robinson ("The tragedy is that . . .") quoted in Cecil Blye, "The Box Seat," *Louisville Defender*, October 19, 1967, C-2.

58. "Abernathy Meets Minister Ali," *Louisville Defender*, April 6, 1967, A-5; Pan African Press, "Champion Takes Greatest Struggle," 9; Bevel quoted in "Chicago Fans Rock Stagg Fieldhouse with Applause for World Heavyweight Champ," *Muhammad Speaks*, May 19, 1967, 26.

59. Ali quoted in Clarence Matthews, "Matter of Sports," *Louisville Defender*, April 27, 1967, B-8.

60. Ali quoted in "Muhammad Ali Speaks His Mind on Riots," *Los Angeles Sentinel*, August 31, 1967, B-3.

61. McKissick quoted in Bill Nunn, "Change of Pace," *Pittsburgh Courier*, May 13, 1967, 14, "News from the Camp of the Champ," *Muhammad Speaks*, May 19, 1967, 9;

UPI report, "Clay's Sentence Termed 'Incredible,'" *Baltimore Afro-American*, July 1, 1967, 13; Ali and McKissick ("one of the greatest living . . ." and "for being the greatest heavyweight . . .") quoted in UPI report, "Ali Advocates U.S. Apartheid," *Baltimore Afro-American*, July 8, 1967, 3; CORE resolution reported in Pan African Press, "CORE Launches Drive to Support Muhammad Ali," *Muhammad Speaks*, December 1, 1967, 9.

62. Carmichael quoted in "Ali Is 'My Hero' Says SNCC Leader, Carmichael," *Muhammad Speaks*, May 12, 1967, 4; Bingham and Wallace, *Muhammad Ali's Greatest Fight*, 194; Forman and Brown ("black people everywhere . . .") quoted in Martin Waldron, "Clay Draft Trial Opens in Houston," *New York Times*, June 20, 1967, 25; Marqusee, *Redemption Song*, 193; Brown ("SNCC stands ready . . .") quoted in "Black Leaders Blast Unjust U.S. Conviction of Heavyweight Champion Muhammad Ali," *Muhammad Speaks*, June 30, 1967, 7, 9.

63. Patterson quoted in Zirin, *Muhammad Ali Handbook*, 197–198; Williams quoted in "How Black Exile Robert Williams Views World Champ from China," *Muhammad Speaks*, November 17, 1967, 7.

64. Editorial page, "Split Leadership," *Chicago Defender*, April 29, 1967, 10; "A New Role for Rev. King," *Cleveland Call and Post*, April 22, 1967, B-5; "Dr. King's Delayed Action Vietnam Bomb," *Norfolk Journal and Guide*, April 29, 1967, 6; "Dr. King's Leadership," *Chicago Defender*, April 22, 1967, 10; "Fallacies in Dr. King's Stand on the Vietnam War," *Atlanta Daily World*, May 4, 1967, 4; "Dr. King and Vietnam," *Kansas City Call*, April 28, 1967, 15; "Dr. King's Tragic Doctrine," *Pittsburgh Courier*, April 15, 1967, 6; Roy Wilkins, "Wilkins Speaks," *Baltimore Afro-American*, April 22, 1967; Roy Wilkins, "News from NAACP," *St. Louis Argus*, July 21, 1967, 2; Whitney Young, "To Be Equal," *Kansas City Call*, May 5, 1967, 15; Cliff Mackay, "Young Takes Slap at King, Carmichael," *Baltimore Afro-American*, April 29, 1967, 3; UPI report, "King's Dual Role Hurting Civil Rights—Sen. Brooke," *Norfolk Journal and Guide*, May 20, 1967, 1; NAACP statement reported in "Viet, Rights 'Marriage' Hit," *St. Louis Argus*, April 14, 1967, 21.

65. Editorial page, "Cassius Clay's Case," *Pittsburgh Courier*, May 27, 1967, 6; "Champion Rips Illegal Drafting of Negroes by White-Dominated Boards," *Muhammad Speaks*, March 24, 1967, 9; "Kentucky Moves to Mix State's 136 Draft Boards," *Baltimore Afro-American*, June 3, 1967, 1; Hauser, *Muhammad Ali*, 192; Editorial page, "Cassius Clay and the Draft," *Atlanta Daily World*, April 30, 1967, 4; UPI report, "Carmichael Says Refuse to Be Drafted for War," *Pittsburgh Courier*, March 11, 1967, 15; "NAACP Is Supporting Draft Law," *Louisville Defender*, April 13, 1967, B-2.

66. Tape-recorded in-person interview with Bob Moses, Jackson, MS, February 12, 2002; Sellers quoted in UPI report, "Draft Refused by Aide to Stokely Carmichael," *Norfolk Journal and Guide*, May 13, 1967, 2; Michael Ferber and Staughton Lynd, *The Resistance* (Boston: Beacon Press, 1971), 127; Marqusee, *Redemption Song*, 176, 242; Julian Bond interview; "Carmichael Back, Passport Is Seized," *Cleveland Call and Post*, December 23, 1967, A-1; Amy Bass, *Not the Triumph but the Struggle: The 1968 Olympics and the Making of the Black Athlete* (Minneapolis: University of Minnesota Press, 2002), 34; Bingham and Wallace, *Muhammad Ali's Greatest Fight*, 96–99, 194 (Information about FBI interest in Ali's case is on pages 96–99; Claude Pepper quoted on page 194).

67. Alice Lynd, ed., "Muhammad Ali: The Champ," in *We Won't Go: Personal Accounts of War Objectors* (Boston: Beacon Press, 1968), 226–234; European Boxing Union announcement cited in UPI report, "EBU to Postpone Decision on Ali," *Chicago*

Defender, June 24, 1967, 15; "Revenge-Filled White Christian Court Continues Persecution of Muhammad Ali," *Muhammad Speaks*, August 11, 1967, 2; UPI report, "World Council Declares It Won't Mix Politics and Sports, Won't Ban Ali," *Baltimore Afro-American*, May 13, 1967, 10; Ingraham ("The defendant appears . . .") quoted in UPI report, "Clay Will 'Keep Preaching' as Judge Nixes Tokyo Bout," *Baltimore Afro-American*, August 12, 1967, 10; Ingraham ("I am concerned . . .") quoted in "Clay Can't Leave Country Now," *Cleveland Call and Post*, July 15, 1967, B-12; "Muhammad Tokyo Plea Unanswered," *Baltimore Afro-American*, July 15, 1967, 14.

68. Lynd, "Muhammad Ali: The Champ," 228; Ali quoted in Marqusee, *Redemption Song*, 195; "Muhammad Ali Chosen to Head Black Watts Summer Festival in California," *Muhammad Speaks*, August 18, 1967, 4; story of averted Old Town riot based on author E-mail correspondence with eyewitness Thomas Morrissey, June 21, 2008.

69. Ali quoted in "Chicago Fans Rock Stagg," 26; John Lewis, "1,000 Howard U. Students Cheer Muhammad Ali," *Baltimore Afro-American*, April 29, 1967, 1; Marion Jackson, "Views Sports of the World," *Atlanta Daily World*, May 30, 1967, 5; Bud Furillo, "Ali's Plan: Cat, Ernie and Eddie," *Los Angeles Herald-Examiner*, November 11, 1966, C-5; Melvin Durslag, "The Champ: 'A Tool of Allah,'" *Los Angeles Herald-Examiner*, November 13, 1966, E-1; "Clay Jailed in Miami on Traffic Charge; Opens His Mouth about T.S.U. Riot," *St. Louis American*, May 25, 1967, 21; Hauser, *Muhammad Ali*, 181; Bingham and Wallace, *Muhammad Ali's Greatest Fight*, 148, 155.

70. John Wilson, "Can Big Cat Show Cassius Has Feet of Clay?" *Houston Chronicle*, November 6, 1966, 4:4; Wells Twombly, "Clay, Cat Slate Workouts Today," *Houston Chronicle*, November 7, 1966, 2:2; John Hollis, "Brown to Help Clay in Training," *Houston Post*, November 8, 1966, 4:1; Bingham and Wallace, *Muhammad Ali's Greatest Fight*, 138, 152; Joe McLaughlin, "Clay Has New 'Dance' for Title Fight," *Houston Chronicle*, November 8, 1966, 3:1; AP report, "Jim Brown Aids Clay," *Los Angeles Herald-Examiner*, November 8, 1966, D-1; AP Wire Photograph, "Autographs Don't Come Easy in Houston," *Newark Star-Ledger*, November 9, 1966, 22; John Hollis, "Harris Knows Champions Die Hard," *Houston Post*, November 11, 1966, 5:1; Dick Hackenberg, "A Scared Cassius Clay Awaits the Big Cat Williams," *Chicago Sun-Times*, November 13, 1966, 135; Alvarez quoted in Dick Hackenberg, "Clay's Big Win over 'The Image,'" *Chicago Sun-Times*, November 17, 1966, 134; Ali ("I have a million dollars . . .") quoted in David Condon, "In the Wake of the News," *Chicago Tribune*, November 16, 1966, 3:1; Ali ("The Negro will never be recognized . . .") quoted in Jack Gallagher, "He's Trying to Uplift Race," *Houston Post*, February 8, 1967, 3:2; Ali ("You should never cease . . .") quoted in UPI report, "Clay at Bishop College, Jabs at Ignorance, Bias," *Baltimore Afro-American*, April 8, 1967, 10; Robert Lipsyte, "Muhammad Ali Shows Other Side," *New York Times*, February 6, 1967, 36; Red Smith, "Frisked Press Hears Muhammad Ali Preach," *New York World Journal Tribune*, February 6, 1967, 25; John Hollis, "Ali Says Houston Is His Home Now," *Houston Post*, February 5, 1967, 6:3; Furillo, "Ali's Plan," C-5; Melvin Durslag, "Rev. Ali Reaches the Dome," *Los Angeles Herald-Examiner*, November 11, 1966, C-1; "Clay, Eisenhower Trade Quips," *San Francisco Chronicle*, October 1, 1966, 38.

71. Ali ("Although I myself never had . . .") quoted in "Muhammad Ali Gives $10,000 to College Fund," *St. Louis Argus*, January 27, 1967, A-1; Shabazz Information Service, "Muhammad Ali Becomes Biggest Single Black Contributor to UNCF Charities," *Muhammad Speaks*, March 3, 1967, 20; "Muhammad Ali Faces Lack of

Worthy Foes," *Louisville Defender*, February 9, 1967, 1; Ali ("I'm a race man . . .") quoted in Gross, "Curiouser and Curiouser," 77.

72. Shabazz Information Service, "Muhammad Ali Becomes Biggest," 20; "Clay Fight TV for Colleges," *Chicago Daily News*, October 25, 1966, 38; Eddie Muller, "Cold Shoulder for Folley," *San Francisco Examiner and Chronicle*, October 30, 1966, 3:8; Joe McLaughlin, "'New' Cassius Comes to Town Friday," *Houston Chronicle*, November 1, 1966, 5:4.

73. Davey quoted in "Ali Exhibition: One for the Road?" *Chicago Defender*, June 10, 1967, 16; Ali quoted in UPI report, "Ali Advocates Apartheid," 3; "Clay Wants to Fight for Children," *Los Angeles Sentinel*, July 6, 1967, B-2; "The Woes of Muhammad Ali," *St. Louis Argus*, July 20, 1967, 18; Berman quoted in "California Nixes Ali Poverty Plea," *Baltimore Afro-American*, July 22, 1967, 10; Sam Lacy, "Boxing: So Many Governed by So Few," *Baltimore Afro-American*, July 22, 1967, 9.

74. Terrell ("his comments about the draft . . .") quoted in UPI report, "Terrell Raps Clay, Vows He Will Muzzle Champ," *Baltimore Afro-American*, March 15, 1966, 15; Terrell ("I feel sorry . . .") quoted in Jim McLaughlin, "Terrell Calls Clay 'Very Confused Young Man,'" *Houston Chronicle*, June 15, 1966, 4:4; Jimmy Cannon, "The Day Terrell Slapped Clay Around," *Los Angeles Herald Examiner*, December 11, 1966, D-1; "Terrell Denies Fouling Clay . . . Wants Rematch," *New York Daily News*, February 21, 1967, 113; Steve Cady, "Fight Films Show Rule of Thumb," *New York Times*, February 21, 1967, 58; Ernie Terrell interview; Robert Lipsyte, "Champion Labels Foe 'Uncle Tom,'" *New York Times*, December 29, 1966, 38; John Hollis, "Ali Apologizes to Terrell for Name Calling," *Houston Post*, January 11, 1967, 4:1; "Terrell Is No 'Uncle Tom,'" *Los Angeles Sentinel*, February 2, 1967, B-3; Exchange between Folley and Ali detailed in UPI report, "Zora to Ali: 'Hi, Muhammad,'" *Los Angeles Herald-Examiner*, February 16, 1967, C-1; Ali ("I know what they're telling Folley . . .") quoted in Al Buck, "Fight Getting Closer, Folley Getting Fiercer," *New York Post*, March 18, 1967, 74.

75. Ali quoted in Lipsyte, "Clay Puts His Affairs in Order," 54.

PART III

1. *Malcolm X*, directed by Spike Lee, with Denzel Washington, 201 min. (Warner Brothers, 1992); *Unforgivable Blackness*, directed by Ken Burns, 220 min. (PBS Paramount, 2005).

2. Ali quoted in David Remnick, *King of the World: Muhammad Ali and the Making of an American Hero* (New York: Random House, 1998), 88.

3. Ali and Davidson quoted in Dave Kindred, *Sound and Fury: Two Powerful Lives, One Fateful Friendship* (New York: Free Press, 2006), 103–107; Howard Bingham and Max Wallace, *Muhammad Ali's Greatest Fight: Cassius Clay vs. The United States of America* (New York: M. Evans and Company, 2000), 104, 183.

4. Ali quoted in Bingham and Wallace, *Muhammad Ali's Greatest Fight*, 181, also see 194; Tape-recorded in-person interview with Bob Moses, Jackson, MS, February 12, 2002.

5. "Clay Indicted; Vows 'I Will Not Weaken,' *Cleveland Call and Post*, May 13, 1967, A-1, A-16; Ali quoted in Kindred, *Sound and Fury*, 131.

6. Bingham and Wallace, *Muhammad Ali's Greatest Fight*, 171, 209–211; Kindred, *Sound and Fury*, 132–134. Muhammad Ali quoted on 134.

7. Bingham and Wallace, *Muhammad Ali's Greatest Fight*, 224.

8. Kindred, *Sound and Fury*, 121, 130.

9. Ali quoted in Kindred, *Sound and Fury*, 123–124, also see 130; Bingham and Wallace, *Muhammad Ali's Greatest Fight*, 230; "Lawyer Sues Cassius Clay for Back Fees," *Cleveland Call and Post*, October 21, 1967, A-1.

10. Ali quoted in Kindred, *Sound and Fury*, 288.

11. Bingham and Wallace, *Muhammad Ali's Greatest Fight*, 193; Kindred, *Sound and Fury*, 132.

12. Thomas Hauser, *Muhammad Ali: His Life and Times* (New York: Simon & Schuster, 1991), 208–209; Dave Anderson, "Pols Spar over the Ali-Quarry Bout," *New York Times*, October 23, 1970, 50; Michael Arkush, *The Fight of the Century: Ali vs. Frazier, March 8, 1971* (Hoboken: John Wiley & Sons, 2008), 16, 60.

13. Ali quoted in Kindred, *Sound and Fury*, 135.

14. James F. Clarity, "Ali Awarded the Red Badge of Courage," *New York Times*, October 29, 1970, 59; Abernathy and King quoted in "Purse for Bout above Estimate," *New York Times*, October 28, 1970, 37; Robert Lipsyte, "Ali Says Frazier Will Be Easier," *New York Times*, October 27, 1970, 50.

15. Kindred, *Sound and Fury*, 137.

16. "Argentine Cast as 6–1 Underdog," *New York Times*, December 7, 1970, 68; Dave Anderson, "Argentine Incurs First Knockout," *New York Times*, December 8, 1970, 64.

17. Hauser, *Muhammad Ali*, 222; Art Fisher and Neal Marshall, *Garden of Innocents* (New York: EP Dutton and Co., 1972), 11–14.

18. Hauser, *Muhammad Ali*, 239; Bob Woodward and Scott Armstrong, *The Brethren: Inside the Supreme Court* (New York: Simon & Schuster, 1979), 160.

19. Hauser, *Muhammad Ali,* 281–282; TWA advertisement, *New York Times*, November 3, 1974, S-4.

20. Kindred, *Sound and Fury*, 199.

21. Ali quoted in *When We Were Kings*, directed by Leon Gast, with Muhammad Ali and George Foreman, 89 min. (Universal Studios, 1996); Muhammad quoted in Gregory Allen Howard, ed., *Ali: The Movie and the Man* (New York: Newmarket Press, 2001), 104.

22. Ali quoted in Howard Cosell, *Like It Is* (Chicago: Playboy Press, 1974), 35.

23. Ali quoted in Hauser, *Muhammad Ali*, 295. See *ibid.*, 293–295 for other Ali quotes.

24. Ali and Cosell quoted in Kindred, *Sound and Fury*, 226–230.

25. Kindred, *Sound and Fury*, 231, 269; Hauser, *Muhammad Ali*, 419–420.

26. Hauser, *Muhammad Ali*, 412–417.

27. Kindred, *Sound and Fury*, 267–269; Hauser, *Muhammad Ali*, 422–425.

28. Hauser, *Muhammad Ali*, 431–432; *Saturday Night Live* [television series], produced by Dick Ebersol (New York: NBC, airdate December 12, 1981). Transcript of *Saturday Night Live* sketch can be found at <http://snltranscripts.jt.org/81/81hnews.phtml> (April 22, 2008).

29. Hauser, *Muhammad Ali*, 432–435.

30. Hauser, *Muhammad Ali*, 435; Kindred, *Sound and Fury*, 272.

31. Young and Bond quoted in Hauser, *Muhammad Ali*, 435.

32. Kindred, *Sound and Fury*, 272.

33. Kindred, *Sound and Fury*, 272–274, 320–321; Hauser, *Muhammad Ali*, 435–439; Lynn Waltz, "Spanish Police Arrest Fugitive from Norfolk; Federal Authorities Will Seek Extradition of Hirschfeld from the Canary Islands," *Virginian-Pilot*, January 31, 1997 <http://scholar.lib.vt.edu/VA-news/VA-Pilot/issues/1997/vp970131/01310544.htm> (September 17, 2007); Mark Conrad, "Ali Sues Former Co-Directors to Nullify 1988 Contract," *Mark's Sportslaw News*, August 28, 1999 <http://www.larryjkolb.com/file/18.html> (September 17, 2007); Larry J. Kolb, "Audio File: Richard Hirschfeld, Telephonically Impersonating Muhammad Ali, Pledges to Help George Bush in Presidential Campaign," <http://www.larryjkolb.com/file/38.html> (September 17, 2007).

34. Hauser, *Muhammad Ali*, 466–469.

35. Hauser, *Muhammad Ali*, 469.

36. Lonnie Ali and Cope quoted in Peter Tauber, "Ali: Still Magic," *New York Times*, July 17, 1988 <http://query.nytimes.com/gst/fullpage.html?res=940DE6DC153AF934A-25754C0A96E948260&sec=health&spon=&pagewanted=1> (September 17, 2007).

37. Lonnie Ali comment reported in Neil Leifer and Thomas Hauser, *Muhammad Ali Memories* (New York: Rizzoli, 1992); Hauser, *Muhammad Ali*, 9–11.

38. Telephone interview with Thomas Hauser, August 25, 2004. Notes in possession of the author.

39. Hauser, *Muhammad Ali*, 517–521.

40. Mike Marqusee, *Redemption Song: Muhammad Ali and the Spirit of the Sixties* (London: Verso, 1999), 299.

41. *Howard Cosell: Telling It Like It Is*, produced by Ross Greenburg, 60 min. (HBO Television, 1999); Howard Cosell with Shelby Whitfield, *What's Wrong with Sports* (New York: Simon & Schuster, 1991), 266; Hauser, *Muhammad Ali*, front cover.

42. E-mail correspondence with Kelly Welsh, publicity assistant for Simon & Schuster, August 26, 2004.

43. For example, *Muhammad Ali: The Whole Story*, directed by Joseph Consentino, 346 min. (Turner Home Entertainment, 1996); *Muhammad Ali: Through the Eyes of the World*, directed by Phil Grabsky, 104 min. (Universal Studios, 2002).

44. Summary of *Muhammad Ali: Through the Eyes of the World* <http://movies2.nytimes.com/gst/movies/movie.html?v_id=255923> (July 11, 2007).

45. For example, John Dittmer, *Local People: The Struggle for Civil Rights in Mississippi* (Urbana: University of Illinois Press, 1994); Harvard Sitkoff, *The Struggle for Black Equality, 1954–1992*, 2nd edition (New York: Hill and Wang, 1993).

46. Thomas Hauser with the cooperation of Muhammad Ali, *Muhammad Ali in Perspective* (San Francisco: CollinsPublishersSanFrancisco, 1996), 8–81; Thomas Hauser, *Muhammad Ali and Company* (Norwalk: Hastings House, 1998), 3–41.

47. Hauser, *Muhammad Ali*, 343–344; Muhammad Ali with Richard Durham, *The Greatest: My Own Story* (New York: Random House, 1975), esp. 52–85. Also see Remnick, *King of the World*, 89–91.

48. Gerald Early, "Some Preposterous Propositions from the Heroic Life of Muhammad Ali: A Reading of *The Greatest: My Own Story*," in Elliott J. Gorn, ed., *Muhammad Ali: The People's Champ* (Urbana: University of Illinois Press, 1995), 70–87; Hauser, *Muhammad Ali*, 343.

49. E-mail correspondence between the author and Thomas Hauser, September 27, 2004; interview with Thomas Hauser.

50. Thomas Hauser, "No! No! No! Don't!," December 2001 <http://www.second-sout.com/USA/colhauser.cfm?ccs=208&cs=3659> (July 12, 2007).

51. Robert Lipsyte, "Back to the Warm," March 8, 2006 <http://sports.espn.go .com/espn/eticket/story?page=ali&num=11> (July 12, 2007); Ali quoted in Thomas Hauser, "Ali: The Legacy," *Observer Sports Monthly*, November 2, 2003 <http://observer.guardian.co.uk/osm/story/0,,1072751,00.html> (July 12, 2007); Thomas Hauser, *The Lost Legacy of Muhammad Ali* (Toronto: Sport Classic Books, 2005); Benedikt Taschen and Howard Bingham, *GOAT: A Tribute to Muhammad Ali* (New York: Taschen, 2004); Kindred, *Sound and Fury*, 319; Dave Zirin, *Muhammad Ali Handbook* (London: MQP Publications, 2007), 356–369.

52. Mark Kram, *Ghosts of Manila: The Fateful Blood Feud between Muhammad Ali and Joe Frazier* (New York: HarperCollins, 2001); Jack Cashill, *Sucker Punch: The Hard Left Hook That Dazed Ali and Killed King's Dream* (Nashville: Thomas Nelson, 2006). For an example of critical scholarly coverage of Ali prior to the publication of the Hauser book, see Jeffrey Sammons, *Beyond the Ring: The Role of Boxing in American Society* (Urbana: University of Illinois Press, 1988), 225–233.

53. The event can be seen at <http://www.youtube.com/results?search_query= ali+opening+ceremony+olympic&search=Search> (October 1, 2007).

54. The ceremony can be viewed at <http://www.youtube.com/watch?v=Y9Ol-mPyjsNU&mode=related&search=> (October 2, 2007). Costas's words are taken from the youtube clip of the television broadcast.

55. Ed Bradley (correspondent). *60 Minutes* [television series] (New York: CBS, airdate August 4, 1996). Bradley's and Lonnie Ali's words are taken from a videotape of the television broadcast.

56. Richard Sandomir, "TV Sports: Here's How Ali Got Up There," *New York Times*, July 21, 1996 <http://select.nytimes.com/search/restricted/article?res=FA0815FD3D 5D0C728EDDAE0894DE494D81> (July 17, 2007); Dave Kindred, "How Muhammad Ali Brought Light to the Olympics," *Louisville Courier-Journal*, July 22, 1996 <www. jeteye.com/jetpak/1e5c4a53–5ee2-424c-b7de-1d733242c479> (April 22, 2008).

57. Lisa Riley Roche, "NBC Chief Says He Pushed for Ali in '96," *Deseret News*, January 30, 2002 <http://deseretnews.com/oly/view/0,3949,65000204,00.html> (July 17, 2007); Ebersol, Bingham, Hauser, and Ali quoted in Kindred, "How Muhammad Ali Brought Light."

58. George Vecsey, "Sports of the Times: Choosing Ali Elevated These Games," *New York Times*, July 21, 1996 <http://select.nytimes.com/search/restricted/article?res =F20B1FFC3D5D0C728EDDAE0894DE494D81> (July 17, 2007); Clinton quoted in Kindred, "How Muhammad Ali Brought Light"; "Adidas Launches Evolution of Impossible Is Nothing" <http://press.adidas.com/en/DesktopDefault.aspx/tabid-11/16_read -7581/> (October 4, 2007).

59. Bloomberg quoted in "United States Olympic Committee—Muhammad Ali Athlete Bio" <http://www.usoc.org/26_603.htm> (July 17, 2007).

60. Thomas Hauser and Muhammad Ali, *Healing: A Journal of Tolerance and Understanding* (San Francisco: CollinsPublishersSanFrancisco, 1996).

61. Davis Miller, *The Tao of Muhammad Ali: A True Story* (New York: Warner Books, 1996); Hana Ali, *More Than a Hero: Muhammad Ali's Life Lessons Presented through His Daughter's Eyes* (New York: Pocket Books, 2000), especially xi, 6, 14, 22, 28, 86, 93 (Muhammad Ali quoted on page 86); Muhammad Ali with Hana

Yasmeen Ali, *The Soul of a Butterfly: Reflections on Life's Journey* (New York: Simon & Schuster, 2004).

62. *Touched by an Angel* [television series], directed by Tim Van Patten (New York: CBS, airdate May 9, 1999). See also *Touched by an Angel*, episode 522: "Fighting the Good Fight," <http://www.touched.com/episodeguide/seasonfive/522.html> (June 27, 2007); *Touched by an Angel*, <http://en.wikipedia.org/wiki/Touched_by_an_Angel> (June 27, 2007).

63. Robert Lipsyte, "Still Floating, Still Building; Ali and His Wife Planning a Center to Celebrate His Life," *New York Times*, March 7, 1999 <http://query.nytimes.com/gst/fullpage.html?res=9407E7DE133FF934A35750C0A96F958260> (December 28, 2008).

64. All of these documents can be found at the Muhammad Ali Center's official Web site: www.alicenter.org.

65. I observed these texts and recorded their contents when I visited the Muhammad Ali Center in June 2007.

66. Carol Slezak, "Owner of Ali's Name Won't Exploit His Hero," *Chicago Sun-Times*, April 18, 2006 <http://www.highbeam.com/doc/1P2-1624327.html> (June 28, 2007); Kevin B. Blackistone, "Ali's Integrity Was Not Compromised in Naming-Rights Deal," *Dallas Morning News*, April 14, 2006 <http://www.dallasnews.com/sharedcontent/dws/spt/columnists/kblackistone/stories/041506dnspoblackistone.215fa692.html> (June 28, 2007).

67. "CKX Partners with Muhammad Ali; Company Acquires 80% Interest in Name, Image, Likeness, Trademarks and Existing Licensing Agreements of the 'Greatest of All Time,'" April 11, 2006 <http://ir.ckx.com/ReleaseDetail.cfm?ReleaseID=192582> (June 28, 2007).

68. Apple "Think Different" ad: <http://www.youtube.com/watch?v=vwtTf6ZvaTk> (October, 15 2007); Adidas "Impossible Is Nothing" ad: <http://www.youtube.com/watch?v=cv9zTzlNu-k> (October 15, 2007); IBM "The Future Is Open" ad: <http://www.youtube.com/watch?v=BesI6NEPWlM> (October 15, 2007).

69. See interviews with Robert Lipsyte and Thomas Hauser in Zirin, *Muhammad Al Handbook*, 286–301, 356–369.

70. Ali ("No wonder we hate . . .") quoted in Ric Flair with Keith Elliot Greenberg, *To Be the Man* (New York: Pocket Books, 2004), 240; Ali ("What's the difference . . .") quoted in Hauser, "No! No! No! Don't!"; Kindred, *Sound and Fury*, 267–328; Cashill, *Sucker Punch*; Hauser, *The Lost Legacy of Muhammad Ali*; Kram, *Ghosts of Manila*; Joe Frazier with Phil Berger, *Smokin' Joe: The Autobiography* (New York: Macmillan, 1996).

71. Editorial page, "Time Could Do for Muhammad Ali What It Did for Jack Demps[e]y," *St. Louis American*, May 4, 1967, 8.

Index

Abernathy, Ralph, 126, 150

Ali, Hana, 183

Ali, John, 95, 114, 144

Ali, Muhammad: as anti-war symbol, 122, 134, 148–149, 170–171; box-office appeal of, 30–32, 35–39, 40–48, 49–50, 51, 58–59, 63, 81, 89, 94, 113–116, 149–153; as corporate pitchman, 171, 184–185, 193, 195–196; cultural image of, 2, 7, 10–11, 15–17, 33, 40, 52–53, 62, 137–138, 154–155; employment of blacks, 17–18; feelings toward Louisville Sponsoring Group, 23, 74–75, 95–96, 114; moral authority of, 2, 8, 12, 47–48, 77–79, 86, 94–95, 134, 138–147, 149, 152–159, 162–163, 170–171, 174, 180–197; name change from Cassius Clay, 3, 86–88, 106, 124; playing the role of villain, 46–47, 50, 52–53, 58–59, 62–63, 94; professional debut of, 12–13; race leadership of, 96, 120–134; refusal to apologize to Illinois State Athletic Commission for Vietnam comments, 100–102; relationship with city of Louisville, 9–13, 15, 24, 31–33, 55, 57–58, 86–88, 124–127, 186; speaking publicly about race issues, 50–51, 53–54, 60, 64, 65, 121, 125–127; worldwide appeal of, 58–59, 85–86, 95, 111–113, 128, 152–159

Ali Story, 2–3, 7, 139, 156, 169, 171, 174, 191

Ali, Yolanda "Lonnie," 164–168, 172–173, 178–179, 191–192, 196

American Broadcasting Company (ABC), 31, 32, 112, 113, 115

American Idol, 191

American Legion, 106–107

Arum, Bob, 95, 102, 106, 114, 118, 211n3, 217n35

Ashe, Arthur, 121

Balaban and Katz (B&K), 83–84, 108, 115

Banks, Sonny, 35, 45

Benny, Jack, 71

Bentley, Ben, 100, 213n16

Berbick, Trevor, 160

Besmanoff, Willi, 32

Bevel, James, 126

Bingham, Howard, 168, 179–180

Bingham, Worth, 67, 68, 72, 75

Black Muslims. *See* Nation of Islam

Black Panther Party, 127, 131

Blackstone Rangers, 131

Bloomberg, Michael, 181

Boeck, Larry, 20

Bonavena, Oscar, 150–151

Bond, Julian, 121, 123, 130, 162

boxing: importance of management, 14–15; promoter turf battles in, 25, 36, 52, 84–85, 93, 107–108, 110, 113–114, 115, 216–217n35; public perception of, 16–17, 33, 34, 77, 113

Bradley, Ed, 177–178

Brenner, Teddy, 51, 217n35

Brooke, Edward, 129
Browitt, Jim, 86
Brown, Drew "Bundini," 73, 158, 182
Brown, H. Rap, 128, 143
Brown, Jim, 95–97, 106, 108, 110, 115, 118, 144–145, 211n3
Brown v. Board of Education, 7
Buckley, William, 127
Burger, Warren, 152
Burke, Frank, 11
Bush, George H. W., 162
Bush, George W., 174
Byrd, Robert, 69

Cannon, Jimmy, 97, 99, 110, 116
Carbo, Frankie, 26
Carlos, John, 155
Carmichael, Stokely, 128, 129, 130, 143
Castro, Fidel, 178
Central High School, 11
Chargin, Don, 107
Cherry, Garland, 78
Chilton, William, 11
Chuvalo, George: bout with DeJohn, 56–57, 74; bout with Patterson, 71; bout with Terrell, 95, 104; box-office appeal in Toronto, 56, 105; pursuit of Louisville bout with Ali, 57–58, 104; Toronto bout with Ali, 104–109; upbringing of, 55–56
civil rights movement: effect on meaning of Liston-Patterson bout, 39; relationship to public perception of Ali, 8–9, 10, 12, 16–17, 21, 33, 50, 53–54, 58, 63, 64, 65–66, 77, 83, 95, 120–134, 170–171, 193
CKX Inc., 191–193
Clark, Frank, 107
Clark, Lamar, 31
Clark, William, 102, 213n16
Clay, Cassius, Jr. See Ali, Muhammad
Clay, Cassius, Sr., 8, 9, 19, 21, 87, 164, 200n17
Clay, Odessa, 9, 21, 74, 76, 164
Clay, Rudy, 9
Clinton, Bill, 180
closed-circuit television: importance to boxing promotions, 36; logistics of, 13, 42, 51, 63, 83–85, 107–108
Coleman, J.D.S., 76–77
Combs, Bert, 13, 20
Congress of Racial Equality (CORE), 33, 89, 127–128, 133
Conrad, Harold, 145
Cooke, Jack Kent, 151
Cooper, Henry, 58–59, 62, 72, 85, 112

Cope, Dennis, 165–166
Cosell, Howard, 144, 157, 159, 169
Costas, Bob, 175–177, 186
Cottrell, John, 23
Cutchins, William, 69, 74–75

Dalai Lama, the, 186, 189
Daley, Arthur, 43, 99
Daley, Richard, 100–102
D'Amato, Cus, 16, 19, 26, 27, 34, 38
Daniels, Billy, 37, 45
Davidson, Gordon, 27, 60, 68–71, 73, 75, 76, 77, 96, 143
DeJohn, Mike, 56–57, 74
Dempsey, Jack, 19, 56, 81, 196–197
Dooley, Edwin, 117
Dundee, Angelo: on Ali's relationship with Nation of Islam, 65; as Ali's trainer, 25–26, 27; matchmaking ability of, 28, 29, 30–32, 56, 71, 74, 104; relationship with Ali, 158; relationship with Louisville Sponsoring Group, 60, 74–75
Dundee, Chris: friendship with Paul Jones, 116; promotion of Ali's fights, 28, 29, 30, 35, 64, 65; reputed links to organized crime, 26–27, 63
Dunphy, Don, 106

Eagle, Dean, 19, 30, 33, 65, 87
Early, Gerald, 171–172
Eaton, Cal and Aileen, 42, 52, 107
Ebersol, Dick, 179–180, 186
Eisenhower, Dwight, 40, 132
Ellis, Jimmy, 32
Eskridge, Chauncey, 76, 95
Eurovision, 85
Evans, Bob, 78

Farmer, James, 89
Faversham, Bill, 20, 22, 24, 31, 32, 34–35, 60, 66, 68–71, 74–75, 77, 87
Federal Bureau of Investigation (FBI), 110, 124, 130, 213n16, 216–217n35
Fleeman, Donnie, 30
Folley, Zora, 38, 43, 52, 105, 116, 134, 167
Ford, Gerald, 155
Foreman, George, 40, 41, 153–157, 159, 181, 182, 191–192
Forman, James, 128
Foster, Archibald, 70–71, 75–76
Frazier, Joe, 40, 41, 87, 150–153, 157–158, 182, 190, 193, 195, 196
Freedom Rides, 33

Ghosts of Manila: The Fateful Blood Feud between Muhammad Ali and Joe Frazier, 174

Glickman, Bernard, 105, 110, 216–217n35

GOAT: A Tribute to Muhammad Ali, 173

Grafton, Arthur, 69, 70, 76–77, 96

Greatest: My Own Story, The, 18, 20, 23, 171–172, 176, 200n17

Griffith, Emile, 34

Guyot, Lawrence, 121–122

Halpern, Nate, 82, 85, 88

Hannah, Wood, 12

Hatch, Orrin, 162

Hauser, Thomas: *Healing: A Journal of Tolerance and Understanding*, 182–183; *The Lost Legacy of Muhammad Ali*, 173; *Muhammad Ali: His Life and Times*, 169–174, 186, 189, 195; *Muhammad Ali and Company*, 171; *Muhammad Ali in Perspective*, 171; on 1996 Olympics, 180; portrayal of Louisville Sponsoring Group in *Muhammad Ali: His Life and Times*, 23; relationship with Lonnie and Muhammad Ali, 167–168, 172–174, 194

Hindman, Arch, 57–58

Hirschfeld, Richard, 162–163

Hoblitzell, Bruce, 11, 12

Holmes, Larry, 160

Holyfield, Evander, 175, 179

Hoover, J. Edgar, 130

Hunsaker, Tunney, 13, 18, 21, 38

Hussein, Saddam, 171

Illinois State Athletic Commission (ISAC), 100–102

Ingraham, Joe, 131

Inter-Continental Promotions (ICP), 78–79, 81–82

International Boxing Club (IBC), 26–27, 34

Johansson, Ingemar, 27, 30, 63, 81

Johnson, Alonzo, 31

Johnson, Harold, 29, 30, 44

Johnson, Jack, 137, 145

Johnson, Leroy, 149

Johnson, Lyndon, 96, 129, 148

Jolie, Angelina, 187

Jones, Alberta, 17–18, 20, 21

Jones, Doug, 51–52, 62, 72, 105

Jones, Paul, 116

Kefauver Commission, 16, 21, 26–27, 34, 35

Kennedy, John F., 38

Kerner, Otto, 97, 99–102

King, Bill, 12, 13, 31, 57–58, 74

King, Don, 155–157, 159, 160

King, George, 18

King, Coretta Scott, 150

King, Martin Luther, Jr., 53, 64, 95, 121, 122, 124, 126, 129, 148, 150, 183

King of the World: Muhammad Ali and the Rise of an American Hero, 80, 169

Kosair Crippled Children Hospital, 12–13

Krulewitch, Melvin, 34–35

Ku Klux Klan, 8, 122

Lamb, Ralph, 116–117

Lavorante, Alejandro, 38, 45

Laxalt, Paul, 117

Life, 31, 50

Lester, Julius, 146

Lewis, Claude, 23

Lewis, John, 122, 128, 130

Lipsyte, Robert, 110, 111, 134, 173, 194

Liston, Sonny: denied boxing license, 35; during championship reign, 42, 47, 50, 52; fearsome image of, 13, 52–53, 58, 59, 60, 62, 82, 157; loss of title to Ali, 3, 40, 41, 43, 66, 83, 94, 108, 114, 181, 182; mob control of, 17, 26, 48; rematch with Ali, 73–74, 75, 76, 77, 94, 107, 114; response to civil rights movement by, 53, 64, 88–89; victories over Floyd Patterson, 38–39, 63, 71, 81–82

Littman, Archie, 49

Loew's, 83–84, 108, 115

Logan, George, 35–36, 37, 47

London, Brian, 112

Louis, Joe, 16, 21, 35, 47, 59, 70, 81

Louisville Defender, 11, 12, 109, 117–118, 126–127

Louisville Sponsoring Group (LSG): aristocratic status of members, 2, 20, 69; fair treatment of Ali, 20–24, 63, 67, 69–79; influence on Ali's cultural image, 7–8, 21–22, 24, 37, 51, 55, 58, 60, 63, 64, 66, 76–77, 85–87, 138; moral authority of, 22–23, 34–35, 64–65, 76–79, 109; profits/ losses resulting from relationship with Ali, 24–25, 31, 50, 61, 67–76

Luftspring, Sammy, 104

MacDonald, Bill, 63, 80–82

Machen, Eddie, 36, 43, 105

Maddox, Lester, 149

Madison Square Garden, 34, 43, 51, 52, 70, 88, 105, 115, 116, 150–151

Mailer, Norman, 154
Main Bout Inc.: attempt to reschedule
   cancelled Ali/Terrell bout, 103–104; black
   sportswriter support of, 97–98, 109–110,
   117–118; economic nationalist aspects
   of, 96, 98, 118, 133; European campaign
   of, 112–113; failed attempt to make 1967
   Ali/Patterson bout, 116–117; formation
   of, 93, 95; promotion of Ali/Chuvalo
   bout, 106–109; promotion of Ali/Terrell
   bout in Houston, 115–116; promotion
   of Ali/Williams bout, 115; replacement
   of Louisville Sponsoring Group, 51–52,
   70–71, 76, 95–96; white sportswriter
   opposition to, 97, 99–100, 109–110
Malcolm X, 65, 66, 80, 82, 114, 131, 134, 137,
   182, 183, 196
Malitz, Lester, 52, 71
Malitz, Mike, 51–52, 71, 95, 105, 109,
   116–118
Marciano, Rocky, 46, 104, 145
Martin, Joe: desire to become Ali's
   professional trainer, 18, 19–20, 200n17;
   influence on Ali's cultural image, 7–8, 87;
   role in Ali's amateur career, 10
Massell, Sam, 149
Maxim, Joey, 44–45
McKissick, Floyd, 127–128
Merchant, Larry, 111
Meredith, James, 54
Mildenberger, Karl, 113
Mills, Wilbur, 69
Mishner, Don, 179
Mister Ed, 71
Miteff, Alex, 32
Mobutu Sese Seko, 155–157
Moon, Henry Lee, 54
Moore, Archie: bout with Alejandro
   Lavorante, 38, 45; bout with Muhammad
   Ali, 40–48; offer to become Ali's trainer,
   25; ring career of, 44–45; stripped of
   light-heavyweight title, 29, 35, 45
Moses, Bob, 129–130, 143
Muhammad Ali Boulevard, 11
Muhammad Ali Center, 141, 170, 172,
   186–193, 195, 196
Muhammad Ali: Through the Eyes of the
   World, 170
Muhammad, Elijah, 64–65, 76, 88, 95,
   98–99, 101, 103, 114, 124, 131, 141, 142,
   144–145, 158, 161, 196
Muhammad, Herbert: interest in Ali's
   financial situation, 70, 144–145, 152, 156,
   159, 160; personal relationship with Ali,
   158, 161, 165, 172; role in Main Bout Inc.,
   95, 97, 114
Muhammad, Wallace, 158
Muhammad Speaks, 101, 109, 144
Murray, Jim, 48, 109

National Aeronautics and Space
   Administration (NASA), 85
National Association for the Advancement of
   Colored People (NAACP), 33, 39, 53–54,
   121, 123, 129, 146
National Association for the Advancement of
   Colored People Legal Defense Fund, 146,
   150
National Broadcasting Company (NBC),
   175–177, 181
Nation of Islam (NOI): economic nationalism
   of, 64, 93; influence on Ali's cultural image,
   32, 48, 50, 54, 58, 62, 64–65, 83, 86,
   89, 99, 120, 131, 137–138, 141–143, 148,
   152, 158–159, 176, 192, 195; Savior's Day
   convention, 101, 103; separatist philosophy
   of, 16
Negro Industrial and Economic Union
   (NIEU), 96
New York State Athletic Commission
   (NYSAC), 34–35, 105, 117, 150, 216–217n35
New York Times Book Review, 169
1996 Olympics, 174–181
1960 Olympics, 1, 7, 9, 10, 11, 16

organized crime: battles with Main Bout
   Inc., 93, 110–111, 216–217n35; control of
   boxing during 1950s, 16, 26–27; control of
   Sonny Liston, 17, 78–79

Palermo, Blinky, 26
Paret, Benny, 34
Parkinson's syndrome, 175, 177–178, 185, 190
Pastrano, Willie, 25, 29, 45, 77
Patterson, Floyd: aborted 1967 bout with
   Ali, 116–117; on Ali's draft evasion case,
   128, 131; first bout with Ali, 73, 80–81,
   88, 94, 105, 107–108, 120, 134, 157–158;
   management by Cus D'Amato, 16, 26, 27,
   34; named as potential Ali opponent, 43;
   support for civil rights movement by, 33,
   121; third bout with Johansson, 30; title
   fights against Liston, 38–39, 63, 71, 82, 114
Payne, Billy, 179–180
Pepper, Claude, 130
Perenchio, Jerry, 151, 187

Perez, Tony, 112
Porche, Veronica, 159, 161–162, 165, 183
Powell, Adam Clayton, 110
Powell, Charley, 49–50, 72
Presley, Elvis, 191–192

Quarry, Jerry, 149–150

Raby, Al, 125–126
Radio-Keith-Orpheum (RKO), 83, 108, 115, 116
Reagan, Ronald, 162
Reed, John, 103
Requiem for a Heavyweight, 47
Reynolds, William, 18–20, 200n17
Ring, The, 35, 52, 55
RKO. See Radio-Keith-Orpheum
Robinson, Jackie, 33, 126
Robinson, "Sugar" Ray, 16, 35, 60
Ruby, Earl, 13
Rudolph, Wilma, 13

Sabedong, Duke, 32, 38, 74
Samaranch, Juan Antonio, 176
Saturday Evening Post, 31
Saturday Night Live, 161
Schoenwald, Irving, 100, 213n16
Sellers, Cleveland, 130
Shafer, Raymond, 117
Sinatra, Frank, 84
60 Minutes, 177–179
Smith, Red, 97, 99
Smith, Tommie, 155
Smythe, Conn, 103
Southern Christian Leadership Conference
    (SCLC), 53, 54, 124, 126
Spinks, Leon, 160
Sports Illustrated, 22, 31, 51, 96, 97, 107, 113
Steindler, Howie, 46
Stokes, Carl, 96
Stoner, Fred, 10, 18, 25
Student Nonviolent Coordinating Committee
    (SNCC): admiration for Ali by members,
    120–123, 128, 143; participation in sit-in
    movement 8, 33; perceived militancy of, 53,
    127, 129–130, 148
Sucker Punch: The Hard Left Hook That
    Dazed Ali and Killed King's Dream, 174
Syufy, Ray, 107

Tao of Muhammad Ali, The, 183
Tauber, Peter, 165
Terrell, Ernie: alleged organized crime control
    of, 75–76, 105, 110–111, 216–217n35; bout

with Chuvalo, 95, 104; bout with Hunsaker,
    13; cancelled Chicago bout with Ali, 76,
    99–100, 104–105, 148, 213n16; ugly rhetoric
    before Houston bout with Ali, 88, 134
Theater Network Television (TNT), 82–83,
    85, 88, 108
Time, 51
TNT. See Theater Network Television
Todd, James, 68
Tomorrow's Champions, 10
Touched by an Angel, 184
Triner, Joe, 101–102
Tyson, Mike, 44, 81

Ungerman, Irving, 55, 104
United Negro College Fund (UNCF),
    132–133
U.S. Department of Justice, 110, 130, 152,
    163, 216–217n35
U.S. Supreme Court, 146, 149, 152, 192

Vietnam War: Ali's stand against, 2, 76–77, 93,
    100–102, 125, 129–132, 148–149; press
    responses to Ali's stand against, 100–102,
    109–110; public perception of, 140,
    148–149, 154, 170–171; reclassification of
    Ali as draft-eligible for, 98–99

WABC radio, 82
Wagner, "Gorgeous George," 32, 37, 50, 63
Ward, Gene, 97, 99, 112
Warner, 83–84, 108, 115
Warner, Don, 35
What's My Line?, 145
When We Were Kings, 154–155, 182, 193
Wide World of Sports, 112, 144, 157
Wilkins, Roy, 121, 129
Williams, Charles, 161
Williams, Cleveland, 43, 105, 114–115, 132
Williams, Robert F., 128–129
Williams, Walter, 115–116
Wilson, Atwood, 11
Wilson, Peter, 58–59
Witherspoon, Tim, 160–161
World Boxing Association (WBA), 57–58,
    77–78, 79
Wyatt, Wilson, 21, 69

Young, Andrew, 162
Young, Dick, 99
Young, Whitney, 129

Zimmerman, Paul, 47–48, 52

Michael Ezra is Chair of the American Multicultural Studies Department at Sonoma State University.